BY CARLA POWER

If the Oceans Were Ink

Home, Land, Security

HOME, LAND, SECURITY

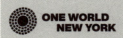

ONE WORLD
NEW YORK

HOME, LAND, SECURITY

DERADICALIZATION AND THE JOURNEY BACK FROM EXTREMISM

CARLA POWER

Published in the United States by One World, an imprint of Random House,
a division of Penguin Random House LLC, New York.

ONE WORLD and colophon are registered trademarks of Penguin Random House LLC.

LIBRARY OF CONGRESS CATALOGING-IN-PUBLICATION DATA
Names: Power, Carla, author.
Title: Home, land, security: deradicalization and the journey back from extremism /
by Carla Power.
Description: First edition | New York, N.Y. : One World, [2021] |
Includes bibliographical references and index.
Identifiers: LCCN 2021011224 (print) | LCCN 2021011225 (ebook) |
ISBN 9780525510574 (hardcover) | ISBN 9780525510581 (ebook)
Subjects: LCSH: Terrorism—Prevention—Case studies. |
Islamic fundamentalism—Case studies.
Classification: LCC HV6431 .P679 2021 (print) | LCC HV6431 (ebook) |
DDC 363.325/17—dc23
LC record available at https://lccn.loc.gov/2021011224
LC ebook record available at https://lccn.loc.gov/2021011225

Printed in the United States of America on acid-free paper

oneworldlit.com
randomhousebooks.com

9 8 7 6 5 4 3 2 1

First Edition

Designed by Debbie Glasserman

At any moment a bomb may fall on this very room. One, two, three, four, five, six . . . the seconds pass. The bomb did not fall. But during those seconds of suspense all thinking stopped. All feeling, save one dull dread, ceased. A nail fixed the whole being to one hard board. The emotion of fear and of hate is therefore sterile, unfertile. Directly that fear passes, the mind reaches out and instinctively revives itself by trying to create.

—Virginia Woolf, "Thoughts on Peace in an Air Raid," 1940

CONTENTS

HOME, LAND, SECURITY

INTRODUCTION

LIKE MANY AMERICANS, I spent the winter after Donald Trump's 2016 election to the U.S. presidency with my blood humming, sensing that some new poison was coursing through both the country and my own body. Nights I'd lie in bed, my hot face cratered into my pillow, my mind turning over the horrors reported that day, of bans and walls and regulation rollbacks. My chest tight and my breathing shallow, my muscles braced for something—I wasn't sure what. Staring at the ceiling, then checking the clock's slog toward morning, I'd feel waves of adrenaline buffet my fury outward, to Trump, to his party, to anyone who'd voted for him. Sometimes the anger curdled into hatred.

By day, I'd begun thinking about writing this book. Even as American politics grew more polarized and American extremist voices grew louder, I read about paths people had taken into and out of violent extremism in Germany, Norway, Pakistan, and Saudi Arabia. My early research focused on young Westerners who'd joined ISIS, and in some of them, I recognized something of my own postelection mental state. If one definition of radicalization is a narrowing of one's worldview, a whittling away of the will or the wherewithal to understand other opinions, I was getting a taste of it firsthand. While the stories I was gathering were of foreign wars and jihadist militants, they bore similarities to the febrile atmosphere in the United States. Describing the project to an acquaintance one afternoon, I was met with disbelief. Surely that was a bit much? he responded. Americans weren't ready to read a book comparing themselves to members of ISIS.

But as happens so often, an idea once deemed radical is now mainstream. In February 2021, the *Ohio Capital Journal* (stated purpose: "connecting Ohioans to their state government") was asking deradicalization experts how Trump-era extremists compared to ISIS recruits. After the attack on the U.S. Capitol on January 6, 2021, Elizabeth Neumann, who led counterterrorism efforts as an assistant secretary of homeland security for three years under Trump, told *Time* that the president's role for the insurrectionists was akin to that of Osama bin Laden's "spiritual leadership" of the 9/11 hijackers. She urged the United States to pursue the insurgents "with the same intensity that we did Al Qaeda."

After 9/11, government and media all but equated violent extremism with Islamist jihadist groups. The story was told, over and over, of how terrorism in the United States had dropped out of a clear blue September sky. It would take another day of national trauma, nearly twenty years on, for many Americans to see what statistics showed, and what people of color had long known from experience: the most serious terrorist threat is not foreign, dark, and Muslim but white and American-made. Like the babysitter in the horror movie who realizes the serial killer isn't in the woods but inside the house, the country has finally begun to recognize the proximity of violent extremists. "Our most serious threats are internal, not external," observed former defense secretary Chuck Hagel. "Politically inspired armed insurgents, extremists, fascist groups and other active destructive forces are now part of the American landscape, as we saw in last week's attack and occupation of America's symbolic cradle of our democracy, the Capitol Building."

AS THE COUNTRY GRAPPLES with how to respond to the problem of domestic political violence, questions abound. How do we balance national security with individual freedoms? Are there ways to teach people to embrace a muscular pluralism or even just tolerance? What should be the role of the government in creating deradicalization programs? What's the line between legitimate political dissent and a threat to society?

Home, Land, Security investigates how people in other countries—and briefly, a handful of American deradicalization pioneers—have grappled with such questions. I talked to policemen and politicians, neurologists and social workers, the mothers of ISIS militants, about what propels people toward violent extremism. I went to Indonesia and Pakistan to see how communities rehabilitated terrorists who weren't foreigners but neighbors and relatives. In Denmark and Belgium, I met police officers who crafted an innovative program for former extremists, dismissed by its critics as "Hug a Terrorist." In Belgium, I interviewed a mayor who was finding ways to stop citizens from becoming radicalized. In Germany, a nation whose reckoning with its Nazi past has put it at the vanguard of rehabilitation efforts, I learned about both the possibilities and the limits of its 720 deradicalization programs.

Along the way, I met people who'd pursued vile plans, whether plotting to blow up the Long Island Rail Road or to knife protesters in a peaceful procession. I emerged having learned new ways to think about terrorism and extremism, but also with a curious yet marked feeling of optimism. Around the world, people are experimenting with humane and innovative alternatives to the traditional remedies of prisons and armed response. Many of the solutions I describe here may seem radical, but as the cultural critic Raymond Williams once observed, "To be truly radical is to make hope possible rather than despair convincing."

But I get ahead of myself.

A WEEK SPENT IN Texas a few days after Donald Trump's inauguration began the journey that would eventually become this book. A Dallas group interested in international affairs had invited me to speak about the subject of my first book, *If the Oceans Were Ink*. I was hoping the evening would be a refuge from all the talk in the news that winter about hatred, high walls, and closed borders, and when I walked in, the first signs were reassuring. In a building designed by I. M. Pei, a soigné crowd picked at cheese and fruit. The group's president, a banker, chatted in French with a Parisian. A Palestinian American doctor and an Algerian American businesswoman conferred about an upcoming fundraising gala.

My book was stacked on Formica tables, manned by a cheerful young bookshop employee with a beard and a baggy T-shirt. *Oceans* told the story of my friendship and studies of the Quran with a traditional Islamic scholar; it had been an attempt to trace where my own worldview as a secular American feminist converged with and diverged from that of a madrassa-trained conservative from rural India. Much to my surprise, the two of us had found common ground—a spacious plot of shared morals. We both believed in the value of democracy, science, reason, pluralism, and human rights, and we had the same commitment to raising strong and curious daughters. A yearlong exercise in listening had yielded surprising alignments with someone whose worldview differed radically from my own.

I wrote *Oceans* to illustrate that Islam is a just, humane faith, a far cry from the intolerance and violence of militant groups that make news headlines. I'd been challenged on the thesis before, but surveying the cosmopolitan crowd that night in Dallas, I hoped I'd be spared.

As it turned out, I was mistaken.

In the Q and A session that followed, an elderly man, rail-thin, raised his hand. "You have not once, in your whole talk, mentioned jihad," he said accusingly. "I have here, from the internet, a list of things Islam says about it." He unfolded a sheaf of papers and proceeded to read a quote from the Quran: "Then kill the idolaters wherever you find them—"

"Yes," I cut him off briskly. "That's the so-called Verse of the Sword. Islamophobes and jihadis both love to use it, since it seems to legitimize violence."

Reader, I must confess, I went all schoolmarm on him. I'd heard this argument before—a handful of phrases cherry-picked from the Quran, thrown down triumphantly.

"The verse is all too often taken out of context, both historically and textually," I intoned, my face pinkening. "If one were to read the entire passage, not just the lines you quoted, one would actually find that, like so much of the Quran, it counsels mercy." What's rarely mentioned, I continued, is the verse's second half: "But if they repent and keep up prayer and give alms, then let them go free; for God is Most Forgiving, Most Merciful." In other words, make peace if your enemy does.

Moreover, I continued, the verse shouldn't be read as a blanket statement about how to deal with non-Muslims; both the Quran and the Prophet Muhammad's sayings contain repeated entreaties for tolerance of Jews and Christians. The Verse of the Sword was revealed to the Prophet at a particular moment in Islamic history, when the early Muslim community was facing off in battle against a very specific group of nonbelievers.

The man folded up his papers, sighing and frowning, presumably, at my naïveté.

"Next question?" I asked, a shade too eagerly.

I DROVE BACK TO the hotel, swearing at red lights, foot too heavy on the brake. I'd faced similar questions before, from those who asked why "the Muslim world" produced so many terrorists, and why "they" hated "us." I'd point out that "the Muslim world" was a flaccid mental construct, lumping together a population ranging from Sudanese tribesmen to Texan neurologists, and that armed jihadis remain a tiny fraction of the 1.9 billion Muslims worldwide. Moreover the "they hate us" formulation crumbled on recognition that the vast majority of the victims of these armed jihadis were themselves Muslim. But these arguments rarely swayed minds that were already made up.

When anyone asked why Islam was inherently violent, I'd tell them that its core teachings preach peace and mercy, but that like all the major monotheisms—indeed, any large population—it had some followers supporting violence. I'd then mention the long history of warmongers and terrorists claiming inspiration from Christianity, from the Crusaders to the conquistadores to the Ku Klux Klan to the IRA. Whether it was Buddhist monks promoting the ethnic cleansing of Myanmar's Rohingya community or Meir Kahane's Jewish Defense

League, most faith groups had tiny minorities who harnessed interpretations of their faith to pursue political goals through violence.

As on that night in Dallas, audiences would often bring me a question on jihad, which I'd try to put into context. The word means "struggle," not "war," I'd say. The Prophet Muhammad said the most important form of jihad was not taking up arms but the *jihad al nafs*— the struggle to conquer one's own darker inclinations. Strict rules of engagement, I'd point out, limit Islam's concept of armed jihad. Only legitimate Islamic leaders, not self-appointed freelancers or militant groups, are allowed to embark on military campaigns. Women, children, and civilians are to be protected. According to classical Islamic teachings, even the enemy's crops and fields are to be left untouched.

What's more, I'd continue, fears of jihadi-inspired terrorism in the United States are wildly overblown. Between 2008 and 2015, the annual chance of dying in a terrorist attack was one in thirty million, while the chance of being killed by an animal was one in 1.6 million. By 2019, Americans faced a one in ninety-two chance of dying from an opioid overdose during their lifetimes, and a one in 107 chance of dying in a car crash. Besides, we in the West are relatively safer from terrorist attacks than we were in previous decades. Political violence has dropped significantly since the 1970s and '80s, which saw the Troubles in Northern Ireland, the Red Brigades in Italy, and the bloodiest years of the Basque separatist movement in Spain.

I'd then point to the dangerous bias of Western media coverage. Though white supremacist terrorist acts began to receive increased media attention with the election of Trump, coverage of terrorism has overwhelmingly focused on jihadis. Between 2006 and 2015, U.S.-based terrorist acts committed by Muslims received 357 percent more press coverage than those committed by non-Muslims, as a 2018 study from the University of Alabama found. Foiled jihadist plots received seven and a half times as much coverage as foiled far-right ones, found another 2018 study.

Jihadist violence is undeniably real, but for Americans, right-wing extremist violence is far more dangerous and became ever more so during Trump's tenure. Far-right terrorists killed more Americans in 2018 than any time since 1995, when anti-government extremists bombed a federal building in Oklahoma City, killing 168 people. The Anti-Defamation League found that right-wing militants were responsible for every 2018 murder linked to extremist beliefs.

Despite the statistics, a surprising number of audience questions at my talks seemed framed by fear: "Isn't it true that Islam is spread by the sword?" Or "Wasn't Muhammad a military leader?" Bias and bad faith lurked behind carefully worded variations on the question "Why are Muslims so violent?" Yes, some people commit violence in the name of Islam, but people foment violence in the name of all sorts of causes. Extremist violence attaches itself to any number of beliefs. In societies where Muslims are minorities, the obsession with "jihadist violence" remains a racist reflex. It's also an inherently dangerous one, allowing other extremisms to mushroom, largely unexamined, until they erupt into violence.

Western security officials have been criticized for enforcing a double standard, using one level of scrutiny for suspected extremists who are foreign or nonwhite, and a far lower one for white ones. Discussing the security failures leading up to the breach of the U.S. Capitol by "Stop the Steal" insurrectionists on January 6, 2021, R. P. Eddy, a former counterterrorism official and diplomat, told *The New York Times,* "There was a failure among law enforcement to imagine that people who 'look like me' would do this." An official inquiry into the 2019 Christchurch massacre in New Zealand, in which a white supremacist killed fifty-one mosque worshippers, found that the country's counterterrorism strategies were flawed by an "inappropriate concentration of resources" on the jihadist terrorist threat.

IN THOSE EARLY DAYS of the Trump presidency, I'd lay out my argument suggesting that a propensity for extremism and violence exists in all faiths, groups, and nations. Invariably, I'd leave these discussions feeling I'd failed. My manner can't have helped. The election had made me, like millions of fellow Americans, pricklier than usual. Brusquer. More defensive. Particularly in a season of rising rage, polarization, and intolerance—both my own and my nation's—I didn't much want to engage in conversations about jihadis. We'd just elected a president who'd ridden to power sowing fear and discord. The week I visited Texas, he'd signed an executive order blocking Syrian refugees and citizens from seven Muslim-majority countries from entering the United States. Extremists of all stripes feed on one another, gaining energy from one another's hard-line statements and stances. Islamic State social media accounts welcomed what one post called the "blessed ban." Trump's discrimination would fuel feelings of alienation among Muslim populations and boost their recruitment, declared ISIS commentators, delighted. One declared Trump "the best caller to Islam."

Why would I want to talk about jihadis when the number of hate crimes against Muslims and other minorities was spiraling? Discussing Islamist terrorism, or even nonviolent extremism claiming inspiration from Islam, seemed only to amplify the discourse of the Islamophobes, with their bile-filled screeds about beheadings and creeping sharia. I wasn't going to give this bigotry any credence by focusing on the few Muslims who might embrace hate. So I batted the topic away.

Over drinks one day, a friend from grad school who worked in her country's security establishment was incredulous: "You're not going to give me that pat line about 'Islam being a religion of peace' again, are you?"

In fact, I kind of did. As much as it rankled to reduce fourteen hundred years of a global faith to a single message, it felt far better, in such fraught times, to train my eyes on the tolerance and justice I'd found in Muslim teachings. With polarization growing both in my birth country and in my adopted one, the United Kingdom, it felt more urgent to point to the peaceful majority rather than to the militant fringes, to speak of tolerance rather than violence, of shared humanity rather than hatred. It seemed wrong to talk about jihadis when a man who'd declared that "Islam hates us" had just moved into the White House. Far better to speak of the Quranic verses celebrating pluralism, or the Prophet's promotion of tolerance.

THE DAY AFTER MY talk in Dallas, I flew to Austin to give another speech, this time at the University of Texas. Much as in Dallas, the crowd was cosmopolitan: many in the lecture hall were studying Islam, international relations, or world history; a few women wore hijabs. After I finished, a young student raised her hand. Why is it, she mused aloud, that many Muslims, and the liberals who defend them, can't seem to understand that the concepts of jihad and sharia are genuinely very scary for some non-Muslims? "When the defenders of Islam don't engage with these concepts," she continued, "don't they just leave the field to the extremists?"

Once again I found myself flummoxed. It was gutsy of her to ask the question in a university hall in Austin, a city known for its liberalism, in an audience that included Muslims, and in a season in which they'd been made targets of hatred. Standing there, I realized that she was not just provocative, she was also right: the loudest voices on violent extremism are generally extremists themselves. One could try to counter them by speaking of peace, or by parsing just why their interpretations didn't reflect Islamic teachings, but what hope did nuance have against violent action? Groups like Al Qaeda, Boko Haram, and the Islamic State framed the terms of the argument with their bombs and beheadings—and all too often Western governments took the bait and responded by imposing hard-line surveillance on their Muslim populations at home and by mounting invasions abroad.

After Al Qaeda's destruction of the Twin Towers seared itself into the American imagination as a primal scene of terror, the United States and its allies responded by invading Iraq and Afghanistan. A little over a decade afterward, the self-styled Islamic State's propagandists honed their own shock-and-awe strategy, cranking out made-for-prime-time videos of immolations and beheadings in order to burnish their credentials as brutal zealots. Simply by covering these atrocities, the Western media found itself an unwitting mouthpiece for ISIS horrors. Together ISIS propaganda and its coverage helped cement the image of the jihadi as monster. After 9/11, it became conventional to frame terrorism as an otherworldly scourge, unconnected to the sociopolitical conditions that incubated it.

In a video that came out of Saudi Arabia in 2017, three old men clamp their hands around a glowing globe as a crowd of dignitaries look on respectfully. The king of Saudi Arabia and the presidents of Egypt and the United States face a "command and control center"—

banks of screens streaming newsfeeds, videos, and data on terrorism. The lights dim, so that the leaders' faces are lit from below by the glowing globe, as they gaze at the "system of systems" designed to monitor extremists. A pulsing, pseudo–*Star Wars* theme swells, amplifying the occasion's Death Star aesthetic.

The 2017 opening of Saudi Arabia's Global Center for Combating Extremist Ideology seemed to render the problem of violent extremism an inhuman one. The command and control center's targets appeared not even as mug shots, but merely as data points. President Trump's address earlier that day, on fighting terrorists, dehumanized them even more. "Drive them out," he thundered. "Drive them out of your places of worship. Drive them out of your communities. Drive them out of your holy land. And drive them out of this Earth." The battle against terrorism, he intoned, "is a battle between good and evil."

Branding terrorism an existential threat to civilization has a bracing simplicity about it, at once soothing and rallying. In 2001 I was a correspondent at *Newsweek*. In the panic and grief after the planes hit the World Trade Center and the Pentagon, the magazine's journalists exchanged memos, trying to understand why the United States had been attacked. While various staff members ventured explanations that were historical, political, religious, and social, one editor was brazen: "Can't we just call it what it is—evil?"

Two decades on, evil remains a blunt and blunting concept, choking off inquiry about why people resort to violent extremism. It blocks out the possibilities of change or redemption, and it seals off routes to a deeper understanding as to why these acts occur. Hannah Arendt may have shown us the banality of Nazi evil, but the motives ascribed to the modern jihadist terrorist remain otherworldly. He is denied banality, denied the context that might allow him reason, and that might explain, though not excuse, reasons for his cause. Headlines present jihadist terrorism in a manner hinging on spectacle. Free-floating, unmoored by circumstance or grievance, its meaning is simply destruction. The 2015 tragedy in Paris, in which Islamist militants killed 130 and wounded over four hundred, was "the work of the devil," said the Australian prime minister. Two years later, after an attack at London Bridge, British prime minister Theresa May blamed "the evil ideology

of Islamist extremism that preaches hatred, sows division and promotes sectarianism." And when a suicide bomber killed twenty-three
people at a concert by the singer Ariana Grande in Manchester, the
British tabloids duly pumped out the bomber-as-monster narrative.
PURE, began the headline above the image of the bombing's youngest
victim, an eight-year-old girl. The word next to it was EVIL, above a
blurry shot of the suicide bomber: PURE EVIL.

FIGEN MURRAY DIDN'T SEE evil in the suicide bomber's face, even
though he had killed her son Martyn and twenty-two others. For days
after the Manchester attack, she didn't watch or read the news, so as to
avoid seeing the bomber's mug shot. But two days after Martyn's
death, she caught a glimpse of the killer's face by mistake, accidentally
walking past a stack of newspapers with his picture on the front. She
instinctively turned away, but even then, she said, "there were only
three words in my mind: 'You foolish boy.'"

The face she saw didn't look evil, just clueless. "They may have
chosen a really rubbish picture of him, but honestly?" said Figen, when
we spoke on the phone a few months afterward. "He looked a bit
gormless. As though he wasn't all there. I just kept wondering, 'What
on earth were you thinking?'"

The police she talked to insisted the bomber knew what he was
doing, but the mother of five disagreed. "I've got kids," she said.
"Twenty-two years old? They don't know what they are doing at that
age. Although he murdered my son, I cannot be cross with somebody
who blindly followed some rubbish they were fed, and then was stupid
enough to die for it."

Where did Figen's sense of understanding come from? Perhaps it
helped that she was a thrice-over immigrant who had been raised
the daughter of Turks in Germany, then later settled in England. Perhaps her work as a counselor had trained her to pick her words carefully. In any case, she resisted using the language of division from the
start.

A few weeks after the bombing, when a top counterterrorism officer visited her house, Figen was saying something about the twenty-

three people who'd died that night, when the officer corrected her: "No, it was twenty-two people who died."

"Well, the terrorist died too," Figen responded.

"Oh, we don't count perpetrators in the police," the officer said.

"Well, he was still a human being," said Figen. "He was somebody's child."

"It's very noble of you to think that way," she remembers being told. "But we don't think that way about them."

THEM. ANOTHER WORD OF division, another favorite of the more excitable press. (NOW THEY KILL OUR LITTLE GIRLS! screamed one front-page headline, despite the fact that the bomber, Salman Abedi, was Manchester-born.)

Even in death, the terrorist is rendered invisible, uncounted, ignored.

In the weeks following the bombing, Figen continued to step over the border between Us and Them. She deliberately flouted it after another terrorist attack occurred just a few days before Martyn's funeral. A man drove his car into a crowd near a London mosque, screaming that he wanted to kill all Muslims, and he succeeded in killing one person. A crowd surrounded the culprit and beat him until the mosque's imam and worshippers formed a cordon, protecting him until the police arrived.

Figen saw a photo of the scene, and moved by the men's unwillingness to let anger descend into mob violence, she decided to forgive the man who'd killed Martyn. A public display of forgiveness from a mourning mother, an immigrant who was born a Muslim, would undermine the tidy Us versus Them narrative being pushed by zealots and populists. A month after the bombing, she called the BBC and went on a breakfast show, forgiving the suicide bomber during the broadcast. The best response to the bombing, she told me later, was refusing division and bitterness. "Terrorists want anger and chaos and hate," she said calmly. "I refuse to give it to them."

She has paid for her restraint. Online trolls told her she didn't look like a grieving mother, because she smiled too much. One Twitter user wrote, "With that attitude, your son deserved to die." In the years since the bombing, Figen has gone on to study for a graduate degree in counterterrorism, eager to understand why people join militant groups, not least because "we have all taken part in creating these monsters, as a society."

THE CREATION OF MONSTERS became a growth industry after 9/11. Between 2002 and 2017, the U.S. government spent 16 percent of its discretionary budget—around $2.8 trillion—on counterterrorism efforts, including its wars in Iraq, Afghanistan, and Syria. It expanded its powers of surveillance and imprisonment at home, and its rights to assassinate both its own citizens and foreigners abroad. The securitized response to terrorism hasn't worked: between 2000 and 2014, global deaths from terrorism increased ninefold. The number of jihadist militants tripled, from 32,200 to over 110,000, according to the State Department and Stanford University's Mapping Militant Organizations project. The seven countries the United States invaded or bombed during the so-called War on Terror suffered a 1,900 percent rise in terror attacks, compared to a mere 42 percent rise in other Muslim-majority countries, found analysts A. Trevor Thrall and Erik Goepner in a study for the Cato Institute.

On both sides of the Atlantic, a polarized view—dividing the world into *pure* versus *evil*—has metastasized. No longer is it applied simply to those deemed foreign enemies, but increasingly to fellow countrymen and neighbors as well. During the month after Britain's 2016 vote to leave the European Union, racially and religiously motivated hate crimes rose by 41 percent. Divide and divide and divide again: we see it in our cities, and suburbs, in privatized police and fire forces, in gated communities. We see it online, in Tweet-size shrieks and Facebook posts that bay and carp. We see it in Washington. Increasingly, we think like census takers or focus group facilitators, flattening our fellow citizens to single dimensions: Black, Latinx, or white, native-born or migrant, members of the 1 percent or of the other 99, Republican or Democrat. Like our elected representatives, we stick more closely to our political tribes than ever.

We all have our own Other, our personal version of Them. Would I, for instance, listen as closely and hard to the story of a neo-Nazi, or to that of an End of Days cultist, as I would to that of a jihadi? I'd like to think I would, but I'm not so sure. My own complicity in the creation of everyday Others struck me on a visit one day back to my hometown, St. Louis. At a grocery store, my fourteen-year-old daughter Nic and I ran into an acquaintance from my old neighborhood. After we'd exchanged pleasantries and moved on, Nic leaned over and murmured: "Do you think she could be a Trump supporter?"

I paused, considered, and guessed, "She might well be."

Nic turned to stare at the woman's receding form, her eyes as wide as if she'd seen a golem lurking in the frozen foods aisle.

Since the attacks on the World Trade Center, the Islamist terrorist has been framed as the *ur*-Other, a catchall receptacle for free-floating anxieties about everything from migration to globalization to waning Western power. Whether as a Guantánamo inmate, or a target of American drone airstrikes, or an Islamic State fighter, the jihadi lives—in law as well as in the imagination—beyond the boundaries of civilized society. The Bush administration's use of the term *unlawful enemy combatant* allowed it to detain and interrogate terrorist suspects without being hamstrung by Geneva Convention rules. After the destruction of ISIS's so-called caliphate, countries around the world debated whether the fifty thousand–odd foreign fighters in Syria should be repatriated or left to fend for themselves in refugee camps. The frank language deployed by some Western leaders stripped the fighters of any humanity, as when Britain's defense secretary announced that his government should "bring destruction" to anyone fighting in Syria, on grounds that "a dead terrorist can't cause any harm to Britain." Even the spectacularly urbane Rory Stewart—a former British government minister who speaks nine languages, taught human rights at Harvard, and set up a nonprofit for artisans in Afghanistan—responded to the threat of returning foreign fighters from Syria thus: "Unfortunately the only way of dealing with them will be, in almost every case, to kill them."

When I read that statement, all I could think of was those infamous four words from Joseph Conrad's *Heart of Darkness*. At the end of his report on Africa for the (fictional) International Society for the Suppression of Savage Customs, the onetime sophisticate Kurtz scrawls: "Exterminate all the brutes."

DEFINING *TERRORIST* HAS ALWAYS been an inherently politicized process, of course. Who gets called "terrorist" and who is deemed, say, a "freedom fighter" depends on who is doing the calling, and when. The U.S. Army once tallied over one hundred definitions of *terrorism,* which makes sense when one glimpses the ways that the powerful use or abuse the term. Jonathan Powell, a lead negotiator in the Northern Ireland peace process, observed that terrorism is "something used by governments to instill fear at home, or support the enemies of their enemies abroad." Back in the 1980s, Osama bin Laden was among those "freedom fighters" whom Ronald Reagan praised so effusively for battling the Soviet empire in Afghanistan. During the struggle against apartheid, the South African government imprisoned Nelson Mandela as a terrorist. In 2020, Saudi Arabia's terrorism tribunal found Loujain al-Hathloul, an activist who'd campaigned for women's right to drive, guilty under its counterterrorism and terror finance laws.

The words *extremist* and *radical,* too often carelessly tossed together with *terrorist,* have suffered similar deployment for political causes. From 2017 to 2019, the FBI fashioned the new category of "Black Identity Extremist" to target activists they claimed were fomenting violence. Russia has banned the Jehovah's Witness sect on grounds of being "extremist." Chinese officials claim that the million Uighur Muslims in mass internment camps are enjoying so-called deradicalization. In 2019 the UK government, having tried for years to nail *extremist* as a legal term, finally had to give up, so elusive was the definition.

In 1963 the Rev. Martin Luther King, Jr., despairing of how white moderates had labeled his actions "extremist," pointed out from his cell in the Birmingham jail that extremism had an honorable legacy. If he was an extremist, then Paul, Martin Luther, and Jesus were, too. What's more, King's so-called "extremism" was a response to a Southern regime that relied on terrorist bombings and lynchings, an apartheid system girded not just by custom and law but by the ever-present threat of violence. Nearly all extremism is relative; what you define as extreme depends almost entirely on where you stand.

And when. Today's statesman is often yesterday's terrorist plus time. Reflecting on how Realpolitik can make former militants respectable, the mid-twentieth-century British politician Hugh Gaitskell once quipped, "All terrorists, at the invitation of the government, end up with drinks in the Dorchester [Hotel]." To be sure, not all terrorists turn into statesmen, as the historian Michael Burleigh has observed: "If you imagine Osama Bin Laden is going to evolve into Nelson Mandela, you need a psychiatrist rather than a historian." Still, the case of the former IRA leader Martin McGuinness shows that former terrorists can craft lives with second acts. The IRA chief of staff became a peacemaker in the 1990s and, eventually, Northern Ireland's deputy first minister. On his death in 2017, the man who'd once commanded paramilitaries killing British soldiers received tributes from world leaders, including Queen Elizabeth herself.

Former enemies may be allowed makeovers, but current ones are rarely portrayed as capable of reform. After every terrorist attack in the West, the media tell the story of the perpetrator's journey—a bildungsroman that inevitably ends in violence. When a boy joins Al Shabab or Al Qaeda, or when a girl sneaks off to join ISIS, they are effectively dead to us. Having joined a listed terrorist organization, they are no longer dynamic human beings but static targets. Unless they become the subject of a manhunt or a court case, they are forgotten. Once a terrorist, always a terrorist, goes the dominant narrative, until they're killed or jailed.

THINKING ABOUT THE QUESTION that the young woman posed that day in Austin, it occurred to me that I'd been willfully dainty about terrorism, radicalism, and extremism. I had first gone into journalism to write stories that make the purportedly alien less so. In a world shrunken by migration and technology, I'd always wanted to try to understand not just those constructed as Others but the systems and assumptions that went into their design as such. I was less interested in arguing certainties than in teasing out processes and complications. Above my desk, I had tacked a Post-it note with the filmmaker Jean Renoir's observation: "The truly terrible thing is that everybody has their reasons."

So why had I stopped short of inquiry when it came to people drawn into militant Islamist groups? If I truly wanted to chart similarities between people with a range of worldviews, surely I should search for common ground not merely with a kindly, quietist Islamic scholar, as in my first book, but with those who engaged in violence. To avert my eyes from the ugly or troubling was to shut down true exploration. It created a closed system of certainties, a liberal's version of Vice President Dick Cheney's hard-ass dictum: "We don't negotiate with evil; we defeat it."

Worse, by refusing to engage fully with terrorists—or even with those who weren't violent but were considered "radicalized"—I was feeding the monster. By turning away from people who fomented discord, I was leaving their "evil" intact. Unexamined and unexplored, the people who got flattened into "terrorists" remained unexplained, their monstrousness unchallenged. And it had become increasingly clear that we had entered an age where conflicts no longer consisted of disputes among quiet practitioners of faith and ideology. If we didn't reckon with the extremists on all sides, we abandoned any hope of bridging conflict in this radicalized age.

Unnerved enough by the young woman's question to feel an inchoate dereliction of moral duty, I thought about an earlier trip to Texas, when I'd visited the Rothko Chapel in Houston, a space for contemplation for people of any and no faith. Inside are Mark Rothko's famous fourteen black paintings. The day I visited, it was bright outside, so that walking in, I found the paintings to be merely huge blocks of plum or black. It took a while for my eyes to adjust, to start to see the depth and movement in paintings that had at first seemed flat, even oppressive. Rothko, who described the six years of working on the paintings as "torment," said he wanted to paint "something you don't want to look at."

To look at something I didn't want to look at—that was imperative,

I decided as I fell asleep. What would I learn if I turned to face these monsters, if I engaged with people who had been cast as the ultimate Others? What could encounters with those who'd embraced intolerance teach us about our own intolerances, our own imaginative limits? Could learning about their paths into extremism suggest ways we might fix our own polarization and extremisms?

The first step in trying to humanize the dehumanized, I decided, would be to talk to mothers of young Westerners who had joined the Islamic State. Hearing about their paths toward violent extremism, I hoped, would begin to complicate my understanding of what makes a jihadi.

Readers who are searching for a book that takes a rigorous academic approach should look instead to the voluminous work on extremism and counterterrorism that is now coming out of think tanks and universities. For those wanting a book on radicalization and counterterrorism policies around the world, search elsewhere. This book is simply an attempt to interrogate what we mean when we talk about Islamist terrorism, by talking to jihadis and to those who have worked to help them leave violence behind, whether parents, parole officers, counselors, or mentors. And while the focus of my investigation is on jihadist militants, it's also a broader, more urgent quest: to see how the Other gets made and—sometimes, with luck—unmade.

The year after I left Texas, a vandal daubed paint outside the Rothko Chapel, scattering leaflets with white supremacist slogans near a sculpture dedicated to Martin Luther King, Jr. The executive director decided to send staff outside to "tell the story" of the vandalism to visitors while the white paint was being scrubbed off, he told the *Houston Chronicle*. By choosing to stay engaged and frank in defiance of hatred, he defended the chapel's mission as a place for contemplation and dialogue. Moreover, he honored the spirit of the paintings within. Much of the dynamism derives from being, as their creator said, "something you don't want to see."

PART I

CHILDREN WHO LEAVE, MOTHERS WHO WAIT

THE LOST BOY

UNDER A NOVEMBER SKY, damp and gray as a dirty dishrag, I traveled from my home in Brighton up to Birmingham, in the British Midlands, to meet Nicola Benyahia, the mother of a young man who'd fought for ISIS in Syria. I was nervous. In the days leading up to the meeting, Nicola's image had grown to mythic proportions in my mind. As the militant group intent on establishing a caliphate had gained land and followers, I'd been drip-fed horrors about hardened warriors who had put a Jordanian pilot in a cage and set him alight, who had made Yazidi women into sex slaves, who had tossed men off buildings for being gay. What kind of woman could have raised one of these fighters?

As the train rattled through the English countryside, I steadied my cappuccino and tried to concentrate on the reading in front of me: a short tract by a British law professor on the need for new ways to talk about terrorism, both in the courts and in public life. Formulating terror laws, wrote Newcastle University's Ian Ward, required "an ethics that properly understands the vitality of human emotions." Ideally, we needed "an alternative jurisprudence, one that owes at least as much to feeling and compassion as it does to reason and the pretense

of certitude," Ward wrote. "We have far less need of a 'law' of terrorism than we do a better developed sensitivity to the tragedies that it
engenders."

I underlined the quote, scrawling a messy star beside it. If law is the
only lens through which we view terrorists, we are training our eyes
on a barren landscape, stripped of any clues as to what made people
into terrorists in the first place.

Motherhood seemed to me the most direct route into an emotional
understanding of the terrorist threat. It was the only thing I imagined
I'd share with this woman, and I figured it might be a way toward some
sort of humanization, perhaps even understanding, of people who'd
been dehumanized and misunderstood. One generally doesn't think
about ISIS fighters as people with mothers. Monsters and demons
tend to be motherless, as nothing humanizes a person more than a
mother. War propagandists know this well, pushing the fiction that We
have mothers and They don't. A British government ad selling bonds
during World War II shows a Blitz-era Madonna cuddling a baby—
a pink, white, and blond vision of hearth and home. From the side of
the frame, monstrous gray claws branded with a swastika paw at the
mother, under the slogan "Keep these hands off!"

The fact of having a mother telegraphs an earlier dependence, a
reminder that the individual wasn't always in charge of his own destiny. This is why adolescents prefer not to be seen with this living proof
that they were only recently babies. Test this assertion, if you like, by
checking with any child who's ever been dropped off at the school
dance by their parents, or with any parent who's ever endured a curt
"Okay, bye now . . . please just go. Please? Now?" through their child's
gritted teeth. To spare my own offspring the shame of being seen as
people with mothers, I have, at various school gates and street corners,
willed myself to look invisible. Ask your own mother: I'll bet she did it,
too. Mothers are living, breathing reminders of our mewling infant-
hood, of humanity at its frailest.

I went up to Birmingham in search of a terrorist's origin story,
which inevitably put me in the company of his mother. Nobody has a
bigger stake in making the case for their child's humanity. No security
agency could wish for a more zealous investigator than a mother pac-

ing and thinking back over a child's past, looking for clues as to why they did what they did. We're good at retracing steps, we mothers: I know it well from personal experience, having lain awake nights, staring at the ceiling, trying to figure out just what I'd done, or what I'd missed, that led my children to a particular misery or mistake. Of course, maternal love doesn't necessarily make for an objective witness. Indeed, it can blind. ("Al, he's a good boy," the mother of the American gangster Al Capone reportedly murmured on her deathbed.) Still, if I wanted to understand how one boy became a terrorist, and how he might have been stopped, meeting his mother felt vital.

In recent years, counterterrorism experts have seized on motherhood as a potential weapon for fighting violent extremism. The United Nations has called for more explicit attempts to include women in counterterrorism work. An Austrian NGO, Women Without Borders, started Mothers Schools around the world, training women from England to Palestine to spot signs of extremism in their families and communities, and to feel empowered enough to speak out about it. At a conference on counterterrorism, I once heard the founder, Dr. Edit Schlaffer, explain to a roomful of security experts why mothers could be so effective at what she called "the first line of defense against extremism." It came down to time and love. "A mother will never give up," she told the crowd. "She'll invest as much time as necessary, and won't clock the hours when it comes to protecting her children."

Not everyone is convinced. Critics point out that the trend simply reinforces traditional gender roles, casting the mother as the docile caregiver, the sentry of her child's soul. "Policy makers in Washington, London, Baghdad, and New York want to mobilize an army of mothers to fight their cause," wrote Sanam Naraghi-Anderlini, founder of the women's rights, peace, and security group ICAN. "But they want mothers who do not challenge them. The motherhood paradigm packages women in apolitical and non-threatening ways according to traditional, and even biological norms of femininity—it is the image of the lioness protecting her cubs. . . . [By] pressing them to act as frontline whistleblowers, governments are using women. As one Iraqi woman notes, 'the government wants women to mop up their mess.'"

At its worst, the motherhood vogue in counterextremism recalls the go-to neoliberal solution to other problems in society: Mom will fix it better. Like childcare or looking after aging parents, it's seen not as a collective problem but rather as something families—read women—can figure out in the privacy of their own homes. As one mother joked to me, "I work full time, and now I have to fight terrorism, too?"

If the official interest in mothers as counterterrorism tools buys into an essentialized vision of mothers as keepers of the home and hearth, I was guilty of it too. It rankled me, as a feminist, to endorse motherhood over fatherhood as the emotional ground zero for families. But from a reportial angle, this bias is unavoidable, because it is usually the mothers of the young Western jihadis who seek help and speak out. "Sixty-five to seventy percent of the time, it's the mother that makes the first contact with us," says Claudia Dantschke, who works with Hayat, a German organization supporting families whose children had joined Islamist violent extremism groups. Mothers are generally the ones who have called hotlines, formed international support networks, sought counseling, and talked publicly about their children's paths into militancy and their own pain.

If grief has propelled a handful of mothers of ISIS fighters to speak out, it seems to have had the opposite effect on fathers, who seemed to sink into silent depression. As one grieving mother told me, "If it was up to me, I would have spoken out about it a long time ago. I was so passionate about the fact that we have to change how we're talking about this. But I had to be very sensitive to my husband, who went off into his cave and would just go numb."

"Fathers," another bereaved mother explained, "want to forget."

Mothers may have spoken out more than fathers, but in truth, few parents are willing to speak in public at all. As my train pulled into the Birmingham station, it occurred to me that the silence surrounding these young people worked to seal their image as terrorists. Talking to Nicola Benyahia, I hoped, would help me complicate that image.

BIRMINGHAM'S TRAIN STATION OPENS into a vast concrete square. Businesspeople paced while waiting for their Ubers. Pairs of graying matrons picked their way across the slick pavement, arms linked. Knots of high-ponytailed teenage girls chattered, heading for the mall in the station. Scanning for Nicola, I instinctively fell back on stereotype and found myself looking around for someone severe and unsmiling, perhaps in a black burqa. But then I saw a figure across the square waving cheerily and clipping briskly toward me in stiletto heels.

Nicola was a pretty middle-aged woman with precise features, wearing a tightly belted trench coat and a long string of pearls over a cobalt-blue button-down shirt. Her cream-colored hijab was fastened by a diamanté brooch, with a few strands of blond hair escaping from it. Around her neck, a tiny diamond dangled from a delicate chain. Later that morning, she would recount how not long before her son Rasheed left for Syria, she'd found a neatly wrapped box on her bed with the pendant inside and a note: "Mama—no matter how much gold and how many precious stones are used, it's never enough to show how precious you are to me." This ISIS fighter had bought his mother an ethically sourced diamond as a goodbye present.

At Nicola's home, a rowhouse in a working-class neighborhood, her living room was pin neat. Photos of her husband and five children hung on the walls, and a pink and white bouquet of fresh flowers brightened the fireplace. On the mantel, a single framed photograph: of Rasheed, a grinning boy with tousled chestnut hair and bright brown eyes.

Propped up beside it was a photo album filled with copies of the texted correspondence between Rasheed and his family during his time in Syria. While Nicola made tea, I flicked through it. "I love you loads and loads," Rasheed had texted. "Your [sic] the strongest person I've ever met." Nicola's texts veered from the emotional ("I love you and you will always be my little boy") to the self-consciously jaunty ("Hope you are being careful on that bike and following mama's health and safety instructions!").

The bike had led to one of Rasheed and Nicola's most surreal conversations. He had called from Raqqa, asking permission to ride his commander's motorbike. The nineteen-year-old loved motorcycles but knew his mother worried about their dangers. "Mama, would it be okay if I rode on the motorbike?" he asked her. "My commander said he'd let me."

At first Nicola was speechless. Three months earlier her only son had sneaked off to fight with the Islamic State, but here he was, calling to see if she was okay with him riding a motorbike. To hear him ask for permission over the phone was to hear the old Rasheed, the biddable boy who'd call her if he was going to be even ten minutes late coming home, who would still kiss her cheek goodnight, teasing her about the weird taste of her face cream.

In the months after Rasheed ran away, Nicola learned to make her voice sound calm whenever he managed to call, and to bear the silence when he didn't. She'd trained herself to tamp down the panic in her voice. "Stay even-keeled," she'd tell herself. "Not frightened, angry, or any other emotion that might spook him."

But when the motorbike request came, she had to stifle a laugh. "Well . . ." She hesitated. "I suppose you can ride it . . . as long as you're wearing your helmet."

Silence from Syria. Then she heard the beginnings of that full-throated chortle she knew so well.

"Oh, and your kneepads, of course," she added, warming to her theme. "And a high-visibility jacket."

Now they were both laughing, sharing in "the absurdity of it," recalled Nicola, "this little white blond boy out there in Raqqa, with bombs falling, finding a helmet and kneepads to ride a motorbike."

No histories of the war against ISIS will record this moment (save this one), but Nicola regards the motorbike incident as a minor assault on the Islamic State. By making her son laugh, she drove a paper-thin wedge between him and ISIS. That he had asked her for permission, that they had laughed together—what was that if not proof that she hadn't lost him entirely? For Nicola, it showed that they were still a family, and it meant that ISIS hadn't won him, not yet. Laughter yokes people together, even if one of them is in a Syrian war zone and the other is in an English living room. Late-night comics lob witty barbs at presidents, knowing laughter pokes the swollen bladder of certainty. Listen hard enough, and you can often make out a distinct hiss beneath a laugh, the sound of air escaping from a belief system after the pinprick of hilarity.

As Nicola recounted the motorbike anecdote, I found myself smiling. It took a beat or two—we were meeting to discuss her son the ISIS fighter, after all. But for the first time that morning, I laughed, if perhaps a bit too high and hard.

RAISED IN A WELSH village by an alcoholic mother and a violent father, Nicola had sought her own independence early. By fifteen, she was out working in retirement homes. She converted to Islam in her early twenties and married her Algerian-born husband shortly afterward. She had three girls before Rasheed was born, followed by a fourth daughter. "Because of what I'd seen as a child, being a mum and getting it right as a mother was so important," she said in her lilting accent. "I so wanted to get it right." Now she works as a counselor for young people with psychological disorders, and she radiates the kind of calm required for a job where a client once threatened her with a kitchen knife.

Talking about her son, Nicola set out her words carefully, as though she were launching a paper boat on a pond. Rasheed "was an absolute joy." Easygoing. Sensitive. Terrible with money. Not a star student, but happy as an apprentice at a local electronics firm. A jokester who loved to make his family laugh, he'd sometimes squeeze into his mother's clothes, reducing his sisters to giggles. Or he'd coax them to try prank sweets he'd ordered on Amazon. As a teenager, he took up free running—acrobatics practiced on urban streets and buildings. He clambered sideways up walls, flipped in midair off benches, used concrete boundaries as launchpads. He often crashed down to earth and spent so much time in the emergency room with broken bones and bruises that Nicola joked he should take out a lifetime membership.

Rasheed's physical daring was matched by his rashness. "He'd get so excited about something or other that I'd have to pull him back and say, 'Hey, Rasheed, let's think about this.'"

Once he came home determined to invest in a business opportunity he'd heard about, selling energy drinks. "Yeah, yeah, Mama!" he enthused. "You put in so much money, and then you'll make lots more!"

"Rasheed, I might be long in the tooth, but I've seen this before, back in the nineties," she responded, as she recalled. "It's a pyramid scheme. A scam."

"No, Mama! You pay like one hundred pounds, and then—"

"Rasheed, listen to me. I'm telling you now. It's a scam, and you're not doing it. It's only people further up the chain who maybe get something out of it. Little people like you aren't going to get anything."

A few days later Nicola was picking him up from school. Rasheed got into the car and leaned over and kissed her on the cheek. "Mama, thank you."

"Thank you for what?"

"You were right, about that energy drinks thing. It was a scam."

Nicola paused. "That's how he was," she said. "Very trusting, very naïve. There was a vulnerability about him."

During the summer of 2014, stories about a fast-growing movement in Iraq and Syria appeared on the evening news, captivating the eighteen-year-old. Born of the remnants of Al Qaeda in Iraq in response to the 2003 American invasion, the group, which called itself the Islamic State, had profited from the chaos in Iraq and Syria during the intervening years. Nicola remembered when the ISIS leader Abu Bakr al-Baghdadi declared a caliphate and how her son enthused about the possibilities of a state governed by Islamic laws rather than by a brutal dictator like Bashar al-Assad. In Al-Baghdadi, he saw a strong leader, able to restore order to chaos. "Rasheed would start talking about what was going on in Syria, and we'd have to say, 'Hang on, we don't know who this guy is. He's come out of nowhere.' But I could see there was a little bit of excitement in him."

I couldn't square Nicola's description of Rasheed with the media images of ISIS fighters. By her account, he was drawn into this group not by ideology or even a particularly keen interest in politics but by magical thinking. Unlike the warriors I kept seeing in the news, he reminded me of Peter Pan, or rather one of the Lost Boys in Never-Never Land: a kid who'd wanted to fly, who'd run away from his mother, whose guileless love of risk seemed to keep him in a Pan-like state of perma-adolescence. Like recruiters for other militant jihadist groups, those working for ISIS often targeted youth who had little or no knowledge of Islam—all the easier to fill their heads with twisted fairy tales of the most dangerous kind, of caliphates and *kafirs* and world domination. In its own propaganda, ISIS painted itself as a land beyond the pale of the international order, out of reach of Western rules and despots' powers. On reflection, I could see how it might be a powerful draw for a credulous boy like Rasheed.

I thought of my own two teenagers, with their freshly hatched ideals, their doodled plans for the future. The younger dreamed of life in a loft in Berlin, where she'd raise children and pursue a music career; the older talked of being a high school English teacher and mental health psychologist who won Academy Awards. Grandiose plans and the quest for thrills are simply part of youth. A few weeks before, my daughter Nic had insisted on showing me an online video of a grinning American teenager filling a bathtub with Jell-O, then diving in. She watched, gripped, and asked to try it on her own, drowning out my bleated protests about waste and corporate sponsorship.

To compare such decadent excesses to the motivations for a violent extremist group might seem a stretch. And yet Nicola's account of her son's feelings, so intense that they deafened him to reasoned arguments, felt familiar to me as a mother, close enough to compare in motive, if not in outcome. The neuroscientist Robert Sapolsky has written about how a teen's attraction to risk, novelty, and passion is hardwired in brain development, a function of the adolescent's still-immature prefrontal cortex. One's teens and early twenties, Sapolsky writes,

> are the times when someone is most likely to kill, be killed, leave home forever, invent an art form, help overthrow a dictator, ethnically cleanse a village, devote themselves to the needy, become addicted, marry outside their group, transform physics, have hideous fashion taste, break their neck recreationally, commit their life to God, mug an old lady, or be convinced that all of history has converged to make this moment the most consequential, the most fraught with peril and promise, the most demanding that they get involved and make a difference.

RASHEED BENYAHIA LEFT HOME for Syria on May 29, 2015. It was a Friday, and as on all Fridays, he worked a half day, and then went to mosque, returning home at night after the last prayers. "He had a routine; he never missed it," recalled Nicola. "He'd come in from the mosque and, without fail, come into the bedroom to kiss me goodnight."

That night she was in bed, but instead of her son, it was her husband leaning over the bed, clutching the headboard, and looking pale. "I can't get hold of Rasheed," he said.

On Monday morning Nicola received a text, allegedly from Rasheed, telling her she wouldn't hear from him for thirty days. The tone was so stilted and formal, she knew the words weren't his:

> I am very safe and in good hands. . . . I ask Allah to protect you and reward you with the highest paradise. Please don't worry. I love you more than ever and again I am sorry.

Nicola and her husband jumped into the car and drove straight to Birmingham's main police station. It was early Monday morning, the waiting room was full of people, and the attending officer behind the counter looked bored. Nicola slid the phone with the text from Rasheed toward him. "We've just heard from our son," Nicola told him, "and we're worried." As the man read, "I could see all panic stations going off inside of him," she recalls.

Nicola didn't hear from Rasheed for ten weeks. When, one morning, his ID picture came up on her ringing phone, she started shaking. At first it was relief, and then "I literally felt like I was going to have a stroke. I couldn't get the words out."

"Where are you?" she asked.

"I think you know."

"Where are you?" she repeated. She knew, but somehow she wanted to hear the words from him.

"I'm in Raqqa. I knew you'd be worried," he said. "I kept saying to my friends here, 'She's going to be so panicked.'" He was sorry he hadn't called, but there'd been no way to phone from his training camp.

"You don't understand what you've done," said Nicola. "The devastation you've left. Your sisters are in bits. We're frantic."

Nicola told me the story fluidly, without fuss, but I could tell the shock still felt fresh. She had waited ten weeks for this phone call, knowing he might be dead. But as she recounted that first conversation from Syria, I recognized an uncanny banality in her particular strain of pain. Parenting manuals describe adolescence as a time when children are careless about their parents' feelings, when they have a surly certainty, a febrile self-righteousness. It was unsettling to discover this ordinary dynamic lodged in Nicola's extraordinary story.

Spooky, too, was Rasheed's phone patter, as Nicola recounted it. He sounded to me like someone calling home from summer camp, brimming with news about the cool kids in his cabin. "He began talking about his friends in Raqqa, how great they were," Nicola recalled. "How there were so many people there, how they'd come from all over, from different nations. The poor, the rich. How millionaires had given up their lives to come fight."

"I wanted to scream at him, 'They're not your friends!'" said Nicola. "But he would have got his guard up, so I simply said, 'They might be your friends, but we're your family.'"

He didn't seem to understand the hurt he'd left behind. "You're going to get blessings, Mama!" he assured her.

Nicola recounted all this without pausing for a beat or a breath, and when she repeated the word *Mama*, my throat tightened, not just because Rasheed had said it but because Nicola remembered their exchange, word for word.

In subsequent talks with her son, Nicola grew scrupulous about keeping her conversations light. After she reported that first text he sent from Raqqa, officers from the West Midlands Counterterrorism Unit had been in regular contact with her, and they told her to ask Rasheed to come home.

Nicola knew instinctively she couldn't press too hard. "I asked him in the beginning, but then I stopped," she said. "I had to keep him emotionally bonded with me." Knowing that ISIS had taken his passport away, and figuring new recruits were closely watched, she reasoned that by suggesting escape, she'd have overwhelmed him. "So I'd just say, 'Whenever you're ready, I'll do whatever it takes,'" she told me. If he ever, by some miracle, managed to come back without his passport, he'd serve time in prison. She could live with that, as long as he came back.

Nicola longed for his WhatsApp calls, but she dreaded them, too.

She wanted to know he was still alive, while the police wanted detailed information on his location and activities. Every time he called, she found herself having to act simultaneously as mother, counselor, probation officer, and intelligence investigator.

"I don't know how to do this," she told her sister. "I can't do this anymore."

"What would you normally do?" her sister asked.

"We'd banter. We'd joke."

"Just do that. Be who you are."

Sometimes Nicola and Rasheed would laugh so much that when she hung up, it would take her a second to remember where he was. On some calls, she would take care to weigh down the levity with some reminder of what he was missing at home. She sent him a picture of himself as a boy, holding his baby sister, with the caption, "I may only have held you briefly in my arms, but you will always be in my heart."

Rasheed sent a photo of himself on the front that Nicola couldn't bring herself to look at for long. "He's smiling," she recalled. "But his eyes, they're sad. I know that face. It was the face he'd give me when he'd come to me and say, 'Mama, I'm sorry. I was wrong.'"

And as the months went on, she felt the tug-of-war for his soul intensify. When Rasheed's commander began pressuring him to get married, Nicola cautioned him against it: "If you die, and there's a grandchild out there—a part of you out there, forever—I wouldn't be able to cope with that." Then, forcing herself, she switched back to banter. "Besides, you've got to be careful—you never know what they're going to look like, what with all those veils!"

NICOLA WORKED TO STAY cheerful on the phone with Rasheed, but some conversations were darker. "We talked about death, and him dying," she said. Out in Syria, his commanders had convinced him that his death would bring a reward to his sisters and parents. "He was sold this fantasy that blessings would rain down on us," said Nicola, shaking her head.

"Mama, don't worry," he told her one day. "When I die, you're going to have so much good luck. Like, I've heard stories, about when someone's died, the whole family get good luck."

"You mean like blessings?"

"Yeah! There are so many people here, whose families, back in their home countries, had no friends. No money. Nobody knew them. And then when they died or were martyred on the battlefield, they suddenly had all these people knocking on their door! They weren't lonely anymore!"

"Rasheed, that family didn't suddenly get a bunch of new friends," she snapped. "Those were probably people from the media and the police. I hardly think that was a blessing."

HEARING ABOUT RASHEED'S GULLIBILITY, so bald that it gleamed, unsettled me. Not only did it complicate my image of ISIS fighters, but it suggested that this young man—now deemed "a person of interest," suspected of taking up arms in a foreign civil war, an offense under Britain's counterterrorism laws—had an inchoate yearning for something, he was trying to fill some nameless hole, one that I suspect neither he nor Nicola really knew how to name. His trip to Syria felt less like a quest powered by faith or political conviction than like a basic human need for—what? Wholeness? Purpose? If running away to fight jihad filled that kind of void, it explained why the reasoned counter-arguments that Nicola and her husband deployed had stood no chance.

In less than an hour on her couch, Nicola had dismantled my preconceptions of what had driven her son to join ISIS. Where I'd expected a boy motivated by Quran-thumping righteousness, I'd found dreamy naïveté. I'd long known that Islam itself wasn't a cause, seeing as there are countless interpretations of the fourteen-hundred-year-old faith, of which the vast majority caution Muslims to steer away from extremism and violence and toward moderation and peace. But I'd always assumed that those who volunteered for jihad were lured by some sort of extremist ideology, its ideas cherry-picked from Islamic texts, then twisted by opportunistic groups. That was the salient political discourse about the Islamic State in Britain. The former prime minister David Cameron warned of a generational battle against ISIS's "poisonous ideology," while his successor, Theresa May, called for the need to defeat "the single evil ideology of Islamist extremism."

But soundbites about dogmatic jihadist beliefs are deceptive, it turns out. Later, I read that academics who study terrorism have a long-running debate about how important religious ideals are in motivating jihadist militants. Some scholars see religiosity as the major engine of motivation, while others argue that the root cause is more likely a search for identity, belonging, or purpose. As with so much about violent extremism, the importance of ideology varies widely from case to case.

It can even wax and wane within one individual. Religious belief clearly didn't drive the young men who bought *The Koran for Dummies* from Amazon before leaving for Syria. But it might have become important to them later on, in ISIS boot camp or under fire. People frequently join an extremist group for personal reasons, embracing its dogma only afterward. "Ideology is one of the big issues we haven't properly cracked," John Horgan, a prominent expert on radicalization, told me in a telephone interview from his office at Georgia State University. "It's hugely relevant if it gives a group character, direction, or a sense of meaning. But things become more confusing and obscure at an individual level. You might have someone who is a true believer—but those in my experience are very, very few and far between. The reality is that people by and large don't join for ideological reasons. They join for adventure, excitement, or camaraderie."

ALL THAT SUMMER NICOLA worked closely with the police, telling them about her talks and text exchanges with Rasheed. The best she could hope for, she knew, was getting him back home, where he'd face years in prison for joining a terrorist group. "I get it," she told the officer assigned to her case. "He did something wrong. He made the wrong choice. If I'm lucky enough to have him back in this country, I know he'll go to prison. I just want him back here."

During the six months Rasheed was in Syria, Nicola told virtually nobody about his whereabouts, besides the police. "It was tactical, because I didn't know how people were going to react," she explained.

"Being the child of an alcoholic, I know that shame is something you can tap into very quickly." Guilt compounded the shame. "I just felt 'What have I done? Am I a bad mom?'"

She kept going to work, kept glancing at her phone, kept picking it up when Rasheed called. "I felt like a freak," she recalled. "In most situations, no matter how traumatic—like a car accident, or cancer—someone will be able to identify with you. But the political ideology around radicalization means that this is not something you can talk openly about. There's nothing out there for you, so it isolates you even further."

She asked the policewoman whether there was a support group of some sort, a place where she could talk to other parents facing similar problems. A few weeks later the officer assigned to her case returned triumphantly—"really excited," said Nicola. There was a local women's group, she said, where women did coffee mornings, even spa days. Of course, Nicola couldn't discuss anything about the situation with Rasheed with them, but it might give her a break from thinking about it.

Nicola was incredulous. "I've got friends," she responded. "If I want a coffee, I'll go to Costa Coffee." What she needed was people whose children had joined terrorist groups, people who wanted to help their kids, while also doing the right thing by the law.

One day when the isolation grew nearly unbearable, Nicola was searching the internet for support groups for the families of terrorist suspects when she discovered the work of Daniel Koehler, a deradicalization expert in Germany. When she emailed him, he wrote back immediately, with a reply that was "a godsend," she said. "Simple. Plain. He said I wasn't to blame, and that there was no way I could have seen it coming."

Koehler put Nicola in touch with Christianne Boudreau, a Canadian woman whose son Damian had been killed in Syria the year before. She got in touch.

It was comforting, talking to someone else who'd lost a child to Syria. Better still, both Christianne and Koehler gave Nicola practical advice on how to talk to Rasheed. They prepared her for certain turning points, such as his return from his first battle. The trauma of combat might make him more aggressive, they warned. To Nicola's surprise, the opposite proved true. Instead of pushing her away, Rasheed sounded even more desperate for his mother, even "clingier," she recalled. He asked whether she'd had any of her "funny dreams" about him, then made her promise to come back on the phone after he spoke to his father. "It was like he wanted my voice to be the last in his head. Like he'd seen stuff, and it scared him. Like he felt death was near him."

When Nicola told Christianne and Daniel about these conversations, they were unnerved by how much Rasheed talked to her, and by how open he was about how much he missed her. "He'd even turn around to his friends while we were on the phone, telling them how close we are, how amazing our relationship is," she recalled.

Christianne worried that the boy's openness could put him in a vulnerable position with his commanders. "The link between you two?" she told Nicola. "That's the link ISIS wants to break."

Despite their closeness, Rasheed kept certain details of his life from Nicola. He told his father about the battles, and only after one of his sisters asked him whether he'd seen a beheading did he admit to her that he'd witnessed one in Raqqa.

By not giving up on Rasheed, by continuing to talk about everything from bike helmets to British football, by believing that he might have a future after terrorism, just as he had had a childhood before it, Nicola was defying the language of the absolutists on both sides. ISIS saw him as a fighter for the cause; most Britons would write him off as a terrorist. Nicola, however, could look back and see a boy whom she'd watched learn to walk and to read and later to leap off sides of buildings. She could look forward, too, and hope that he might be allowed to grow into a man who could learn from his terrible mistake.

Thinking about the photos of the mischievous boy in her living room, it occurred to me that parents are the historians and prophets of their children's lives, the ones who look both to the past, searching for early signs of the people they're growing into, and to the future, wondering what they'll become. As parents, we have no choice but to believe in their growth. It's our job, surely, as we escort them toward independence. In it for the long haul, we have to maintain our faith in the suppleness of the spirit. To raise a kid from diapers to adulthood, we've got to believe people can change.

This expansiveness of spirit, this belief that any person contains multitudes, is the vision that both violent extremists and populist hard-liners want to extinguish. The "lock 'em up and throw away the key" crowd defines a person by one moment of his life. Even the politician who blames terrorism on a "violent ideology" reduces a complex process to a set of beliefs. The parent tries to look beyond a single act toward a lifetime. Nicola's decision to keep talking, to refuse to believe that a very stupid choice defined someone forever, was the action of a desperate mother, of course. But hearing about her dialogue with Rasheed during a season of rising rancor and division in the public sphere felt particularly poignant. Real conversations and offers of redemption felt in such very short supply.

FOR MONTHS AFTER RASHEED left, Nicola couldn't bear to go into his bedroom. One day she felt a nameless pull and went in. For some reason, she found herself sitting on the floor, looking through a flat plastic box of playthings he had saved. A toy car. A Ninja Turtle figurine. Toys from McDonald's Happy Meals. Then she saw a stack of cards, many from her, some for birthdays, and others that she occasionally got for him and her other kids just to tell them that she loved them. "I'd put them on his bed with a little gift, like a bottle of aftershave or something," she said, smiling at the memory. "He'd kept them all."

In the middle of the stack sat another card. On its blue-bordered envelope was printed "My Death." Inside, a short message:

> Death can strike at any time. Give all my money to Mama. My bank card is in the case in my phone. Remember me in your prayers, and remember that death will take everyone. Now is the time to turn to God. I love you all for the sake of God. Remember to treat Mama and Baba with respect and honor.

Not long after Nicola found the note, she got a Skype call from Rasheed. He was sitting on a curb in Raqqa, holding his phone. Two small kids, the youngest just a toddler, kept trying to get into the frame. "They were very cute, but I'll never forget, one had a black eye," she said. "In both their eyes, there was an emptiness. A vacant look. You could see they'd been traumatized." Rasheed said he'd been asking around the neighborhood, trying to find out what had happened to the boy with the black eye. Nobody seemed to know.

As they were talking, an old lady dressed in black hobbled up next to Rasheed. She pointed at his gun, lying beside him on the sidewalk, and then she pointed at the sky. Rasheed, nodding, tried to understand her torrent of Arabic. She pointed at the sky again. "My son," she said. "They've killed my son. Can I borrow your gun? I want to shoot those planes down."

As Nicola watched, Rasheed shook his head and tried to communicate in broken Arabic. "Too high." He pointed upward. "It's too far."

In this triptych on a cellphone screen were three generations of pain, on two continents. Nicola, trying to reach her son through the power of her voice. The elderly Syrian woman, asking the teenager to shoot the U.S.-led coalition planes that shot her son. And then the bruised, burnt-out stare of the kids.

Nicola smiled at the memory of how earnest, how gentle, Rasheed had been with the mourning mother. "My gun won't reach them," he had told her. "Look how high the planes are. It won't reach."

"It will reach," the woman insisted. "It will reach."

THE LAST TIME NICOLA spoke to Rasheed, she kept saying, "Look after yourself, and remember that I love you." To which he kept saying, "Mama, I love you, I love you."

"It just wouldn't stop," she told me. "Neither of us would let go. I felt he didn't have long."

Afterward she sent him a text message: "I won't see you again here, in this life, but hopefully I will in the next life."

One night in late November, when Nicola came home from work, her husband got up and kissed her. When she pulled away, he pulled her back again, tighter.

"I've had the call," he said. He didn't have to say anything else.

Later, he told her more. On a bad line, in broken English, a man said that their son had been killed ten days before. Hit by a coalition drone strike on the Syria-Iraq border, Rasheed had died instantly.

After his death, Nicola paced back over the past, trying to sift innocent moments from clues of his radicalization. The Benyahias had never been didactic in their approach to Islam, but in hindsight, she now recognizes clues that Rasheed was becoming more rigid in his practice. One day he told his father he wasn't going to the "boring" mosque the two of them had attended together all his life. He was switching to the Green Lane Mosque across town, which attracted a younger and, said some, a more radical crowd. Another time he asked his mother to shorten his trousers to the ankle-length style that many ultraconservative Salafis wore. "People are going to think I can't dress you properly!" Nicola said, before giving in and hemming them.

Another time he suddenly refused to cut his hair. And he wanted to join a *halaqa*—a Quranic study circle—that met at ten P.M. "What kind of a study circle," wondered Nicola, "starts that late at night?" In hindsight, perhaps the gym he joined might also have been a clue. It was shabby, but he still wanted to go. Nicola had heard that certain gyms in Birmingham were associated with recruiting grounds for drug dealers and gangs. Why not, she later wondered, for potential ISIS recruits?

As Nicola told it, Rasheed's story was one family's tragedy, not a national security issue. "On a human level, it's no different from grooming," she said. "We call it radicalization. The narrative is different, but the process itself is no different from what pedophiles do in grooming people online. You could say the child had a choice, in whether or not they went to meet the person. You could say Rasheed had a choice, in going over to Syria. My child had a choice. But he had no idea what he was getting into."

Something that is routinely framed as a threat to the West, Nicola framed as victimhood. This was the first time I'd heard the concept of grooming applied to recruitment to a violent extremist group, but police and security services had long noted similarities between the tactics of sexual predators and violent extremist groups. In both cases, as Britain's former chief crown prosecutor Nazir Afzal wrote in *The*

Guardian, "perpetrators take teenagers who feel misunderstood, show them propaganda about a better world and a better life, and distance them from their family and friends. Then they take them."

Whoever groomed Rasheed probably could see that the boy was vulnerable. In 2014 Nicola and her husband had separated for a few months. Though temporary, the separation had upset Rasheed. Could a recruiter have sensed his fragility and in it a possibility for a potential volunteer? Being sympathetic to a militant group is one thing; joining one is another. To move from toying with extremist ideas to actually joining an extremist group frequently takes not just interest but also some sort of grievance. A life event, trauma, or victimization can make a young person particularly receptive to the messages of revenge and retribution preached by the extremist group. Searching for such a grievance in her son, Nicola feared that one trigger might well have been her own stress.

Nicola had been on the board of a local public school with a large Muslim student population. After newspapers stoked fears that some Birmingham schools were promoting hard-line Islamist teachings, the national educational authorities launched an investigation of twenty-one schools, including the one where Nicola volunteered. Known as the "Trojan Horse Affair," the case was national news, and the months of tension were tough on Nicola, the board's only woman member. The skin on her legs broke out in a stress-related rash. Things grew tense with her husband. She eventually resigned, along with the rest of the board, even while maintaining that the government's charges were unfounded. Looking back, she wondered if someone might have used the case to encourage Rasheed's anger against the government. "Someone could easily have said to him, 'Look at what they're doing to your mom,'" she said. "He'd always have tried to protect me." And therein, she suspected, lay Rasheed's "grievance."

Set against Rasheed's stressful present would have been his memories of a past adventure in a faraway Muslim land. When he was two, the Benyahias had lived in Yemen for four years. It had been a golden time, of simple living and day trips to sunny seaside coasts and medieval castles. Once they ordered fish at a restaurant, only to have the waiter get into his boat, row out in it, and catch lunch in the Red Sea.

In Yemen, power cuts might mean the air conditioning was switched off for hours a day, but at least Rasheed's parents hadn't been stressed about work. "There weren't the massive expectations of you that we have in British society," explained Nicola. "It was just about being together. Nobody expected that you have fancy holidays, that the more stuff you have, the better things could be." Once the family returned to the gray British Midlands, those years in Yemen gradually became burnished into family legend.

Memories of Yemen, Nicola suspects, played a part in Rasheed's decision to join ISIS. It isn't only kids leaving for Syria who long for a simple life, she says. Running away from it all remains a near-universal daydream. "Why do we have so many reality TV programs, putting people in jungles or on desert islands, giving up all their tablets and phones, just going back to talking, and living simply?" she said. ISIS propaganda expertly tapped into this modern nostalgia, saying, in effect, *We'll give you a house, and a purpose, and you won't have to deal with this capitalist materialism.*

When Nicola put it that way, I began to see that one strand of ISIS's narrative was not so very different from stories being spun elsewhere. Rasheed's quest for a simpler world with easy answers about where to live, what to do, and how to pray sounded a lot like the hopes of Americans who voted for a president who promised to "make America great again." It chimed with the desires of Britons who voted to leave the European Union as a way to "take back control." A 2018 poll found that nearly three times as many English believed their country had been "better in the past" than thought it had a bright future.

I could hear echoes of Rasheed's state of mind in stories from my own country, of the teen alone in his bedroom, certain of only one thing: an uncertain future. He knows he won't do as well as his dad or granddad did, not with the local coal mine or car factory or steel mill shut. On a friend's recommendation, he watches the YouTube videos of Jordan Peterson, who urges him to look beyond today's "chaos" and back to the days when "masculine" order—the true way—prevailed. Online algorithms and curiosity might push him toward groups blaming Blacks, gays, and feminists for the plight of modern America. (A 2016 internal report at Facebook found that 64 percent of people who joined an extremist group on the platform did so only in response to a Facebook algorithm.)

Like the American teen drawn into the white supremacist orbit, a young recruit to the caliphate glances backward to an imagined utopia. Invariably, the extremists' golden ages hearken to the past and the future, promising power and control for those who feel they have neither in the present.

Rasheed's bad decision had other echoes in the zeitgeist. In a world being remade by mass migration, people have a strong yearning for origin stories. Extremist recruiters can easily lure youth whose parents migrated to the West and who are curious about their Muslim heritage, young people who perhaps feel estranged both in their ancestors' countries and in their own. But as Nicola pointed out, that sense of being caught between cultures and unsure of where one belongs doesn't afflict only the children of immigrants. "Everyone seems to have a fascination with their history, with where they come from," she said. "Why do you think we have so many websites about finding your ancestry?" Purity may be the stated goal of both right-wing and jihadist extremists, but it reverberates in more benign hungers for authenticity—a yearning tapped into by companies selling products from popcorn to shampoo.

Nicola also found an overlap between Rasheed's radicalization and other forms of extremism. Four months after he died, she attended a workshop for counterterrorism practitioners in the Netherlands, on the invitation of the German deradicalization expert Daniel Koehler. In one session, Koehler screened a video showing militant animal rights activists radicalizing a recruit. He'd warned Nicola beforehand that the session could feel fairly intense and suggested she leave if she found it too distressing. But she stayed and watched as the single-minded militants wore the recruit down. "The person became quite ill, not eating or sleeping," she recalled, shocked to see a political belief manifest as physical illness.

The recruit in the video reminded her of Rasheed. In the weeks before he'd left for Syria, he hadn't slept, hadn't eaten much, and had stopped going to the gym. He had seemed so zombified that she and her eldest daughter had worried he was on drugs. In fact, a period of extreme lethargy is often part of the radicalization process. "They get to this low point, when they're really tired," Nicola explained to me. "Then the recruiter will come along and say, 'I've got the answer to this. You don't need to feel like this anymore, if you just do this one thing.' So now they have this avenue, knowing they'll go to Syria, and believing they'll feel better." After making the decision to join ISIS, Rasheed began eating better and exercising again.

Nicola also recognized a similarity between the animal rights activist's state and that of some of her clients struggling with mental health issues. "It was almost like when someone's been really depressed and suicidal and doesn't want to live," she said. "When they've finally decided they want to kill themselves, there's almost a calm about them."

Understanding the relentlessness of the recruiters, as well as the psychological journey that radicalization could take, helped Nicola feel less guilty. "When I saw how clever they were at indoctrinating this person, I realized that, with what I knew at the time, it would have been impossible for me to do anything else," she said.

GIVEN THE STIGMA OF having a child go fight in Syria, Nicola could have simply retreated after Rasheed's death, letting her grief close over her. After all, that was what most mothers in her position did. It's what her own husband did. But as a professional counselor, she wanted to lessen the stigma around talking about radicalization, much as conversations about sexual and domestic abuse have ceased to be taboo in recent decades. "The only thing I think could have saved my son, was if I had somewhere to go to air stuff, in a safe space," she said. "A place where I could talk about changes I saw, and say, 'Do you think I'm being stupid?'"

When she said this, I inadvertently found myself thinking of an old friend named M. C. Raj, who lived in the Indian state of Tamil Nadu. I'd met him while I was reporting a story on the social and political organization of Dalits, members of the caste once disparaged as Untouchables. A local organizer working for Dalit empowerment, he and fellow Dalits had faced decades of exclusion and prejudice and were denied entrance to schools, houses, neighborhoods, and jobs. For decades Raj, as everybody called him, had operated out of his house.

Then one day he received a grant to buy some land. Ambitious and well versed in leftist theories of resistance, he developed huge plans for building a Dalit empowerment center.

I asked him what the community needed most urgently. A conference room, for leadership training? A soup kitchen?

He shook his head. "A gossip center," he said. "A place for people to come, sit, and gossip."

I laughed, assuming he was joking.

"No, I'm serious," he continued. "True change in society is built on gossip!"

I thought of Raj as Nicola spoke of the need to carve out places for people to talk in new and different timbres about social issues. "Playing it safe doesn't always get us the real solutions," she explained. "Maybe we need to come out of our safety boxes and do something different. That's how we will get real change."

TO CHALLENGE THE SILENCE around extremist recruitment, Nicola founded Families for Life, a counseling service for people and their families affected by radicalization. She rented a space in two rooms in a business park, located on a street of dull redbrick Victorian buildings on the outskirts of Birmingham. It's overwhelmingly women who phone to talk to Nicola, most with a gnawing sense that something's not quite right. A mother whose son is becoming more withdrawn, or whose daughter has grown more belligerent. A girlfriend coping with her boyfriend's curious obsession with a Quranic study group across town.

Often the signs that worry the callers are so subtle that they can't put into words why they're phoning. In their incoherence, Nicola sees her attempts to understand Rasheed. "I know exactly how you are feeling," she'll tell them. "You feel like you're babbling, just clutching at straws." Much of what she does is listen, without judgment. Given the confusion in many communities about reporting possible terrorist suspects, just that service is valuable. "You need to have a very open-door policy with the family," she says, "where they can come forward, and be educated with the skill set for detecting signs of possible radicalization."

And yet that's incredibly difficult. Those who study the process of radicalization say the only certain thing about it is that it's highly complex. Over and over, literature on the prevention of violent extremism suggests that holding radical beliefs doesn't necessarily lead to terrorism: there's no conveyor belt that begins with sympathy for a cause and ends with acts of violence. People who hold extremist beliefs may not support violence; and some people commit terrorist offenses with no knowledge of extremist ideology. As Marc Sageman, a former CIA officer and a counterterrorism expert, states bluntly, "Despite decades of research, we still don't know what leads people to engage in political violence."

Over the years, in various countries, I'd heard such a broad range of explanations for the causes and cures for violent extremism that I felt like the proverbial blind man trying to figure out the shape of an elephant. Or rather, herds of elephants, since the reasons a French student might travel to Syria would be vastly different from those of an Afghan tribesman who agrees to fight with the Taliban. There was huge variation even within particular countries. In the mid-1990s, I'd sat in a madrassa in Northwest Pakistan talking to children who were being prepared to fight jihad in Afghanistan. Many had been sent there because their parents couldn't afford to feed them or send them to another school. I returned to my hotel, convinced that the key to eradicating radicalization was decent education, free to the poor.

I was partly right. But neither poverty nor lack of education explain the radicalization of the Pakistani army major I met a few years later. He was wealthy, living in a colonnaded white house in a fancy Lahore suburb, with a daughter who was studying English literature. Trained by the Green Berets to fight the Russians in Afghanistan, he'd used some of his wealth to set up a jihadist training camp in Kashmir. His commitment to militancy didn't even come from particularly strong feelings about the conflict between India and Pakistan over Kashmir. When I asked him whether he'd stop fighting if the Kashmir issue was resolved, he said no. He'd keep fighting until all the world was Muslim.

Religious ideology was a driver to militancy for this Pakistani major, but it clearly wasn't for a young man I met after 9/11, in Birmingham. He admitted he'd been into drugs and clubs before becoming inspired by Osama bin Laden as sort of anti-imperialist hero.

To get a glimpse of just how manifold the drivers toward militancy can be, one need only look at the *Plan of Action to Prevent Violent Extremism* issued by the United Nations in 2016, which attempted to list them. People could be susceptible to "push factors," including lack of socioeconomic opportunities; marginalization and discrimination; poor governance; violations of human rights and the rule of law; prolonged and unresolved conflicts; and radicalization in prisons. They could also be susceptible to "pull factors," including individual backgrounds and motivations; collective grievances and victimization stemming from domination, oppression, subjugation, or foreign intervention; distortion and misuse of beliefs, political ideologies, and ethnic and cultural differences; and leadership and social networks.

On reading it, I thought there were nearly as many reasons people were drawn to jihad as there were jihadis.

KNOWING HOW INDIVIDUAL EACH case is, Nicola does what any good counselor would do: she draws clients out and tries to sketch "the whole map of the person," from their relationship with their parents to their life at school. Only then might they be able to recognize signs of genuine radicalization and distinguish them from fleeting phases or moods. Many callers to Families for Life want to challenge their children's new theological interpretations of Islam, but Nicola invariably counsels against it. "Don't go down that rabbit hole," she tells them. "We did it with Rasheed. Believe me, you can argue till the cows come home. Remember, they got into this because it was an emotional issue for them, and the ideology came much later. Go to what it was that brought them on that journey."

In 2003, Britain instituted a program called Prevent to identify people at risk of becoming radicalized or committing acts of terrorism. But confusion reigned over what the program meant by "radicalization" and "extremism," and in 2011, an official government paper overhauling it admitted that "some parts of the country"—read: Muslims—"felt that they have been victims of state 'snooping.' "

More controversy followed in 2015, when counterterrorism legislation vastly expanded Britons' responsibility for monitoring one another. Ordinary citizens like teachers, social workers, and doctors were supposed to report people who seemed at risk of being drawn into terrorism or even just "extremism," whether violent or nonviolent. After spending a few hours doing online training about radicalization, everyone from nursery school teachers to heart surgeons suddenly had counterterrorism added to their list of duties. The 2015 law meant that "everybody tiptoes about, rather than talking about extremism," Nicola told me. "There's now a culture of wanting to cover your back, so they pass concerns on like hot potatoes."

While the government framed the legislation as a matter of safeguarding vulnerable individuals, some saw it as an extension of state surveillance and an erosion of individual freedoms. Human rights groups protested, as did university professors, students, and teachers, arguing that the beefed-up reporting laws risked stigmatizing Muslims and chilling free speech. The broader dragnet turned up absurd cases: in Staffordshire, a master's student who was reading a textbook on terrorism in a college library was taken aside for questioning about his beliefs on homosexuality and Al Qaeda. Nursery school staff reported a four-year-old for saying its father was preparing a "cooker bomb," when in fact the child had meant "cucumber." University conferences on Islamophobia and Islam were canceled over concerns that they breached Prevent guidelines.

The United States saw similar panic-induced incidents. In 2015, a fourteen-year-old Muslim from Texas was handcuffed and taken into juvenile detention after his English teacher mistook a clock he'd built for a briefcase bomb. Human rights groups warned that the vague indicators were being used to spot people suspected not just of terrorism but of simply being somewhere in the all-too-spacious "pre-criminal" space. A 2014 questionnaire from the National Counterterrorism Center asked police, social workers, and teachers to rank people in the communities where they work according to categories that included "connection to group identity" (race, nationality, religion, ethnicity), and expressions of hopelessness and futility. At the Department of Homeland Security, researchers were developing something called Future Attribute Screening Technology. It would use algorithms to monitor a person's heart rate and the steadiness of their gaze, among other things, to determine whether they were planning a crime.

Minority Report, the 2002 Steven Spielberg movie based on a short story by science fiction writer Philip K. Dick, is set in Washington, D.C., in 2054, when mere thoughts of criminal behavior can get you arrested. Using the psychic powers of clairvoyants, the elite police unit PreCrime arrests people before they commit murder. Many analysts have pointed out the parallels between the plot of the Tom Cruise thriller and post-9/11 counterterrorism efforts in Britain and the United States. In 2006, in a sting operation in Miami, the FBI arrested seven men on grounds that they were planning on committing acts of terror, including blowing up Chicago's Sears Tower. Apprehended after an agent posing as a terrorist infiltrated their group, the "Liberty City Seven" had no contacts with terrorist organizations, the FBI admitted, nor had they acquired explosives. Their plans to attack the Sears Tower were "aspirational rather than operational," said the FBI's deputy director. Despite this, four of the seven were convicted of providing material support for terrorism, with the man deemed the group's "leader" receiving a prison sentence of thirteen and a half years. The *Minority Report* mindset gripped some local law enforcement forces, too. In 2018, the Brennan Center for Justice, a nonpartisan law and policy think tank, produced a chart of the indicators that police and sheriffs' offices across the country used as indicators of potential radicalization. In Boston, "frustration at U.S. policy and events around the globe" merited suspicion. In Lincoln, Nebraska, the only risk indicator listed was "paying debts prior to a terrorist attack." In Oakland, according to the chart, those "searching for a sense of meaning and community" were deemed suspect.

Just scanning the list is chilling; the purported indicators of radicalization lie as much in the eye of the beholder as do beauty, evil, and patriotism. I'd been guilty of many of these indicators. Had I been Muslim, I could so easily have wandered into a precriminal space.

ON THE TRAIN HOME from my meeting with Nicola, I kept thinking that the most surprising thing about her story was that so much of it felt ordinary. Rasheed's path from free-running enthusiast to ISIS fighter wasn't a straight one, but as best as Nicola could make out, the emotions that had powered him along it were pretty mundane: youthful idealism, gullibility, and an emotional vulnerability that someone had found easy to exploit.

On reflection, the ordinariness—or maybe more accurately, the familiarity—of Nicola's story was not accidental: after all, I'd sought out a mother and one who was, like me, white. Nicola is a native English speaker, born in Wales, and she shares my daughter's given name. Few British mothers of ISIS fighters were as willing as she was to speak publicly. That she was the only person I'd found willing to speak to me may reflect the fear that Prevent had instilled in many immigrant communities.

Then again, why hadn't I started my reporting by hopping on a plane and going to talk to Afghan, Iraqi, or Nigerian mothers? With their countries ranking in the top three in the world for 2019's Global Terrorism Index, they'd be statistically far more likely to have children who'd joined militant groups.

The answer I finally came up with, as the train pulled into London: I'd fallen into the default framing of terrorism for Westerners. Terrorism is something that happens to Us here, not to Them over there. It's palpably false, when you look at the numbers. But unconsciously, I'd used that lens. Buried deep in my focus on Western recruits was a lump of latent Orientalism. It wasn't just that a kid from Birmingham or Brooklyn joining ISIS hit closer to home. Rather, the construction of the terrorist as the Other meant that Westerners who joined Islamist militant groups were deviations from the norm. For their mothers, it was a true tragedy, lying outside the realm of ordinary griefs. But the template of the Muslim Other casts Afghans or Iraqis or Nigerians who join militant groups less as tragedy than as a reflection of the chaos reigning in regions clumsily lumped as "over there."

A corollary discovery was how much my cultural proximity to Nicola dictated my understanding of Rasheed's actions. As a white mother, it was easy for me to see her as a victim, and her son Rasheed as an ordinary teen with Lost Boy aspirations. Our ability to determine what extremism is often hinges on how we relate to the people who are deemed extreme.

"YOU'RE THE MOTHER OF A TERRORIST"

No one can tell a mother how to act:
there are no laws when laws are broken, no names
to call upon.

—RITA DOVE, "PERSEPHONE ABDUCTED"

THE FIRST DAY I talked to Nicola, what struck me was her loneliness, how walled in she was by shame and silence. Rasheed had joined ISIS in May 2015, when it was claiming responsibility for carrying out spectacular attacks in Europe, and when Western politicians were framing it as an existential threat to civilization. To have any allegiance to an ISIS fighter, even if it was just emotional, brought stigma and legal risks.

The people who had assured Nicola that "I was not a freak," as she wryly put it, were Daniel Koehler and Christianne Boudreau. Christianne, a Canadian woman, had trained with Koehler as a family counselor focusing on radicalization after her elder son, Damian, was killed in Syria. She later established herself as a mentor and advocate for parents who were worried about their children joining militant groups. Networking by phone, social media, and in person, she had become a vocal advocate for more transparency around radicalization and for the rehabilitation of violent extremists.

I wondered about these conversations between the families of radicalizing youth. Did they reveal patterns in what had led these Westerners to go fight in Syria? And did they help, in some way, to challenge the stock ways we talk about terrorism?

Two years after Damian left to fight in Syria, Christianne and her twelve-year-old son Luke left their native Canada to stay with her retired parents in a village in the Dordogne, where they would try to put their lives back together. Hoping to find out what Christianne had learned through her own ordeal, and through counseling other families, I booked a ticket to France.

I WOULD STAY OVERNIGHT in Toulouse and travel the next day to Christianne's village. Picking me up at the airport, my Uber driver asked me where I'd come from. When I told him England, he swiveled around to look at me, as though I'd said I'd caught the red-eye from Xanadu. "What is your country thinking?" he asked, incredulous. "How on earth do you think it's a good idea to leave the European Union?"

I told him I was as mystified as he was. That I was shocked, not just by the vote in favor of Brexit, but by how it had revealed there were two Britains, since none of my friends had voted for it either.

"But why would you want to be stuck on that tiny island, cut off from Europe?"

"Beats me," I said. "I've been trying to figure out what possessed those people for months."

"And?"

I stammered something about the campaign slogan "Take Back Control" and the Brexiteers' promises of a neater, simpler world, a world before migration, before globalization.

He snorted. "Those days are gone, if they ever existed in the first place." For him, they never had. He was of Moroccan Jewish ancestry, he told me, born and raised in Spain. He'd moved to France and had a great kid with an Italian woman. He'd moved to Belgium, because the wages were better. He'd moved back to Spain for much of the winter, because he hated the rain and missed his family.

"You're a walking, talking Mediterranean region!" I said.

"Hey, there are worse things to be." He shrugged.

By the time he'd dropped me off at my Airbnb, we'd agreed that this new mania for walls and strict borders and cultural purity was folly.

And yet millions of people around the world seemed to be yearning not for dialogue and pluralism but for something rather less messy. Purity and certainty: that's what the men promising walls and sovereignty were hawking. That's what some young people joining militant groups were craving. And that's what the Islamic State would deliver, its propaganda promised. In 2015, ISIS's English-language magazine *Dabiq* celebrated the death of "the gray zone," a place between cultures where Muslims were stranded when they didn't join either ISIS or the "crusaders," as ISIS called its Western enemies. Gray zone residents were weak, refusing to take sides in the great civilizational battle cleaving the earth. But *Dabiq* had good news to report. The gray zone was "critically endangered," its propagandist assured readers.

> Its endangerment began with the blessed operations of September 11th, as these operations manifested two camps before the world . . . a camp of Islam . . . and a camp of kufr, the crusader coalition. Or as [Osama bin Laden] said, "The world today is divided into two camps." . . . Bush spoke the truth when he said, "Either you are with us or you are with the terrorists." Meaning, either you are with the crusaders or you are with Islam.

If refusing to take sides in a phony civilizational showdown made you a resident of the gray zone, then I'd been living there for years. So too, I suspect, did Nicola, who knew her son had done wrong but loved him all the same. So did the other parents, whose personal loyalties to their terrorist children smeared the thick black lines drawn by zealots and nationalists. The Western parents of the jihadist recruits I met had lingered in the gray zone longer than most. They reject the Us and Them rhetoric, the demands for division and suspicion, the reliance on stereotypes or essentialism. Their losses have made them acutely aware of the tangled, sometimes snarled interconnections between the world's people, cultures, and countries. Loving their children, yet knowing they did wrong, these parents understand the hollowness of righteousness. Their world is ordered not by passports or borders or laws but by private loyalties. "Our passion comes from emotion and hurt," Christianne would tell me. "It doesn't come from power, money, and political directives. When it does come from those things, you can control it. But with us, it's emotion, and governments or caliphs cannot control it. That's what makes us dangerous."

THE NEXT MORNING I took the train from Toulouse to Eymet, the village where Christianne and Luke live with her parents. Sitting on a sunny terrace, sipping coffee and smoking cigarettes, she reminded me of a character in a Tennessee Williams play, a weathered and heartbroken beauty pitted against small-town bigots. Her voice is stained with nicotine and sadness, and she has fine lines around her fine eyes. She claims she looks awful, but she doesn't. There's a force field of determination around her, so when she tells me she was into bodybuilding back in her twenties, I'm not surprised.

During the cold first months of 2013, Christianne lived a double life, split between Calgary and Syria. Every night she'd tuck Luke, then ten, into bed and descend to the basement of their house. Switching on the computer, she would log on to jihadist websites or watch YouTube videos posted by militant groups fighting Bashar al-Assad's forces in Syria. She would scan the fighters in every frame, straining for the details of their faces, poring over images of men in black waving triumphantly at the camera, brandishing AK-47s, running through smoke after bomb blasts. Every now and then she'd stop to peer closely at a particular face. Then she'd scroll through the death announcements to make sure that the name she was terrified she'd see wasn't listed, at least for one more day. The face she was looking for was that of twenty-one-year-old Damian, who'd left that fall to fight in Syria.

The half-lit nights at the computer were followed by stressful days glued to her phone screen. When she woke up—if she'd been lucky enough to fall asleep—her first thought would be her phone, and whether there might be a text from Damian. When she showered, she'd take the phone into the bathroom with her, the volume turned up, in case he called. During meetings at the nonprofit where she worked as an accountant, she would put it on the table in front of her, in case it vibrated with a message from her son. "You're always wondering what's happening," she told me. "Has he been captured? Has he been tortured?"

And throughout, she would ask herself a less immediate question: why would a Nova Scotia–born boy, raised Catholic, decide his destiny was to fight a war in Syria? He'd always been sensitive, the sort of boy who defended weaker kids against bullies in the playground. He was exceptionally bright, with an IQ of 154. Ever since kindergarten, school had been pretty much a bore. Against Christianne's wishes, he'd dropped out at sixteen, though he remained intensely interested in learning, particularly about global politics and social justice. He was suspicious of authority, dismissing politicians as fools.

Christianne's home life wasn't necessarily a refuge from her worries about Damian. She and his father had divorced when he was seven. She had lost a baby son to cot death and was a victim of domestic abuse by a new partner.

In his teens, Damian had struggled with depression, with his world shrinking to the size of his computer screen. He rarely left the house, and at seventeen he attempted suicide. When he converted to Islam soon after that, Christianne was relieved, hoping it would bring him direction and peace. For a time, it did. He got a full-time job stacking boxes in a warehouse and lived at home with his mother, who'd drive him to the mosque.

But he soon left his job, scraping by on a disability pension he received for his mental health issues. "He had an inner struggle with who he was," said Christianne. "He wasn't getting enough from the life he was living. He was frustrated and bored."

When Damian turned twenty, he moved into an apartment in downtown Calgary with three other young men, all of whom attended the same Islamic study circle and storefront mosque. He grew more aloof from his family, no longer bringing friends back to the house. He disapproved of Christianne's lifestyle, loathing having to watch his family "indulge in fornication and infidelity legally and limitlessly and stagger around poisoned on intoxicants," as he put it in a Facebook post. He espoused 9/11 conspiracy theories. When his phone rang while he was at Christianne's, he would take the call outside. At dinner, when she opened a bottle of wine, he'd leave the table.

Then one day in November 2012, Damian left for good, telling his family he wanted to train as an Islamic scholar and that he was going to Cairo to study Arabic. But two months later, in January 2013, two agents from the Canadian Security Intelligence Service knocked on Christianne's door. They'd been following him and believed that he had never gone to Cairo but to Turkey, where he went to a military training camp run by militants. From there, they said, he crossed the border into Syria and began fighting for Jabhat al-Nusra, a Syrian affiliate of Al Qaeda.

ANGRY, DEPRESSED, AND DESPERATE to find meaning for his life, Damian—in Christianne's telling—sounded more like the young men I'd assumed were drawn to jihadist groups than had the enthusiastic, naïve Rasheed. Decades of headlines about "Islamic rage" and "jihadist fury" had conditioned me to assume that anger and alienation, more than idealism, drove individuals toward militancy. If one were looking for a pat profile of someone who'd want to run off to fight in Syria, Damian seemed to fit it. He was a child of divorce who suffered from mental health issues. He had watched his mother suffer the loss of a child and domestic abuse. On the phone, Damian told his mother he had come to Syria because he wanted to defend suffering women and children. Joining the jihad, Christianne said, had partly been his "way to fight back symbolically." He'd taken the fight he couldn't win at home to Syria, where presumably he thought he'd find order, purity, and purpose.

Moreover, Damian was a Western convert to Islam. Exact numbers are hard to come by, but studies have shown that converts, who form a small percentage of Muslim communities in the West, are overrepresented in extremist groups. Scholars debate why this might be. Some say that a recent convert's zeal leads them to groups embracing rigid and righteous interpretations of classical texts. Others suggest that not growing up in a Muslim household is more apt to leave a convert without a solid knowledge of Islamic practice to counter jihadist recruiters' claims. Every academic studying radicalization I'd read or interviewed stressed the fierce complexity of factors pushing and pulling someone into violent extremism.

After years of talking to scores of worried parents, Christianne concurs. "Everyone wants a neat profile of the terrorist: that the father is missing, or that there's something tragic in their life driving them. There's the hunt for something concrete, so we can put it in a box and make it easy to solve. But people aren't easy, they're complex."

On hearing that the Canadian security services had suspected Damian was radicalizing for two years before his departure but hadn't told her, she felt betrayed. Not only did she feel she might have been able to help; she also grew suspicious of their motives. Did they really want to help her son return? Were they using Damian's movements to track other suspects? After the security agents told her not to tell anyone where her son was, she began to suspect that she, too, was being "played," that the officers were trying to "extract as much information from me as possible" about Damian's associates. (Adhering to its rules on speaking publicly about its cases, the Canadian Security Intelligence Service refused to comment on Christianne's account.) Looking back, she's convinced that intelligence agents were "grooming" her to get information—names, addresses, and contacts—from Damian's computer. "I gave it to them." She shrugs. "They kept dangling a carrot, saying 'We're going to help, however we can. We're trying our best to get him home, but you have to have patience.'"

Her lack of trust for the authorities was compounded by fear. The agents warned her that the men who recruited Damian may have known where Christianne lived with Luke and her daughter Hope, and even where her children went to school. "You were always looking over your shoulder," she said. They cautioned her against speaking to the press. This secrecy, she suspects, was less about her security than about maintaining Canada's image as a place without a homegrown terrorism problem.

She sensed that she was losing him. In one conversation in particular, she felt him slipping away. "He was alive, but his voice was cold. Hard. Empty." On his Facebook page, she wrote about how bereft the family he'd left behind felt: "The thought of never seeing you or holding you again has broken my heart in pieces."

Damian—whose fellow fighters now called him Abu Talha al-Canadi, "the Canadian"—texted back:

It would be better for you to accept this so that we would be able to speak without there being the same "we all miss you you are breaking my

heart" thing which fails to cause guilt and kills all forms of conversation.
I am finally where I belong.

For six months, Christianne told few people about Damian's situation. As time wore on, she frayed from the strain. Luke had always seen Damian as a father figure; now watching him talking on the phone with his brother twisted her heart. He still thought Damian was studying Arabic in Cairo; his mother couldn't bear to tell him the truth. Luke would rock on the floor, begging his brother to come home. "I need you," he would say.

Raised a liberal Catholic, Christianne had taught her children to be open to other faiths, but she now found herself wracked with bouts of Islamophobia. "I went through a period of extreme hatred for Muslims," she recalled. At the supermarket, if she saw a woman in a hijab, she had an impulse to run her over with a shopping cart. On the road, the sight of a hijab made her want to steer toward the woman wearing it. "I just didn't know where to put my anger."

When I was twenty-six, my own father died after a break-in at our vacation home in Mexico. Though the police were never certain who killed him, the best explanation for the murder came down to a case of mistaken identity. We'd had a tenant who'd got mixed up with some drug dealers. My father had gone to the house to do some repairs, and the dealers must have assumed that he was the tenant, who owed them money. They came to call one day, tied my father up and beat him, demanding he pay them what he owed. A week later he died from internal injuries.

It was a random piece of bad luck, and yet for a couple of years I'd fashioned monsters from the too-sturdy materials of fear, pain, and laziness. In my head, Mexico shrank to a terrifying place, where every Jesus statue in every cathedral wept blood, where knocks on the door heralded not a friend, the flower salesman, or the tortilla lady, but assassins.

Years went by before I'd return to Mexico, before I'd stop reducing it to the site of my own sadness. Like Christianne, who was shocked at her own split-second flash of Islamophobia, I remain horrified at my prejudice, even though it's passed, and I remain ashamed at how I let grief poison my feelings. I think of the women made targets of Christianne's anger, the fallout from a foreign conflict raining down on them like toxic ash from a distant fire.

AS CHRISTIANNE'S ATTEMPTS TO get professional support for her family foundered, she felt increasingly isolated. When she asked the intelligence agents for a referral to someone Luke could talk to, she alleges, they'd brush her off. "Not right now, we have to get the right person," they'd say, or "It's not in the budget." So she cold-called child psychologists herself. She'd start to explain, "My eldest son has joined a terrorist organization, and has gone to fight in Syria, and I don't know how to help my younger son deal with it." But nobody wanted to touch her case. "They either didn't respond, or went, 'Yeah, okay,'" she said, miming putting down a phone receiver. "Click."

Seven months had passed since she'd learned that Damian was in Syria. Increasingly distraught, she went against the intelligence agents' advice and broke her silence by speaking to a reporter. The piece was published on June 23, 2013, in the *National Post,* quoting her, but not by name. That morning she was at work. While she was on the phone with a child counselor's office, attempting to make an appointment for Luke, she got a text from the agent in charge of Damian's case, saying he needed to talk to her right away. Another text followed, asking to speak to her at once.

"I lost it on them," says Christianne. She texted back, "Unless you are finally coming forward with some sort of counseling for my family, nothing is that important. Otherwise, you can back off." She says she never heard from the agent again.

One night, nearly a year after she'd learned Damian was in Syria, her phone rang. It was a reporter asking for a recent picture of her son. When she asked why he wanted it, he told her: Damian was dead.

CHRISTIANNE DRAGS DEEP ON her cigarette and puts on her oversize sunglasses, like a woman recovering after the night before. She's moved to France in part to grieve but mostly because she feels alienated from her home in Canada, where Damian's departure left her unsupported, unemployed, and broke. Her situation, she feels, is a result of her having continued to speak out, breaking Canada's silence about home-grown extremists. She was frank about what she saw as the government's ham-handed response to the problem, and she insisted that young people were vulnerable to exploitation by recruiters.

After she went public, the judgments rained down on her. She rattles off the list of accusations: "You must have done something wrong," "You didn't raise him right," "Maybe it was your belief system." Online comments were even harsher. "There were people who said I should be dead, too," she tells me, her mouth tightening. "Complete strangers, hiding behind a computer screen."

Back in Calgary, when her contract at the nonprofit where she worked as an accountant ended, Christianne tried to find another job. After every application, she'd get a call from someone at human resources, right before the interview. Invariably, as she recalls it, the position was unexpectedly filled, or the job specs had changed. Finally, a sympathetic headhunter told her that the human resources departments had probably Googled her and, when they learned of her backstory, had worried about whether her past would damage their reputation. "You're seen as a mother of a terrorist," the woman explained.

Christianne thanked her for her candor. Unable to find work, and deep in debt, she eventually lost her home to the bank. "That's what honesty gets you," she shrugs, "a kick in the ass. And they say they need more mothers of ISIS fighters to come forward. Really?"

The phrase the headhunter had used to describe Christianne—"mother of a terrorist"—hangs over us, an unholy mix of nurture and menace. Dictionaries gloss the phrase "the mother of all _____" as descriptive of something that is the biggest, most basic thing of its kind. Nobody ever refers to "the father of all evils" or "the father of all battles." To be a mother of a terrorist is to be the source, the fount of something evil. When a youth joins a jihadist group, it's inevitably the mother who's on the front line of criticism, Christianne says. "Nobody looks at the father," she says. "Nobody asks 'Where was he? What did he do?' It's all about the mother."

I nod, mentally adding terrorism to all the social ills mothers have been blamed for over the years. "Mothers of terrorists" can join the line, right next to the mothers Freud said caused their children to be schizophrenic; the midcentury American "refrigerator mothers" whose chilly parenting was blamed for their children's autism; and the hundreds of mothers—mostly Black—prosecuted in the 1980s and '90s for supposedly creating "crack babies" by taking drugs during pregnancy.

MOTHERS GAVE BIRTH TO these children, but others used their anger, anxiety, or trauma to pave the routes into extremism. Daniel Koehler, the bearded and bespectacled director of the German Institute on Radicalization and De-Radicalization Studies, began thinking about the problem of violent extremism while he was still in his teens, watching the neo-Nazi skinhead cliques at his Brandenburg high school. He began his career working with right-wing violent extremists, and when he later expanded his work to include jihadis, he found striking similarities. Recruiters, whether speaking the language of religious extremism or of white supremacy, encourage a narrowing worldview based on intolerance, Koehler has said, a "de-pluralization of political values and ideals." They persuade the people they target that their own problems are linked to larger, fictitious struggles, like the "global struggle against Islam by the infidels . . . or the destruction of the pure Aryan race through immigration." A deft recruiter can braid someone's loneliness, or his struggle to find a girlfriend or a job, into an extremist's worldview. Slowly the target's isolation, disappointment, or anger melds in their mind with the larger struggle. The pitch, explained Koehler, is that by building a caliphate or an Aryan society, "then all of these problems would go away."

The year after Damian's death, Koehler came to Christianne's house in Calgary to begin training her as a counselor for families coping with a radicalized member. For Christianne, trying to piece together why Damian left, it rang true to hear Koehler talk about the process of depluralization as "being slowly backed into a corner, so that they only have tunnel vision," she said. "He helped connect how important the emotions and motivations were, and how they can get twisted." Together they set up Mothers for Life, a virtual organization designed to act as a hub for parents whose children had joined jihadist groups.

AT LUNCHTIME, CHRISTIANNE AND I walked down the hill from her parents' house to a neighborhood restaurant. We ordered two prix fixes and a large glass of house red for Christianne. As we ate, she tried to explain how one person's radicalization could spread alienation to those around them. How the pain it caused seemed to spread out in ever-larger circles, rippling through families.

Over the years, she'd fielded calls and messages from families who feel isolated. She's heard stories of siblings who wanted to follow their brother or sister to Syria. Parents who grew increasingly alienated from the police and security systems they hoped would help them: "They lose their faith in the system, their faith in humanity." One French couple whose grandchildren had been taken to settle in the Islamic State were planning to move themselves to Raqqa to be reunited with them. Christianne had seen the stress end marriages and start drinking problems. Families left behind often have to cope with mental illness. One mother, on the death of her son, paid smugglers to take her across the border from Turkey to try to see where he died. She went, spent a week there talking to his fellow fighters, and returned. The trip didn't provide the closure she'd hoped for. Soon afterward the woman unraveled and lost touch with reality. She now talks as though her son were still alive.

WE'D BEEN TALKING FOR two hours. Our coffee cups were drained, the restaurant was empty, and the waitress asked us to lift our feet so she could sweep under the table. "Knowing what you know," I asked, "what would you do to counter violent extremism, in a perfect world?"

Christianne raised her eyebrows and barked a short laugh. "In a perfect world? We'd start rebuilding communities, families, and youth. We've forgotten about the importance of human relationships. We keep cutting away at the places that support them—youth groups, community centers. Trying to take shortcuts with technology."

That's it? I thought. *Boys' clubs? After-school sports? Scouts and skate-*

boarding? Town halls, community barbecues? That's the solution to what has long been presented as a shadow threatening civilization? Christianne's proposed fix seemed so ordinary—chillingly so. I wasn't entirely convinced that these recruits were simply victims of the breakdown of Western societies.

Along with allowing social connections to languish, she continued, we'd allowed fear to block out inquiry and stunt dissent. Take the very word *radicalization,* which could be such an engine for change, even for good, she said. "We've taken this word and bastardized it," she said, leaning back in her chair and raising her hands resignedly. "We now think of all radicalization as wrong. People are putting up walls, blocking themselves in with this fear. That fear is squelching hope, and we have to replace it again." That fear showed up in how resources were allocated, she added. Fear was one reason that her work, counseling families, was largely pro bono, while budgets for bombs, for drones, and for jails only grew.

IN THE SPRING OF 2015, the women of Mothers for Life decided to write an open letter to their children who'd joined the Islamic State. Posted on Facebook on Mother's Day, it was a plea for their children to come home from Syria, a paean to pluralism, and a rebuke to the Islamic State:

> We are all sisters and do not know any borders or nationalities. We currently come from seven different countries and have yet experienced the same story. We speak the same language of motherhood, and we are waiting for your return, but waiting in vain. . . . We, your mothers, taught you many things but most importantly justice, freedom, honor and compassion for all of God's creation and for every human being.

The letter closed with criticism of their own governments and the suggestion that the blame for the rise of violent extremism lay not just with individuals and their families but with global leadership:

> To those in charge of making decisions we say: We are the mothers left behind and we must be heard. We need to be supported, and our stories

prove that many things have gone wrong. We have been lied to, left without help, and sometimes it was possible for those taking our children
away to do so, because you were turning a blind eye.

The letter was swiftly translated into ten languages and was
covered in over fifteen hundred press articles, but it received no official response either from Western governments or from the Islamic
State.

A year later, like a chorus in a Greek classical drama reminding
powerful men of moral truths, the group returned to the public stage.
Their second annual Mother's Day letter was a frank attempt to do
what governments are fond of saying they'd never do: talk to terrorists.
Marked "Attention: Abu Bakr al-Baghdadi," it stated baldly that their
children had been "tricked by those who only follow their own greed,
sin and lust for power."

When I asked Christianne whether she was frightened to speak so
directly to the ISIS leader, she gave a strangled laugh. "What are they
going to do to me?" she asked. "I've already lost my son."

Loss can isolate you, can make you build walls and barriers. But it
can also spur fearlessness, a willful disregard for man-made conventions and laws. It can give you the courage to challenge accepted codes,
to ignore propriety or convention in search of a larger truth, or a more
profound connection with others, even with those frequently cast as
the Other. It took an act as shattering as a son's death for these mothers
to find new ways to talk about and to terrorists—an index of just how
rigid and entrenched we've rendered the discourses of silence and security.

GRIEF MADE FIGEN MURRAY daring. On May 22, 2017, her son Martyn
Hett was killed, along with twenty-two others, in the Manchester
Arena attack. As I mentioned in the introduction, she forgave the suicide bomber on national television a month after Martyn's death. Five
feet tall, with a preternaturally direct manner, she has a slightly otherworldly mien.

The day we meet in Preston, a city in Lancashire, she is clothed entirely in black, her jet hair hanging down, bone straight. The inside of her wrist is covered with a tattoo of a bee—the symbol of the city of Manchester—and under it, the slogan: #BeMoreMartyn.

We meet the day Figen is due to speak to a counterterrorism graduate seminar at the University of Central Lancashire. She'd always been terrified of public speaking, she tells me, but since Martyn's death she's no longer nervous about it. "The worst that can happen, has happened," she explains. "So I've become rather fearless." She had been a counselor, but after the bombing, she had decided that her work lay in speaking out against hatred. The bomber "unleashed something in me that's growing bigger and bigger," she says. "It's really powerful, and it comes from being a mum. There is nothing I won't do to resist and defy this. I'm not scared. I'm thinking, 'No, I'm going to kick ass.'"

We're walking through a crowded shopping street on our way to the university when she stops short, bends down, and picks up something shiny on the sidewalk. Opening her palm, she reveals her treasure: an ordinary household screw. "Martyn's with me," she says.

The bomb that killed Martyn was homemade, packed with nuts, screws, and bolts. Standing directly behind the suicide bomber when it was detonated, Martyn was found with sixteen screws lodged in his body. Since his death, Figen has been finding screws everywhere she goes. At home in England, in her ancestral Turkey, in Prague, in Brussels, she's picked up screws. The day we met, her collection numbered one hundred and fifty. "They're always shiny." She beams. "Never, ever rusty. It's a little thing, picking them up, but for me it's important." As soon as the bombing inquest is over, the police have promised to give her the screws found in Martyn's body. She plans to have them melted down and made into a heart, a thing of beauty, and thus, she says, "a big 'up yours' to the terrorist."

She pockets the screw, her gray-green eyes shining, and we walk on.

FIGEN NEVER VIEWED HER son's murderer as a monster. From the first time she'd seen a screenshot of his face in a newspaper, she saw simply a "foolish boy." She'd learned early on in life how vulnerable young people can be drawn in by groups promising simple, prepackaged answers. She'd been groomed herself once, when she was sixteen.

Born in Turkey, Figen was raised in Germany, south of Frankfurt. Her alcoholic father verged on violence, one night even threatening to kill both Figen and her mother. As a teenager, she escaped the fear and loneliness she felt at home by working part time in a tea shop. The owners belonged to the Jehovah's Witness sect, which some consider a "high demand" group, dictating individual members' decisions. Her employers took a particular interest in the teenager. "They gave me hugs. Attention. Warmth. A friendly welcome. And safety, in a time when home felt so unsafe that I was terrified I would die." They invited her to join them at Bible study, then a Jehovah's Witness convention. "I was in a bad place, and they found me," she said. "Bit by bit, I got brainwashed."

Within a few months, they had convinced her that she should marry a forty-year-old man. One afternoon, she dropped by the tea shop to tell the owners she was quitting, and the couple refused to let her leave. "You're not of sound mind," the man said. "We need to keep you here for a few days." His wife showed her the spare room, telling Figen she could stay there while they looked after her. Suddenly the spell broke: "I thought, 'They're trying to force me, to lock me up. They can't be good people.'" Luckily, Figen's older sister was due to pick her up, and after a bit of shouting and threats of calling the police, the two young women escaped. A few days later, Figen went back to the tea shop, bringing with her several Bibles they'd given her. Setting the pile down on a table, she placed the engagement ring the man had given her on top.

The memory of that summer helped Figen forgive and to whittle down the image of the bomber from monstrous proportions: "I can't be cross with a little fish, although the little fish murdered my son." In the months following Martyn's death, she continued to sidestep hatred. "I don't see myself as a victim," she said, "because that's what the terrorists want."

That September Figen attended a conference on Women for Peace in Cheshire, England. Well known as the mother of a Manchester victim, she was ushered to her seat by a young woman assisting with the conference, who then sat beside her. A woman in hijab, pearls, and stilettos began her speech, telling how her son had joined ISIS and died fighting for them.

The young woman kept glancing at Figen, watching her reactions intently. *What the hell are you looking at?* Figen wondered.

At the end of Nicola Benyahia's speech, many in the audience were in tears. The woman sitting by Figen peered at her: "How do you feel?"

"I want to go up on stage and give her a massive hug," replied Figen.

She didn't rush up to the stage immediately, figuring people would think she was attacking the mother of a terrorist. Instead, she waited till the crowd around Nicola thinned, then approached her. Nicola stretched out her hand to shake it.

"I don't shake hands," Figen told her. "I do hugs now." And she gathered a slightly stunned Nicola into her arms. "She was a bit off with me," recalls Figen. "Not cold, just a bit off."

Nicola, for her part, recalls feeling stunned, even "shellshocked," by meeting, for the first time, someone related to a terrorist bombing victim. The encounter triggered "a little bit of me that sometimes doesn't go away, which is the guilt."

Despite the awkwardness, Figen tracked down Nicola's phone number and called within the week. "We were both bleeding inside as mothers who have lost sons," said Figen. "Both boys had been out there grabbing at life. Both boys ceased to exist because of one little act."

The two women began talking by phone, sharing their experiences as children of alcoholics, professional counselors, and grieving mothers. The friendship was transgressive, crossing the very lines that extremists—and many in Britain—want to draw. Both had spoken out publicly against the Us and Them rhetoric after terrorist attacks. Both had strangers popping up on social media, castigating them for speaking out. People bayed for a show of hatred from Figen and expected silent shame from Nicola. "Mother of Satan," some troll called Nicola. Another said he hoped her son died screaming for her, in pain.

A few months after they met, they agreed to appear together on a popular British current affairs show. Sitting on the morning show's set, with its requisite coziness—coffee cups, a blond interviewer tilting her head just so to listen—Figen and Nicola spoke about a shared experience. "We lost our sons to the same monster," said Figen. "It doesn't matter in which way—it's the same organization, the same ideals that both our sons died for."

"Are either of you angry?" asked the interviewer.

No, each woman responded, refusing to follow the script demanded by populists and militants.

Did they have a message for ISIS?

Nicola paused. "You're not going to silence me," she said. "It was actually a really risky thing I did, going public with this. But if I was silent, this was going to continue, they would keep instilling the same fear."

"They've killed the wrong mothers' children," agreed Figen. "They picked the wrong people to kill."

When Nicola later told me that the cameramen were crying after filming, I wasn't surprised. But what struck me was how radical it was to proclaim that their losses were linked. A terrorist wants to damage the status quo, but he also wants to rearrange alliances, to force people into camps created by mutual fear. Figen and Nicola refused to be confined to the categories created both by terrorists and by those who cast terrorists as entirely unconnected to "Us," save that they want our destruction.

Mourning women publicly transgressing the lines drawn during war is a theme as old as the Greeks. In *The Suppliants* by Euripides, mothers of two cities form an alliance in the cause of a larger civic right: to allow the mothers of the vanquished city of Argos to give their sons a proper burial. In *Antigone* by Sophocles, the heroine argues against King Creon for a proper burial for her rebel brother, and she is rendered a pariah.

Timeless, too, it seems, is the opprobrium that grieving women get when they challenge the accepted customs of conflict. When the British tabloid the *Daily Mail* wrote on Figen and Nicola's joint appearance, it headlined the article with Figen's quote about losing their sons to the same monster. "Except one was an innocent victim, and the other one was a murderous barbarian," responded one reader online. On Facebook, television viewers who saw the show rushed to defend the status quo—the lines chalked out both by violent extremists and by those who refuse to see any connection between extremism and the societies they live in. "The terrorist scrum [*sic*] deserved death how can you compare?" read one post. "No similarities whatsoever." Another viewer "felt sorrow for the mother of the lad murdered but nothing but contempt for the scumbag who died fighting for daesh [*sic*]."

Many readers saw Figen as the parent of a martyred innocent; many dismissed Nicola as just the mother of a terrorist. "It sat with me for a few days afterward and made me feel quite sad, the difference in the way we were viewed," Nicola said.

Both women have continued to speak out, lecturing at schools and conferences about their experiences. But Nicola can tell she makes institutions nervous; high schools want to vet her speeches before she gives them. "Figen's voice is instantly seen as that of a victim of terrorism and is instantly taken as credible," Nicola told me. "With my voice, people get a bit nervy about supporting me. It'll be 'Oh, this is a mother of an ISIS fighter.'" No matter how many times she tells her story, how plainly she lays out how she worked closely with the police and the counterterrorism officials, some still see her as complicit with terrorism. "Sometimes I wonder, just how much more do they want of me?" Nicola said. "How much more do they need me to share?"

Figen's son Martyn achieved folk hero status in his native Manchester, where crowds gathered to watch his coffin be pulled through the streets by white horses wearing plumes. But Nicola never had a body, a death certificate, or a funeral for Rasheed. "When I met with Figen, it did open my eyes on how many things I'd missed out on," she said. "How many things I'd pushed away and buried. How much I hadn't had." At the time, "I figured I just had to get through, and survive," she said. "But listening to her, I thought, 'Why should I have to have been so alone?'"

The stories of Nicola and Christianne suggest not only the complexities of radicalization but its fallout. Too often, the story we tell ourselves is about a single event: a bomb blast or a lost son. The mothers' stories shine a light not just on the nuances of radicalization but on the long tail of a terrorist act: how violence works to silence dissent, to build suspicion, and to spread through societies.

In the wake of 9/11, Western societies saw an increase in securitization. Coined by political scientists in Copenhagen, the term refers to how politicians, citing some existential threat to a nation's safety, link political decisions or populations to national security. In many countries in the West, the securitized reaction to terrorism rendered the everyday life of Muslims suspect. Police forces surveilled Muslims in mosques, malls, and immigrant neighborhoods. Beards, skullcaps, and hijabs were suddenly signs not of diversity but of danger. Clicking on the wrong website, or making the wrong comment in a high school classroom, could make a Muslim into a suspicious person. The isolation faced by Nicola and Christianne, as well as their initial reluctance to speak out, was nurtured by a culture of securitization. They resisted its attendant suspicion and fear by steadfastly sharing their stories, over and over, and by counseling other mothers, helping them to do the same. They told their stories, but as the reaction to Nicola's television appearance suggests, many people simply didn't want to listen.

THE GODMOTHER AND HER GODDAUGHTERS

IS UNDERSTANDING THE PATHS into and out of violent extremist groups simply a matter, then, of listening? Another mother, another story, would show me that it was much more than that. During our conversation in France, Christianne had mentioned a Belgian mother of a fighter in Syria who'd sent her son money for medical bills, which meant she ended up in prison for supporting terrorism. A few months on, I made contact with her and later took the train from London to Brussels to meet her.

We go to a café, the woman I'll call Charlotte and I, on a quiet street in Brussels. It's a neighborhood of gracious residential buildings of dark brick and gray stone, built in an era of confidence fueled by colonies overseas. Charlotte and I speak in French, then English, eat croissants, sip café crèmes, and vainly try to wave away cigarette smoke from the neighboring table. The setting couldn't be more European, but the conversation is a story of profound alienation from it. Like Christianne, Charlotte is well known in her own country. Shop assistants and waiters routinely ask her to wait a second, while they try to place her face. Blue-eyed and blond, she's in her late fifties, a big-boned, slightly blowsy woman. "All the time, they'll say, 'I know you,'" she tells me. "Then they'll be like—'I remember! I know! Syria! You're the mother on television!'"

There's a "tattoo" across her forehead, she says dryly: "I am a mother of a terrorist."

While researching this book, built as it is on other people's tragedies, I kept telling myself that I'd been respectful of their losses, even as I probed their wounds. As journalists, we often comfort ourselves with that palliative half truth about giving the voiceless a voice. It can be true, but not in the case of a woman like Charlotte, who has recited her story to various ranks of police, both Belgian and Turkish, to diplomats and security services, to judges, lawyers, prison wardens, a playwright, and the press. When I interview Charlotte, I'm not giving a hearing to the unheard. My questions make her cry several times every time we meet, and speaking publicly has already lost her three jobs. Once an accountant, she's now retraining to be a teacher. That a Muslim can be blond and native-born confounds some of her fellow Belgians. "When I say, 'I'm Charlotte, and I've been Muslim for over twenty years,' they jump back one meter," she explained. "Then when I tell them I live in Molenbeek"—a heavily Moroccan neighborhood in Brussels with well-publicized ISIS recruits—"they jump back three meters."

The radicalization of Charlotte's son, whom I'll call Kareem, was spurred by this sort of prejudice. If Nicola's son left for Syria largely due to his naïveté, and Christianne's son was spurred by personal anger, Charlotte's son was radicalized because of the broader difficulties of being brown, Muslim, and European. Kareem left for Syria when he was eighteen, mostly because he was unable to see a future for someone with his skin color and surname. He spoke French, Dutch, English, and Arabic, but still he couldn't seem to find a job. Neither his father's Morocco nor his mother's Belgium felt like home. "Where am I going to work?" he'd ask Charlotte. "Where can I make my home?"

He became obsessed with the struggle of the Palestinians, but when his parents spoke against his going to Gaza, he turned his attentions to the civil war in Syria. Bashar al-Assad was murdering and imprisoning his own people, he told Charlotte. Even the Belgian government condemned the Syrian leader. Though he'd not been particularly diligent about his prayers or fasting during Ramadan, Kareem now argued with his father about the meaning of being a good Muslim. For him, it meant going to Syria to help fellow Muslims in peril, whether they agreed or not.

Charlotte and her husband begged him to talk to returnees from the conflict, or to the imam. But Kareem scoffed at the imams at Belgium's big mosques, saying they were soft and weak, "like Care Bears."

Knowing Kareem was going to try to leave, Charlotte and her husband went to the police station to tell the authorities of his plans. The officer assured her that he'd put a note on Kareem's file, so he'd be put on a no-fly list. He wouldn't be allowed out of the country. In fact, he was. On January 22, 2014, Charlotte got a call from an unknown number, with a man informing her that Kareem was in Turkey, heading for Syria. She hung up and immediately dialed the police inspector to tell him. That's impossible, he said.

It wasn't. Because Kareem was a few months past his eighteenth birthday, he was no longer a minor, and so he hadn't been stopped. To this day, Charlotte blames the authorities for his departure. "I did my job," she said. "But the Belgian security services didn't do theirs."

When she reached Kareem by phone, he assured her that he was in Syria to help Muslims. Besides, he told her, if he died, the doors of Paradise would open for her.

She made him promise not to become a "kamikaze," a suicide bomber.

"I'm not crazy, Mom," he reassured her. "I won't give them the chance to make me do that." A true Muslim would never do such a thing, he said, and he was a true Muslim.

Later, when Kareem was wounded, Charlotte sent him €1,000 to cover medical care and living expenses. She entrusted the funds to a young French woman, a friend of Kareem's who was leaving Europe for Syria, and who had plans to marry him there. Charlotte tried to dissuade her from going, but when she couldn't, she gave her the money. "My son didn't have money, and was wounded in a war zone," she later explained. He might have starved to death or been bombed. She saved him from starving; when he did die, in February 2015, it was in combat, during the U.S. attack on ISIS at the Deir Ezzor airport.

The money Charlotte sent to Kareem landed her in jail. The year after her son's death, Belgian authorities charged her with financing terrorism. Because she gave the cash to the French woman to take to Syria, she was also charged with terrorist recruitment. Police came to her house at five A.M. one day and took a mug shot and her fingerprints, then carted her to a jail cell and detained her "as a very big terrorist in a very small room," she said.

The judge agreed to her release after a day, but the indignity of the arrest still rankles, particularly whenever she sees Kareem's recruiter walking freely around in her neighborhood. "He is living, he is eating," she says bitterly. She's reported the recruiter's whereabouts to the police twice, but they say there's not enough evidence to convict him.

For a time, she drew strength by being active in a Molenbeek group for families of people who had gone to Syria. It was called Les Parents Concernés, but mothers were the primary advocates for their lost children—only one father ever joined. "The fathers want to forget, because it's so shameful for them," says Charlotte.

It was a story I heard again and again in my travels. Women tend to be better social networkers about family issues, but Charlotte has another theory. Recruiters and militant commanders actively try to break young people's bonds with their fathers, telling them that it is their father's fault that they weren't raised as proper Muslims, she says. "But ISIS knows that it's hard to break the tie with the mother. They know that it says in the Quran that 'paradise lies under the feet of the mother.'"

Kareem was buried by the Deir Ezzor airport, near where he was shot. Charlotte couldn't travel there and was pretty sure there wouldn't be a grave there to see in any case. To get as close as she could, she traveled with two other mothers of dead Belgian fighters to Kilis, the Turkish city on the Syrian border. "I wanted to walk the same streets he did," said Charlotte. Without a body, funeral, or gravesite, it was a comfort for her to pray where Kareem had prayed, in a blue mosque at the top of the hill, high enough that she felt she could just make out Aleppo in the distance. "It was one moment I can have with him," she said. "Not at the same time, but at the same place."

That peace quickly shattered: while she was taking photographs from the hilltop, snapping images of Syria, the Turkish police arrived. Once again she was arrested. Hauled to the police station with the other mothers, their phones taken, they were charged with suspicion of espionage. "They thought we were spies, like James Bond," she said. Interrogated for half a day, the women were set to go to prison, until the Belgian ambassador intervened. It was absurd, said Charlotte. "I was like, 'You let ten thousand young people pass over the border, and you take all this time over three mothers?' "

Charlotte had brought a bag of Kareem's clothes to Kilis, hoping to distribute them to Syrian refugees fleeing to Turkey. At the border gates, she met one woman, a former teacher, who had just escaped the war with her son. Charlotte approached her, telling her that since Kareem had originally gone to Syria to help Syrians, she hoped maybe his shoes and clothes might help.

The woman was pregnant and promised to name the child after Kareem. "My son will continue to wear your son's clothes," the woman told Charlotte. "And your son will continue to live within my son."

Charlotte's visit to the border was a series of challenges to the tidy falsehoods of borders, of singular identities, of West and East, of Them and Us. A blond woman standing, scarf on her head, by a mosque, looking over the border into Syria, toward where her son had died. The police arriving, hustling her down off the hill. The frantic calls and pleas on the phone. And finally, the sad symmetry of handing the soccer shirts and shoes to the refugee mother, a woman running away from the war Kareem had run toward.

Stripped down, the story had the structure of a lesson from a holy book: loss, punishment, and grace. In the eyes of the law, she was a traitor. She'd supported her son, who'd fought with the enemy. His death had brought her to a Turkish hillside, with a clear view across the border into Syria. Charlotte had broken from Us, sending love and resources to Them.

It was an unusual vantage point, for a blond Belgian woman born a Catholic. But the Belgian police clearly recognized its value when they approached her to see whether she might be willing to work with youth returning from the Islamic State. She'd understood, as well as anybody could, what sadnesses had made her son leave for Syria; perhaps she could help smooth the way for several young women who wanted to return from it. Most had been imprisoned, immediately upon their return, for joining a terrorist organization, but those sentences were brief. Belgian security forces knew the period after prison would be fraught for these young women. How would they be rehabilitated? Could they reintegrate into mainstream society?

So began Charlotte's mentorship of four young recruits, relationships that grew so close that she took to calling the young women her "godchildren."

They were young, these "godchildren." Three of the girls that the Brussels authorities had asked her to mentor were literally children, in juvenile detention. One had left for Syria at thirteen and a year later had returned to Belgium with a baby. One young woman wanted to leave for Syria to help children there and to have one of her own, a child to help build the Islamic State. Gently, Charlotte tried to anchor the fantasy with a bit of realism. "Okay, you want to be a mother," she told her. "You make a child in a war zone. Bombings all around. What kind of mother would you be, to offer that kind of life to a child?"

When Charlotte met with her charges, she didn't lecture them about Islam or politics but kept the conversations personal. "My son died," she explained. "So they have a lot of respect for me."

Like her son, these girls had left Europe believing that racism made it impossible to live a good life there as a Muslim. That's what the ISIS recruiters had told them, anyway. Pointing to her own life as a Muslim convert, an accountant, a Belgian, Charlotte tried to argue that being Belgian and Muslim weren't contradictory, but were in fact the essence of contemporary Europe and their own birthrights. "Your parents came here in the sixties and helped to build the new Belgium. So it's *your* Belgium. You were born here, only with a brown face."

"It's a racist country," the girls insisted.

"With your name, your skin, it's not easy," Charlotte would concede. "But in fact, you have more value, because you have *two* cultures! You've got to prove to them your name is an advantage. A plus, even!"

She said that to them. But deep down, she saw their point.

Watching the hurdles one goddaughter faced reintegrating, she would grow to share their alienation even more deeply.

———

CHARLOTTE IS SO BUSY, and the arrangements to introduce a journalist to an Islamic State returnee are so delicate, that it takes months to set up a meeting with her and one of her goddaughters. The date we finally choose is a cold and gray December day, just before Christmas. We meet for Sunday brunch in a storefront café in Molenbeek. I know nothing about the goddaughter, a former ISIS recruit I'll call Lucie, except that she and her mother were up at six in the morning to catch the train to Brussels. It's the first time Lucie's probation rules have allowed her to visit the city since she left prison a year ago. She agreed to tell me her story, asking that I not use her real name, or those of her mother and daughter.

Lucie is in her late twenties, with thick dark brows, black-framed glasses set on a strong nose, and a forest-green head wrap matching her sweater. A convert to Islam, she'd gone to Syria with a friend and her five-year-old daughter, Aisha. When I asked her why she joined up, Lucie tells me it was for much the same reason that many new Muslims did: ignorance of what Islam asked of her. In her Brussels neighborhood, the only books in local Islamic bookshops were Salafi or Saudi-style Wahhabi interpretations, notoriously strict and severe. So when she decided she wanted to deepen her understanding of the religion, and she heard about the uncompromising approach trumpeted by the Islamic State propaganda, she figured it was the proper way to practice Islam. She felt an obligation to do *hijra*—emigrate to a Muslim country—and craved "the feeling of being useful."

Lucie and Aisha lasted less than three months in Syria. What Lucie saw in the Islamic State, she said, "wasn't the faith I had chosen at all." She escaped to Turkey, where she and Aisha spent a month in prison before the Turks handed them back to the Belgians. A Belgian judge sent Aisha to live with her father and deemed Lucie a threat.

Lucie's mother Pauline says the fact that her daughter was a white convert to Islam hurt Lucie in court, that it was tougher on her than it would have been had she had an immigrant background. "If you compare her to other girls, lots of them have parents who aren't Belgian," recalls Pauline, solid, deep-voiced, with short-cropped silver-blond hair. "They don't speak French very well, and can't explain things as well as Lucie could. If you can speak, explain things, then you must be dangerous—"

"In the judgment, they said, 'You're too intelligent to be a victim of radicalization,'" Lucie breaks in, "'so you must be a danger.'"

"You need to play a role," suggests Charlotte. "Show them you're not that bright."

"Yeah, maybe I need to act crazy in court," laughs Lucie. "Like have some beef soup or something, dribbling out of the corner of my mouth, so they don't think I'm dangerous."

I was unconvinced by Pauline's assertion that Lucie was disadvantaged by her status as a white woman. We were sitting, after all, in a country whose nineteenth-century violent plunder of the Congo was excessive even by the standards of European imperialism. An imperial superiority lingers in laws and traditions even today. Muslim women are banned from wearing face veils, and the town of Ath still holds a parade featuring "the savage"—a white man in blackface, chains, and a nose ring. As attuned to institutional Islamophobia as she was, even Pauline occasionally lapsed into a slightly xenophobic tone. She tutted to me over how she didn't recognize the city of her birth: "When I come to Brussels, I say, 'I'm going to Marrakesh,'" she says, shaking her head sadly. "Most Belgians have moved away. It's too much." She could never live there now. "It simply feels too foreign."

AND YET BOTH MOTHER and daughter were committed to telling their story as one shaped by victimhood. Mons prison had no deradicalization program; indeed, both Lucie and Pauline suspected that the prison made a concerted effort to stoke her feelings of anger and isolation. "There you couldn't be a Muslim," insists Pauline. "They were trying to make her a Catholic."

As a Muslim, Lucie didn't eat pork, so she'd choose the vegetarian option for meals. But pork would suddenly appear in her rice. "You're in Belgium," one guard told her. "Eat Belgian food." The guards tapped ashes from their cigarettes onto her prayer mat, or dropped her Quran onto the floor. A hijab was against the prison uniform code, but Lucie still tried to dress modestly, wearing long sleeves. The wardens would come by and needle her, asking "Oh, aren't you hot, in all those clothes?" (Asked later about these incidents, the Belgian prison service said it couldn't comment, as it didn't have details on such an old case.)

After the 2016 terrorist attack in Nice, when a man drove a truck into a crowd on Bastille Day, Lucie's life inside prison grew worse. "You happy now?" her fellow inmates asked. "Are you going to get a truck when you get out of here? Are you going to plant a bomb?"

It happens every time after an attack in the West, says Charlotte. "When there is a bombing, people become more racist."

To cheer her daughter up, Pauline had a joke T-shirt made for her, embossed with a decal of a bomb on the front and the slogan I AM A BOMB.

"They kept pushing and pushing me," Lucie says. "So after a while, it was almost like, 'You want a radical? I'll show you a radical.' I held on, but I was about two days away from breaking." Her faith steadied her, though: "I was afraid of God," she says. "If I hadn't been, I'd probably have done something to someone."

It was in prison that she discovered Sufism and began reading the works of Sheikh Hamdi Ben Aissa, a spiritual leader whose work counsels peace and warns against the dangers of anger. "When I found his teachings, I was like, 'Oh, yeah! Is this Islam?'" says Lucie. "This is what I was looking for!"

Pauline was raised Catholic but doesn't practice now. Before Lucie's incarceration, she had no time for religion of any kind, least of all Islam. She hadn't understood Lucie's conversion, or her daughter's need to embrace what Pauline saw as a foreign faith. But seeing how Islam helped Lucie through prison and the loss of custody of her daughter Aisha, changed her mind. "I couldn't understand why religion was so important," Pauline said. "Now I know. If she hadn't had a religion while she was in jail, it would have been catastrophic."

Pauline's loyalty to Lucie has cost her a son. Lucie's older half brother Sebastian is in the Belgian military. After her departure for Syria, Sebastian's commander called him in to see whether he, too, harbored sympathy for the Islamic State. Sebastian asked his mother to cut off ties with Lucie, since it was causing him trouble at work. Pauline refused point-blank. Sad that she no longer sees Sebastian, she is also angry that the military effectively divided her family. "Those people are dangerous," she mutters. "They think all Muslims are bad or dangerous. But it's really those [military officers] who are dangerous, because they don't want to hear what other people have to say."

WE'RE ORDERING *SHAKSHUKA—* **A SPICY** Maghrebi egg dish—when all at once, in a smooth, near-synchronized motion, the women whip their phones off the table and slide them between their backs and the seats of the booth we're sitting in, to muffle the microphones. They're being constantly monitored, they believe, their social media is being read, and their phones are tapped. "See?" says Charlotte, retrieving her phone and showing me that someone—she knows not who—is listed as remotely "connected" to it. "With ordinary numbers, I can just unconnect by pressing . . . here. Not with whoever's listening now."

Charlotte shakes her head. "You know, I was in the police station the other day," she tells Pauline, "and they're asking me all these questions, and I could see, on their screen, that they had the answers, there on their screen. They know everything."

"They can't use it in court, though," Pauline explains. "They have to try to get you to say it."

"Hey, let's take a selfie for them, post it on Facebook," Charlotte suggests, raising her phone defiantly.

"Coo-coo!" someone giggles. We grin for the camera, as Charlotte snaps us at the table.

The surveillance is just one way Lucie still feels she is treated as a traitor by the state, even though she is out of prison. An official tore up her national identity card, she says, making it impossible for her to open a bank account or receive unemployment benefits. She is shadowed by security agents, she believes, even when she goes to the movies. One slid into a seat two down from her in a near-empty movie theater, right after the lights went down.

Lucie enrolled in a secretarial school, but she wasn't allowed to wear her hijab. She wore a headband instead, and when her female classmates found out about the restriction, they joined her, donning headbands in solidarity. Her schoolmates were wary at first but soon warmed, shocked at how "normal" she seemed. Lucie says her probation officer tells her that she's an exemplary example of a jihadi's rehabilitation into society.

And yet she still can't live with her daughter Aisha, who since her return from Syria has lived with her father in Brussels. That's really all she wants now, she tells me: to be back together with her daughter. On her phone, she shows me a picture of herself with a smiling ten-year-old, on one of the ninety-minute visits she's allowed every month.

Pauline and her husband haven't seen the girl for four years. "We have been treated as terrorists," says Pauline, her voice breaking. "They said it in court: 'You're a family of terrorists.'" She is weeping now. "The judge knows Aisha wants to see us again, but still, she says it's too soon. It's a tragedy for us, but for her, too."

Every time they see the judge, he tells them, "Not yet, not yet." "They're supposed to give a reason," says Lucie, "but they haven't. What I'm worried about is that when she's older, when she understands why she's not been allowed to see us, that she'll—"

"Get angry at the state?" I interject. "Get radicalized?"

Lucie nods. "You've got to think long term about these things."

Pauline no longer feels loyal to Belgium. Though voting is mandatory for Belgian citizens, she's so disgusted by how she and Lucie have been treated that she won't be casting a ballot in the upcoming elections. "That's finished for me," she growls.

Pauline's youngest daughter, Laura, angered at how the authorities have treated her family, has made plans to move to Africa. Pauline and her husband are thinking of moving to France or Portugal. She's not much bothered where. "I have only one wish," she says. "To get out of Belgium. This isn't my country anymore."

"And you?" I ask Charlotte, recalling her speeches to her goddaughters about how it's possible to live a happy life as a Belgian Muslim woman. "Do you ever feel the same way?"

"All the time, I'm feeling more and more Muslim," she answers. "More and more Moroccan than Belgian."

"Me also." Pauline nods. "Just the same."

So this, I thought, *is how a young person's departure spreads ripples of alienation.* Where once it was just Lucie who didn't feel at home in Belgium, now it was her family, too. This alienation has even spread to her "godmother" Charlotte, a woman the security services chose to help show young returnees that it is possible to be both Muslim and Belgian.

ON RETURNING HOME TO England, in the interest of journalistic due diligence, I research news stories about Lucie and find that she left out chunks of the narrative. According to reports in the Belgian press, she didn't go to Syria merely to "feel useful" or because she felt it was her Islamic duty to emigrate to a Muslim state. Rather, she left in response to a Facebook post that had been placed by Yassine Lachouri, an Islamic State fighter who was looking for a European wife. Unknown to Lucie, Lachouri was a former drug dealer, a convicted murderer, and a known associate of the mastermind of the November 2015 attacks in Paris.

Moreover, the press reported, after Lucie was released from Mons prison, she was charged again, this time for absconding with her daughter without the father's permission. ("He'd given me her passport!" Lucie had told me over breakfast, Pauline nodding beside her. "He signed a paper, allowing my daughter to go!") She was tried for a second time. Aisha's father told the court that though the girl's mental state was improving, she still talked about Kalashnikovs at school. Lucie had "plunged her daughter into a hell she should never have known," said the prosecutor at the trial. "Contrary to what she wants us to believe, she was a fierce supporter of the Islamic State."

Lucie was acquitted in this second trial, but the press reports evoked a more complex story than the one I'd heard at brunch. If grief gave these mothers a special lens, training the eye away from some details and toward others, my commitment to empathy had done the same. I felt like a bit of a chump. It was dispiriting, having to shift from seeing her as an innocent abroad and a victim at home to someone rather more complex. I'd listened, sure, but listening had its pitfalls.

Not long afterward, I read something the Israeli author Amos Oz wrote about growing up in Jerusalem in the 1940s, in the final years of the British Mandate over Palestine. He'd been "a little Zionist-nationalist fanatic—self-righteous, enthusiastic and brain-washed," he wrote, hurling stones and shouting "British, go home!" at patrolling army cars. But then he befriended a British policeman, an act that led the other children to label Oz a traitor. "Much later, I learned to take comfort in the thought that, for fanatics, a traitor is anyone who dared to change," he wrote. "Fanatics of all kinds, in all places at all times, loathe and fear change, suspecting that it is nothing less than a betrayal resulting from dark, base motives."

I'm no fanatic. But that feeling of mild betrayal, upon reading the news stories about Lucie, alerted me to the dangers of my own desire to believe in her. I'm no fanatic, but my need to believe in a simple, single story contained a hint of fanaticism. I'd used brunch and shared identities—as white Westerners, as mothers, as daughters—to create rickety bridges toward understanding. But in so doing, I'd expanded my ability to understand extremists only slightly. Since it hinged on issues of identity, I'd merely created my own liberal version of Us and Them. It would take real vigilance for me to fight that sort of polarization.

I HAD STARTED WITH mothers for reasons both reasonable and biased; but Charlotte's work with the Belgian government in reintegrating fighters made it clear that the mothers were not alone. Governments were also invested in dealing with these returning men and women. Were there governmental or civil society programs that, like the mothers I'd met, operated from faith in people's ability to change for the better?

PART II
CHANGE
MAKERS

TRUST EXERCISES

IT WAS, I'M HALF-ASHAMED to admit, a fun day. The Security and Counter Terror Expo wasn't sold as fun, of course. London's annual showcase for the business of fighting terrorists drew a crowd of blue-suited executives, swaggering special forces types, police officers, and government mandarins. Even before stepping into the exhibition hall, I could feel the event's vibe: a tense hum, oscillating between fear and control. You heard both emotions in the show's macho motto—"Protect. Prevent. Prepare." You saw them, too, in the looming sign greeting visitors to London's Olympia exhibition space: a photo of worried-looking white men in a briefing room, staring at something. We don't know what that something is, but one man is so nervous at the sight that he's jammed two fingers into his mouth, gnawing away.

Inside, some 350 vendors waited to stoke, then soothe, your fears. Salesmen for ballistics-proof shutters, concertina wire, and "mob-attack-tested" fences stood behind their wares. Men with buzz cuts watched rapt as remote-controlled robots disarmed fake bombs. I loitered at the stand selling "street furniture"—a marketer's attempt to create cozy connotations for the concrete planters and barriers built to stop terrorist attacks. Three Russian businessmen gazed at a demonstration of a Technicolor orange drone that buzzed over our heads like a steroid-pumped soldier beetle. Just down the aisle were stalls selling computer systems to protect people from drones. When terrorist groups like ISIS began loading bombs onto drones, it opened a whole new security frontier, the man selling something called DroneProtect told me, smiling.

It's a neat business model: an arms race to safety. The drone salesmen and the counterdrone salesmen, like the nearby stallholders hawking "The Security of Security," had tapped into a growth industry, powered by a never-ending spiral of need for new ways to stay ahead of terrorists. All the vendors, whether they were peddling drones, holsters, or styrofoam coffee cups with built-in surveillance cameras, were selling one product: safety, at all costs. One company's stall bore a sign reading ANYWHERE CAN BE THE NEXT SOMEWHERE.

All this stood in stark contrast to the rehabilitation efforts that Christianne, Nicola, and Daniel Koehler had described. The Security and Counter Terror Expo stalls touted enemies that were so scary and monstrous as to be invisible. Having now talked to four mothers of these purported monsters, I wanted to look at people and programs who worked with terrorists to change their minds. Was that possible? If so, how? And at what cost?

In an age when extremists are gaining followers around the world, using conspiracies and falsehoods to draw followers into their worldviews, the question of persuasion becomes vital. Whether extremists are sealed into their groups by interpretations of religious texts, or by anonymous conspiracies that defy rebuttal, or by real-world grievances, their convictions can seem implacable. These beliefs may be secondary to their radicalization; as I'd already seen, the embrace of ideology sometimes came after, not before, deeper and more personal motivations—which made logical argument even more pointless. If reason failed in the battle against extremists, perhaps these drones and walls and bomb-defusing robots might succeed? An endless stockpiling of gadgetry, to use on a low-level war against small and scattered armies, some made up of our neighbors, even family members?

———

SIMON CORNWALL IS NOT the type of guy I'd imagined would be calling for befriending terrorist offenders. Ruddy-faced, with a bullet-shaped head and a bluff manner, he's an ex-military man who served in Northern Ireland and the Falklands. When we meet at a near-empty café in North London, a couple of days after New Year 2020, he's headed out to Iraq. And yet when I ask him about the best ways to treat former violent extremists, he sounds uncannily like Christianne and Nicola. To prevent them from offending again, he says, "what you have to do is have a relationship with them, and you have to care about them." He smiles ruefully. "My partner says I sound a bit hippieish on this subject—but I'm the furthest thing from a hippie that there is." After the army, Cornwall went into the UK probation services, setting up its counterextremism program, then working for the national counterterrorism program Prevent. He's now an international consultant, helping governments and NGOs from Norway to Kazakhstan create strategies for terrorist rehabilitation.

We're meeting about a month after a terrorist attack in London killed two people and sparked public debate on the effectiveness of deradicalization programs. On November 29, 2019, a Cambridge University prisoner rehabilitation program held a conference in London. Among the participants was Usman Khan, a British man convicted as a member of an Al Qaeda–inspired group who had plotted to bomb the London Stock Exchange and other targets in London. Sentenced to sixteen years in prison, he served just half of that after an appeal. On the day of the conference, wearing a fake suicide vest and smuggling kitchen knives into the venue, he stabbed and killed two of the conference organizers and wounded three others. He fled across London Bridge and was shot and killed by police.

Campaigning politicians seized on the tragedy, which occurred ten days before Britain's national election. The conservative Tory party championed the "lock 'em up" strategy, and Prime Minister Boris Johnson called for longer prison sentences for dangerous criminals and terrorists. His Labour opponent blamed Tory cuts to prisons and probation services and pointed to the war in Iraq as a root cause of radicalization. It remained a bitter irony that the attack had happened at a conference on prisoner rehabilitation, by a purportedly rehabilitated former prisoner. While an inmate, Khan had participated in two government deradicalization programs. One had encouraged violent extremists to examine their identities, beliefs, and relationships, probing what led them to join militant groups. The second had offered theological and psychological mentoring.

Clearly, neither had worked—a fact pointed to by those skeptical about rehabilitation programs. When it came to deradicalization, Johnson observed, "the instances of success are really very few." *The Times* ran a stark headline: LONDON BRIDGE ATTACK: POSTER BOY FOR REHABILITATION. AND KILLER. But Dave Merritt, the father of Jack Merritt, one of Khan's victims, who had worked for the prisoner rehabilitation charity, wrote in an op-ed that his twenty-five-year-old son would have been "seething at his death, and his life, being used to perpetuate an agenda of hate that he gave his everything fighting against." Jack had fought for "a world where we do not lock up and throw away the key . . . where we focus on rehabilitation not revenge."

I applauded the sentiment but knew the incident was a blow for champions of rehabilitation. Usman Khan had proven to the British public that deradicalization programs weren't foolproof. But nor were the "certainties" of lock-and-key severity. Indeed, prisons—full of traumatized individuals, many looking for identity and belonging—can create "near-perfect" conditions for radicalization, as a 2010 report from the International Centre for the Study of Radicalisation and Political Violence suggested. "Many prison services seem to believe that the imperatives of security and reform are incompatible," it said. "In many cases, however, demands for security and reform are more likely to complement than contradict each other."

Increasingly, I was becoming convinced that investments in reform were actually investments in security. While not as shiny or sexy as drones and robots, they were safer in the long term.

SIMON CORNWALL CERTAINLY EMBRACES this view. He has the CV of a hard-liner but champions solutions that hard-liners dismiss as naïve.

After he set up Britain's central extremism unit in 2008 to work with convicted terrorists on their release from prison, he inaugurated a mentor system, where probation officers would meet with their charges. Much as with pedophiles, with whom he'd worked earlier in his career, the aim was to "befriend them, talk to them, learn their patterns and behavior, and understand where their risks and triggers are," he tells me. The local community was brought in, too, with neighborhood mentors working alongside probation officers to help reintegrate the offender. The process broadened the offender's network: probation helped them find a job, counseling, or education; the police handled security; and a community group—like a soccer team, a mosque, or a youth center—provided opportunities for making new friends. "If you can get them to invest in the community, and the community to invest in them, they're less likely to do bad things," Cornwall says. He likens it to squatters doing damage to property. If a squatter is just passing through, "he doesn't mind kicking holes in the walls of an apartment," he says. "If it's my house, I'm not going to kick a hole in the wall. In fact, I'm going to paint it."

Over the years, though, Cornwall has been dismayed to see the emphasis shift from rehabilitating people to rendering them security risks. Parole work grew to be more about technology and tracking than about talking. He believes the London Bridge attack showed up the limits of what he calls the "tick-box" approach. Assessed as being the "highest level of risk" on release from prison, Usman Khan had been under surveillance by the UK's domestic intelligence agency MI5. Living in a flat in Stafford, he'd been allowed to travel the one hundred fifty miles alone to London on the day of the conference. He was wearing a GPS police tracker on his ankle, but while the gadget could tell police where he'd been, it didn't tell them his state of mind.

For the government to know an offender's mindset, says Cornwall, it's important to keep talking, and listening, week after week, in a manner that can sometimes seem downright parental. As a probation officer, he gets calls from terrorist offenders he hasn't seen for six or seven years. One called him recently, looking for reassurance. His mates from his extremist days had wanted to chat, and he was worried about being pulled back into the gang again. "Quite often these guys have no father figures or structure in their lives, and we can help put it there, and give them some care," Cornwall says. "Good old-fashioned probation methods."

Cornwall's approach sounds simple and humane. It calls for a long-term commitment, patience, and some sort of buy-in from the wider community. For police, whose remit is security, a terrorist will always be seen as high risk. To a probation officer, who may have helped a former terrorist get a job and settle into a community, there is always the chance of change. A probation officer's time frame is different from that of the security services. "Their idea of security is there," Cornwall says, pointing to a single spot in the middle of his palm. "Someone's locked up, and so it's safe. But I'm going, 'Is it safe all the way down there, and there and there?'" He stretches out his arm to suggest an indeterminate point in the future.

"So it's about long-term investment in someone, and betting on their ability to change," I say, thinking of the mothers of ISIS soldiers with their baby pictures.

He pauses. "But it's not what the media want to see around terrorism. They don't want to see someone caring about someone, or looking after them, or holding their hand, or saying, 'He's made a really bad decision; let's try to help him make some good ones.'"

Cornwall's been trolled on social media after his TV and press appearances. "Friends of mine have even said, 'What the hell are you doing? You're apologizing for terrorists,'" he says. "But I tell them, 'Someone has to befriend them.'"

IN MY RESEARCH ABOUT how people are trying to tackle extremism, I find that thousands of people across Asia, the Middle East, Africa, and Europe are working to keep talking with violent extremists. Governments are sinking huge resources into rehabilitating former extremists rather than simply fighting, jailing, or exiling them. The breadth of approaches is bewildering, reminding me of Chekhov's line that "if many remedies are prescribed for an illness, you may be certain that the illness has no cure."

But remedies do proliferate. Around the world, imams, psychologists, and social workers have been dispatched to talk with violent extremists or those in danger of becoming them. Therapists work with terrorist suspects and radicalized youth to tunnel into their pasts, observe their presents, and map out their futures. In Britain, former violent extremists learn to box and play soccer. In a German prison, jihadist and neo-Nazi inmates put on plays and dance. A Somalian program offers classes in history and tailoring, auto maintenance and welding. A Danish youth worker solemnly detailed the activities he organized to keep local youth from flirting with extremism: group weekends for fantasy role-play games in old castles, and a contest involving hurling frozen chickens across the floor of a community center. (I stifled a giggle.) Saudi Arabia's terrorist inmates get painting lessons. A Parisian working with French "formers," as ex-extremists are known, employed a technique she called "Proust's Madeleine"— a childhood memory drawing the terrorist back to who they were before they became one. An Indonesian prison tried to reconnect extremists with mainstream cultural values by staging a show with the country's traditional shadow puppets.

Since so many of these programs bear the imprint of their national or regional cultures, I wondered what an American deradicalization program might look like. At first, I couldn't find any—in part because the United States has had far fewer convicted terrorists than did Muslim-majority countries or even European countries like France and Germany. The U.S. approach to countering violent extremism, experts estimate, lags around twenty years behind that of western Europe. Europe—particularly countries with decades of right-wing extremism and neo-Nazi movements—has had more experience with helping people leave groups behind and has poured resources into preventing people from joining them in the first place. In Austria, France, and Germany, parents concerned about radicalization can call toll-free lines for help. Britain's counterterrorism strategy Prevent has funded freelance mentors for at-risk youth, and drama classes teach grade-school students to think critically about extremist propaganda.

In the United States, the trauma of 9/11 has had the opposite effect: the country chilled funding for creative solutions and embraced securitization. European parents and counselors can set up grassroots efforts, but Americans who don't go straight to law enforcement may be charged with terrorist conspiracy. One rehabilitation practitioner noted that U.S. laws on lending "material support" to foreign terrorist groups could technically even extend to her. "If you're in an off-ramp situation, and you're not someone's attorney, how do you not get charged with lending material support?" she asked.

Framing American Muslims as security risks has stoked toxic mutual suspicion between Muslim communities and the authorities. In 2015 Adam Shafi, a Bay Area twenty-two-year-old, was arrested for trying to support a terrorist organization. He'd become a target of an FBI investigation after a 2014 family vacation in Egypt. One day in Cairo when Adam went missing, his father Sal, a Silicon Valley executive, reported it to the U.S. embassy. A few days later the youth returned, having gone to Turkey to witness the situation of Syrian refugees there.

Back home in California, Sal cooperated with the FBI, meeting with agents and discussing his efforts to help find his son counseling for depression. Unbeknownst to him, the FBI had also had Adam under surveillance, trailing him and tapping his phone calls.

In June 2015 at the San Francisco International Airport, as Adam was boarding a flight to Istanbul, agents stopped him. They allowed him to go back home, but a few days later, came to his house, put him in handcuffs, and arrested him for having "attempted to provide material support to a designated foreign terrorist organization," according to the criminal complaint. The "material support" was Adam himself, who'd told friends by phone about his love for Jaulani, the leader of Jabhat al-Nusra, a Syrian group designated as terrorist by the U.S. State Department, and his willingness to "die with [the group], whatever kills us." Before that, though, he wanted to fight: "I just hope Allah doesn't take my soul until I have at least, like, a couple gallons of blood that I've spilled," Adam said. "How can I meet Allah when my face has no scars on it?"

Realizing that Adam could face twenty years in prison, Sal tried to cobble together a deradicalization program, proposing a team of counselors, an imam, and psychiatrists to work with his son. He attended a Washington, D.C., conference on radicalization, where he met Daniel Koehler, the German deradicalization expert, who agreed to take his case. The Shafis' lawyers were hopeful that law enforcement might agree to a rehabilitation program in lieu of prison, they told *The New York Times* in 2016. But then came the terrorist attacks in Paris and San Bernardino, and their hopes of a rehabilitation program faded.

Shafi's advice to other parents worried that their children might be becoming radicalized suggests some of the weaknesses of a heavily securitized approach: "Don't even think about going to the government."

Adam ended up waiting in prison for his trial for forty months, before a jury acquitted him in 2018. Prosecutors indicted him again, on charges of cashing a fraudulent check to fund travel to join a terrorist organization, but a federal judge disagreed, giving Adam credit for time served, five years probation, and six months of house arrest.

In the eyes of the Department of Justice, Adam Shafi was a terrorist not because he actually fought, or bombed, or killed, but because he planned a trip to Syria to join a terrorist organization. When a government starts locking up young men for boasting to their friends on the phone and buying airline tickets to the Middle East, one must wonder whether it has begun to think from an ideological framework, allowing security to trump a nation's other principles. The logic of securitization renders everyday activities suspect, and can make suspects of ordinary citizens.

A EUROPEAN COUNTERTERRORISM OFFICIAL once told me a story about attending a conference on how to handle returning ISIS fighters. His group of experts consisted of Danes, Kenyans, and an American. While the Danes and Kenyans were comparing notes on how they'd help formers find new jobs and community support, the American stood up and walked out. The United States would simply lock up anyone who'd fought with ISIS, he explained, so the exercise just wasn't worth his time. "We know how to find and finish targets in the terror world; we're really good at that," Frances Fragos Townsend, a former Homeland Security adviser and national security adviser for combating terrorism, observed in 2011. On softer efforts like rehabilitation and deradicalization, she conceded, not so much.

The relative lack of interest in terrorist rehabilitation reflects American penal culture more generally. We're the world's busiest jailer, with just 5 percent of the world's population but a quarter of its prison population. Over the past forty years, American society has become "distinctly more punitive," writes Joseph Margulies, professor of law at Cornell University, with "the angry impulse over the past several decades to purge the community of undesirable elements by dramatically increasing the government's power to monitor, exclude, restrain and imprison those considered a threat." In the mind of the public, this trend has created "a monster-criminal, a beast beyond redemption or reform that is innately hostile to the community." Belief in the monster-criminal, he observed, has spurred "a dramatic decline in the faith of the rehabilitative ideal."

A less sinister reason for American suspicion of official rehabilitation programs is the Constitution's First Amendment, which guarantees freedoms of religion and speech. China may not see any legal hurdles to opening camps to "deradicalize" Uighurs away from Islam and toward a state-sanctioned creed. The autocratic Kingdom of Saudi Arabia doesn't have a constitution that prevents it from teaching inmates that Wahhabism is the only true Islam. Even France could fund programs aimed to make Muslims embrace republic-sanctioned citizenship. But in the United States, at least in theory, the government can't try to repurpose people's beliefs.

From a cultural standpoint, it's odd that Americans are so unwilling to invest in helping violent extremists. To dismiss them as irredeemable feels uncharacteristically static for a country that claims to worship dynamism and change. It seems out of step with the keep-smiling, keep-trying optimism that powers American culture. We embrace the born-again, the comeback, the reboot, the revived and reinvented. We invented the twelve-step program and the blockbuster movie sequel. Our economy and sense of self hinge on hundreds of millions of immigrants eager to remake themselves, and to become American in the process. But why does our belief in fresh starts stop when it comes to prisoners, particularly those convicted of terrorism offenses? When I search online for "American forgiveness," all I get is a bunch of articles on student loans.

The only American deradicalization program I could find—the

country's first—was in Minneapolis, Minnesota. A brainchild of a local organization called Heartland Democracy, it was short-lived and tiny, with a single participant: a Somali American teenager named Abdullahi Yusuf, who had been stopped at the Minneapolis airport trying to make his way to join the Islamic State in Syria. Curious to see this American experiment in rehabilitation, I flew out to Minneapolis.

BY THE BOOK

ON NOVEMBER 9, 2017, I sat in a packed courtroom in the Minneapolis federal courthouse, craning for a glimpse of the man everyone had come to see. He certainly didn't look like a terrorist. Six foot four and skinny enough to be nicknamed "Bones" by his basketball buddies, Abdullahi Yusuf wore glasses and a blue button-down shirt, partially untucked. As the twenty-one-year-old rose to face the judge, he looked like a grad student on a Sunday morning, not someone who'd just served twenty-one months for trying to join ISIS.

When Ahmed Amin, Abdullahi's mentor and tutor during this experiment in jihadist rehabilitation, first met the accused, he thought they had brought the wrong kid in from prison. *This is a terrorist?* he thought. *There's no way this kid was a terrorist—no way!* Abdullahi, then just eighteen, was handsome and friendly, talking about football and basketball with his new mentor with an easy confidence. Unlike some of the other children of Somali immigrants whom Amin taught in Minneapolis high schools, he didn't seem to hold on to the culture of his parents too rigidly, nor did he reject it entirely. To Amin, he seemed an all-American kid.

In many ways, Abdullahi was just that. (A court order against his speaking to the media meant I wasn't allowed to interview him, so I had to learn his life story through court documents and press clippings from interviews before his sentencing.) Like millions of other children of immigrants to the United States, he'd grown up working hard to carve out his identity as a new American. Born to Somali parents in a refugee camp in Kenya, he came to Minneapolis with his mother and brother when he was three. Five years later his father, who'd had visa issues, finally joined them. Abdullahi grew up in a largely Somali neighborhood and taught himself English by watching cartoons. At school, the Somali kids were teased about their African and Muslim heritage. In fifth grade, asked to state his ethnicity on a form, he ticked the box next to "African-American." The terrorist jokes bandied round the playground after 9/11 grated. "The kids didn't mean it like ill will," he told *New York* magazine. "But it put a doubt in my head about who I am and how I fit in."

When Abdullahi was in eighth grade, his family moved from their inner-city neighborhood to the middle-class suburb of Burnsville. On his first day of school, seeing all the white kids in their varsity letter jackets felt like walking onto a movie set. In high school, he played for the Burnsville soccer team, which gave him a sense of belonging and focus. But when the season was over, that camaraderie faded, and he drifted into a group of Mexican American and Somali American boys who skipped school and smoked dope. Abdullahi's grades fell, and his worried father moved the family to another school district.

In his senior year history class, Abdullahi happened to be assigned Syria as a research topic, and he became increasingly obsessed with its civil war. One day on the basketball court, a couple of older Somali American boys invited him to go to the mosque, then dinner. That night the boys stayed till two A.M., passing around their phones and watching videos on a YouTube channel called "Enter the Truth." He binge-watched footage of fighters in Syria and lectures by the Yemeni American firebrand Anwar al-Awlaki, who glorified jihad and urged Muslims to kill Americans. When a friend asked Abdullahi whether he wanted to join a group heading out to fight for ISIS, he readily agreed. The FBI stopped him at the airport in May 2014, trying to get on a flight to Turkey. Later, arrested along with eight other young men, he was charged with trying to assist a terrorist group, eventually pleading guilty.

ABDULLAHI WAS LUCKY, BECAUSE the federal judge hearing his case, the Honorable Michael J. Davis, was the first U.S. judge to explore the possibilities of rehabilitating would-be terrorists. Even before 9/11, the American legal system had taken a stern view of terrorist sympathizers, Davis explained to me when I visited his chambers. Davis is the first Black federal judge in Minnesota history and a longtime champion of making the court system fairer to marginalized groups. He is also a veteran of numerous jihadist terrorist cases.

The suspects who landed in his courtroom were overwhelmingly young men drawn from Minnesota's Somali American community, the largest in the United States. Starting in 2007, teenagers and twentysomethings from the Twin Cities began joining the West African militia Al Shabab; by 2014, there was a new wave of departures from among the Somali American community, this time to fight in Syria. The sentencing guidelines for terrorist offenses were strict; Davis himself had given one Al Shabab recruit 240 years in prison.

Still, as young Minnesotans continued to be arraigned on terrorist charges, he started to wonder whether there'd be merit in setting up a rehabilitation program. Many of the defendants were like Abdullahi: they'd never participated in violence. They'd never even set eyes on a militant group in the field, because they'd been stopped at the airport before leaving the United States. Nonetheless, said Davis, "they were getting the same sentence as if they'd come back from overseas." In fact, those who were stopped before they could leave were getting *longer* sentences than those who succeeded in getting to Syria, a 2018 report found. Nationwide, returnees from the Islamic State were getting an average of ten years—eight if you counted cases where no charges were brought. For suspects like Abdullahi, who were stopped boarding planes as they tried to fly to the Middle East, the average prison sentence was fourteen years.

When Abdullahi and his eight codefendants were arrested in the fall of 2014, they confounded Judge Davis. Until they tried to join the Islamic State, these boys were ordinary teenagers. On the East and West coasts and in Europe, the world of militant networks frequently overlapped with those of drug dealers or gangs. Not so in Minnesota, where the ISIS recruits were young, in school, with part-time jobs, and without criminal records. "If these were hardened criminals, it would make my job [sentencing them] a lot easier," mused the judge. "But these guys had nothing! Nothing! Nothing!"

In fact, most of Abdullahi's codefendants had jobs requiring security clearances. One even worked at the Minneapolis airport. Moreover, the goals of these young would-be jihadis diverged from those of most other criminals. "With the exception of sex offenders, everyone else is in it for profit or revenge," Minnesota's chief probation and pretrial officer, Kevin Lowry, observed. "This is a completely different mindset, where you're not looking for gain, or profit, or retaliation."

With no U.S. program he could look to as a template, Judge Davis started "poking around online, trying to figure out what the rest of the world was doing." Eventually, he sent Kevin Lowry and Manny Atwal, a federal defender and a veteran of the state's terrorist cases, to talk to European counterterrorism practitioners. "There's a river of stuff out there, but it's an inch deep, and a mile wide," said Lowry, a thin man with a Nebraska drawl and a long career in the criminal justice system. "We were looking for practices and procedures in how to deal with these cases, 'under the hood' stuff." On meeting Daniel Koehler, Lowry felt he'd found what they were looking for.

Judge Davis flew to Berlin to meet Koehler, finding the German expert "putting into words and focus all the things that had been going through my brain, but that I hadn't been able to put together." Mentoring and education, Koehler explained to the judge, were two tools to help "re-pluralize" the vision of extremists who'd had their world narrowed to a place divided into good and evil. Listening to Koehler's theories, Davis decided his approach to deradicalization might well be worth trying in Minnesota.

———

AFTER ABDULLAHI'S ARREST, WHEN his attorneys Manny Atwal and Jean Brandl broached the possibility of finding some sort of disengagement program for the teenager, Judge Davis agreed. Jail wouldn't necessarily help Abdullahi, he reasoned. It could even hurt him. Convicted terrorists around the world frequently emerged from prison even more committed to violence, particularly in countries where few prisons had offender rehabilitation programs. Davis gave Abdullahi's lawyers the green light to find a way to "mess with his mind," as he put it the day we met.

But who should mess with it, and how? Approaching Abdullahi's rehabilitation in religious terms was out: challenging his interpretations of Islam could potentially be seen as an encroachment on his religious freedoms. "For a lawyer," said Atwal, "that's just a line you can't cross." Judge Davis, too, believed that the program must shy away from Abdullahi's spiritual beliefs. "I am not the thought police," he told me. "Far from it. We have the First Amendment, and we need to make sure that nobody's religious views are violated. It's about disengagement from criminal activity. That's where I'm at." In hindsight, he even regrets that people kept using the term *deradicalization* to describe Abdullahi's program. "Everyone thought we were bringing people in, putting a hood on their head, and zapping them, getting the germs in their brain, killing all those radicalized cells."

As Atwal and Brandl looked for someone to work with their client, Brandl thought of a mother she'd first met in the playground at her kid's school. Mary McKinley had recently moved back to her native Minnesota after working on security and social issues in New York and Washington, D.C. She headed up Heartland Democracy, a nonprofit that taught civic engagement to youth who'd been involved in drugs, gangs, or crime. In the program, a coach guides young people through a syllabus of poetry and essays using the Socratic method, encouraging them to investigate their own identities, their communities, and their connections to American society. "What Mary does is take kids who are disaffected, and grounds them in the reality of their own strength, power, and ability to change the world," Brandl explained. She called McKinley: would she be able to help a teenager rethink a toxic worldview? "That's what I do," responded McKinley.

It took time, though, to convince legal officials to allow Heartland Democracy to work with Abdullahi. Minnesota's then U.S. attorney, Andrew Luger, had great esteem for McKinley and her work, but "we had just arrested this guy," he explained in a phone interview. "In our eyes, at that point, he was a hardened, radicalized ISIS wannabe." Trying to transform an aspiring terrorist by having him read Plato and Hannah Arendt seemed fairly fanciful. Moreover, there was no infrastructure or precedent for using such programs. "Mary was this one-woman band," Brandl told me—without an office, much of a staff, or any experience working with terrorism recruits. "Davis wanted me to say, 'Of course! We've dealt with thousands of terrorists!'" chortled McKinley. "He wanted me to say, 'And here's what we're going to do, and here's my binder folder, and here's my Terrorist Drop-off Center, and here's the security system for that center.'"

We are talking, that freezing November morning, in what constitutes Heartland Democracy's headquarters: a couch at a trendy co-working space, located in the basement of a pharmacy in Minneapolis. Blond, blue-eyed, and Minnesota-born, McKinley speaks in full paragraphs with impressive precision. I could well imagine her effortlessly capturing the attention of both pissed-off teens and Washington politicos. Perhaps it is because we were sitting in a hive of hipster entrepreneurs, their faces lit by the glowing Apples on their MacBook Airs. Perhaps it's because I was freshly arrived from England. Perhaps it's because of her energy. In any case, the Minneapolis deradicalization experiment seemed emblematic of so much about the United States, a country that historically prizes individual efforts over statist interventions. There were top-down prescriptions from the government, as in France or Saudi Arabia. Abdullahi's program existed not because of a centralized system, but because a handful of people with entrepreneurial energy took risks. Like so much else in our country, our initial foray into terrorist rehabilitation was powered by hard work, luck, and ingenuity.

WHEN THE U.S. MARSHALS brought Abdullahi from prison to Brandl's office every week to meet with McKinley, she didn't much fuss that she was working with someone facing terrorism charges. "I didn't want to be fascinated by him," she said firmly. "And I honestly wasn't. There are a lot of researchers out there that see these kids as guinea pigs. That's not this process." Nor was she scared to expand Heartland Democracy's brief to working with ISIS supporters. "We're forever talking about topics people don't want to talk about, with people who have been ignored and ashamed of things," she said. "So for us to talk about hate and violence and extremism and ISIS, who cares? Just add it to the list!"

McKinley's statement took me aback, since it collapsed the scaffolding holding up the idea of "Islamist terrorism." American public discourse so often framed jihadis as a unique and uniquely threatening menace, visited on us by foreigners from outside our borders. I hadn't been surprised that mothers of ISIS fighters set their sons' behavior on a continuum with more common teenage behavior. But when McKinley did so, it felt quite radical. She seemed able to ignore the weight that terrorist offenses carried in the United States, particularly after 9/11. She saw the process of radicalization as a social problem, akin to drugs, gangs, and crime. Like the youths facing these all-American problems, Abdullahi had taken a series of incremental decisions that led to a life-changing mistake. "It's so common for these kids to get wrapped up in a situation that they don't quite understand," she said. "It's like when kids don't know why they're suddenly dealing cocaine when two months ago they were just buying some weed. It's as though there's a momentum, and they turn off their critical thinking."

When violent acts are tied to an ideology, it magnifies the horror of their violence. When Proud Boys beat up a woman in the street, their actions may be identical to that of a random mugging, but the effect is far more distressing. Harming souls and societies by dint of their intent, hate crimes and terrorism feel far more destructive than ordinary criminality, even if the acts committed, and the physical damage done, are similar. A more workaday—and thus more pernicious—ideologically charged double standard shows up in American schoolrooms, where Black children are about three times as likely to be disciplined or expelled as their white classmates.

In her interactions with Abdullahi, McKinley refused to imbue his offense with its symbolic import in American culture. Still, she had to impress on him the political context in which he was arrested and explain the charged atmosphere he'd have to navigate. "I set out to construct a curriculum and a dialogue around the magnitude of what he was in," she said. "He wasn't just arrested. His situation wasn't like what he may have seen his friends get into, for stealing a car or something. It's unfortunate, but it was much, much bigger already."

In the beginning, Abdullahi had only a hazy sense of the gravity of the legal case against him. "Why do you think you're on the front page of *The New York Times*?" McKinley would ask. "What do you know about 9/11?" At eighteen, Abdullahi's answer to both questions was "Not much."

McKinley had him read the Patriot Act, the post-9/11 legislation that greatly extended the government's powers of surveillance. He read the 2002 memo by George W. Bush's White House counsel Alberto Gonzales, which argued that the Geneva Conventions' rules for questioning "enemy" prisoners no longer applied. Like the other teenagers McKinley had worked with, Abdullahi had a finely tuned radar for systemic bias. "With all of them," she said, "whether it's a personal sense of injustice, linked to their parents, or a larger political injustice, there's a sense that 'Clearly, this system isn't made for me, because I'm not winning.'"

Knowing this, McKinley set about trying to get Abdullahi to think about ways in which he might see a place for himself in American society. She decided he should work his way through Heartland Democracy's syllabus, which included thinkers from Plato to Camus to Ta-Nehisi Coates. She brought him a copy of *The Autobiography of Malcolm X* and called a friend who'd worked in the public school system. "I was like, 'Okay, I need your coolest young Somali teacher,'" McKinley recalled. "And she's like, 'Got him.'"

MEETING AHMED AMIN, I immediately see why he'd be the right man to try to save a boy seduced by ISIS dogma. His head shaved bald and gleaming, the thirty-three-year-old has a whirligig energy, yet at the same time he seems calmly anchored, able to hunker down comfortably wherever he might find himself. That sense of confidence, I imagine, belonged to someone who'd had to carve out his own identity.

He's had to go his own way, he tells me, as a Black-but-not-African-American man and as an immigrant who came from Minnesota's Somali community but was no longer of it. After years of sleeping on floors in refugee camps in Somalia and Ethiopia, he arrived in the United States at twelve without a word of English. Till he started in the Minnesota schools, his only formal education had been a few scattered classes at a madrassa.

Still, he excelled at school, partly because of being "raised in the shadow of a saint"—his father, a well-educated man who pushed his six children to succeed. The Amin household ran on the assumption that the American dream was a reality. Hard work, they were told, could help overcome the challenges of being Black, Muslim, and Somali migrants in the Midwest. Later, Amin would use his "indirect mentors"—James Baldwin and Frederick Douglass—to hone his ideas on his country's history.

Amin now speaks in idiomatic English, without a trace of an accent. He calmly admits to being an atheist, "very ambitious," and unlike many in the Somali American community, "pretty much of an assimilationist." His best friend is white, as are women he dates, and he remains wary of what he calls the "Somali American silo." A social studies teacher before being promoted to vice principal, he coaches debate, and it shows: he slaloms between topics—from Black American identities to Somali tribal culture to postcolonial theory—and weaves through arguments from Franz Fanon, Edward Said, and Homi Bhabha, all without drawing breath.

He'd hold three-hour sessions with Abdullahi, first at the Anoka jail and later at the halfway house where the youth lived during the second part of his sentence. He must have had a dazzling effect as a tutor, I suggest.

"I think he was more fascinated by my story than his own," he admitted, with a grin.

"You're the first person I've seen that made me think of what's possible," Abdullahi told him once.

"How's that?" Amin shot back. "I'm a schoolteacher!"—hardly a profession that teenage boys see as the summit of American success.

Later, Amin reflected that Abdullahi had been referring not just to Amin's job but also to his sense of self. "I think what he was talking about was 'You are American, you are Somali, and you can connect with them both.'"

Abdullahi impressed Amin, too. "What killed me was how reflective he was," Amin said. "I didn't have to build a scaffold for his thinking." What he did have to do, however, was suggest meaningful ways of living that didn't involve terrorism. He chuckled. "Mary gave him Malcolm. I was like, 'Mary, are you sure?'"

But *The Autobiography of Malcolm X* did for Abdullahi what James Baldwin and Frederick Douglass had done for Amin. "It was like, 'Wow! I'm Black! American! Racism is a thing!'" Amin said, recalling Abdullahi's reaction. "For the first time, he was seeing someone who looks like him going through some of the same struggles. Believing that people aren't treated fairly. Going to jail. He got so caught up in the text."

Abdullahi didn't even have a high school degree when he met Amin, but he'd torn through Homer's *Odyssey,* and he loved Greek philosophy. "I was like, what?" Amin recalls. "No terrorist loves philosophy! What do you mean you love philosophy?" So they discussed Plato's view on the unexamined life, which in turn led to a discussion of Malcolm X's struggle for justice. "I told him, when you lead an examined life, that's a painful life," explained Amin. "Malcolm felt the pain of injustice. And he died for it."

Amin hoped to show Abdullahi that despite his feelings of outsiderhood, he still belonged as an American, not fighting some war in a country he'd never even visited. Abdullahi's struggles with belonging, identity, and society's low expectations for men of color were nothing new. Indeed, they were part of a long American tradition for young men from marginalized communities.

Early on, Amin assigned him Sherman Alexie's essay on reading a poem by a Native American writer. Mentor and prisoner spent hours parsing the poem's opening words—"I'm in the reservation of my mind." The line sparked a conversation about the limits Abdullahi placed on his own ambitions, as a teenager from a poor family who wasn't doing well in school, whose parents didn't entirely understand his life, nor he theirs. They talked about what it meant to grow up in a patriarchy, and what it meant to be Black men in America. "Read Ta-Nehisi Coates!" Amin would tell him. "Coates'll tell you—'You're just a black body!'"

So Abdullahi went back to his cell and read Coates on Black manhood. And Michel Foucault on surveillance in prison. And Viktor Frankl on humans' search for meaning. And David Foster Wallace's famous commencement speech, "This Is Water," which warns against "the default setting" of being unconscious of your own context. Real freedom, Wallace wrote, involves "attention, and awareness, and discipline, and effort, and being able truly to care about other people and to sacrifice for them, over and over, in myriad petty little unsexy ways, every day." For Abdullahi, in prison for making a grand and stupid gesture on behalf of the Syrian people, the essay resonated powerfully. It felt liberating for the young man to contemplate the possibility of making everyday choices to frame his own reality, Amin recalled, even in a prison cell.

Amin passed on to Abdullahi some lessons from his own stern, striving father. He wouldn't let him indulge in a victimhood narrative, the storyline so beloved by extremist recruiters. Amin told Abdullahi about how the young Frederick Douglass would bring bread along with him when his mistress sent him on errands. Out on the street, the illiterate slave would go up to white boys and say, "Hey, teach me the letters, and I'll give you the bread."

"I told him, 'Hey, if Freddy Douglass can trade bread for knowledge, then what excuse do you have? You get to sit here, and we feed you? Get reading!'"

EVERY MORNING WHEN HE got up, Amin told Abdullahi, he had a ritual. He'd look at himself in the mirror and run a movie in his head about who he was—or rather, who he could be. The exercise was designed to counter, at least in the bathroom mirror, anybody else writing the script of his life. "There's a narrative about you now," he told Abdullahi.

"Oh my god, I'm a terrorist," Amin recalls Abdullahi responding.

"How are you going to rewrite that?" Amin replied. "What kind of movie are you going to play in your head now? I bet it don't look good!"

Mary McKinley used a Hollywood analogy, too, in her conversations with Abdullahi. Early in their work together, when he was vacillating about cooperating with the government, she told him he could choose between two movie plots to star in. In one movie, he'd emerge from prison and head off to Yale Law School. In the other, he'd do a "long con"—pull off an elaborate swindle—in which he might fool people for a while, only to disappoint them in the end. He could choose, she told him. "Don't allow other people to decide when your story is done."

Both McKinley and Amin worked with Abdullahi for three years for free, except for ad hoc payments for writing the program proposal. "I did think at some point that if I were a man, I would have got paid," McKinley said lightly. "It was the same as it is all over the world: the men were getting paid, and they're not working with the kids. The women—and the young man—are working with the kids, and not getting paid."

Of course, there were other injustices at work besides gender: the only man not paid for his work was a Somali immigrant. "Mary and I made zero dollars," Amin observed. "I told her, 'Do you know anybody else who works three years for no money?'"

THE SHEER DIVERSITY OF its members made Abdullahi's team the very model of an American deradicalization program. There was Brandl—"the lesbian Buddhist lawyer," said McKinley. And Atwal—"the Indian British Sikh, an immigrant two times over. There was the Somali guy, and the blond Catholic midwesterner"—McKinley herself. The mix of people turned out to be a test of Abdullahi's acceptance of difference. When Brandl told him she was gay, she challenged Islamic State values. She did so again by hugging him—"me, a white woman!"—she said, shaking her head at the memory that he'd let her do so. "You're not going to be able to do that if you're steeped in ISIS propaganda."

Though born a Muslim, Amin had become an atheist. A hard-line ISIS ideologue would abhor a fellow Muslim who'd lost their faith, but Abdullahi didn't. "He let me authentically be me, without questioning," said Amin.

I'm charmed by this all-American lineup, just as I'm charmed by pretty much everything about the Heartland Democracy program. It had Abdullahi talking about texts I happened to revere, and raised discussions about values I shared. The program tried to make Abdullahi think critically about his place in the American landscape—rather than, say, guiding him to a more mainstream interpretation of Islam, or poking around his early childhood for signs of trauma. The approach resonated broadly with my methods for making sense of the world. I could see that Amin was trying to build Abdullahi a context out of books, to create a shared experience through talking about ideas.

But I had to admit that my clammily enthusiastic reaction to Abdullahi's transformation was also somewhat suspect. It wasn't simply that I like a good American success story about a bright boy given a second chance. It wasn't just the pleasure of hearing how during his sessions with Amin, he set his sights on getting a high school diploma—not just a GED—and on going to college after that. It wasn't just hearing how he'd dazzled Brandl with his thoughts about Plato's cave, and Atwal with his delight in Mindy Kaling's memoir. Or that he discussed *The Unbearable Lightness of Being* with a prison guard.

I cringe slightly as I type this, but I found myself responding in a particularly keen way, because Abdullahi had been converted to my way of seeing the world, using my kind of texts. My reaction had a whiff of the triumphant Victorian missionary about it. It's always so very satisfying to see someone find the right path, don't you agree? By trying to steer someone away from one worldview and toward another, you risk indulging your own zealotry. Having seen someone else's views move closer to your own, it's all too easy to take that as validation that your vision is the right and proper one. "The fanatic," wrote Amos Oz, "strives to upgrade and improve you, to open your eyes so you, too, can see the light. All the fanatic wants is to take you in his arms and hug you, to raise you from the lowly spot you are stuck in and place you in the sublime place he has discovered, where he has since been basking and to which you must ascend immediately. For your very own good."

INTERROGATING MY OWN REACTION prompted me to think about deradicalization programs more generally. The creation of each new one, whether in the American Midwest or in northern Nigeria, poses an implicit moral question: what norms should people be deradicalized into? Rehabilitation is all very well, but how much should government "mess with someone's mind," as Judge Davis put it? For many programs or practitioners, it's enough simply to get someone to disengage from the terrorist group—to leave it and renounce violence. But other approaches, particularly state-sponsored ones, bear the imprint of the dominant political culture, and with it, a more doctrinaire approach about what normalcy looks like.

Germany's deradicalization programs work to bend the arc of reform back to a very German interpretation of postwar democratic values. France's short-lived program stressed *laïcité,* the republican banishment of religion from the public sphere. Saudi Arabia's state-funded deradicalization program tries to guide convicted terrorists to the official conservative Wahhabi philosophy that has supported the rule of the House of Saud since the kingdom's founding. A report from the RAND Corporation suggested that the Saudi program didn't necessarily want to change the worldview of extremists, just convince them of "the legitimacy and religious rectitude of the Saudi state."

Perhaps because I'm an American myself, it took me longer to see the implicit assumptions underpinning Heartland's identity-focused, faith-free approach. McKinley sent me the results of an exercise she'd assigned Abdullahi, trying to get him to think about how multifaceted his identity was, how it was much more than simply Muslim or Somali. Given the prompt, "I am . . . ," he had written:

I am human
I am an alleged terrorist
I am not sure how that makes me feel, I throw a fit
I am currently drinking a Sierra Mist

I am in a hole
I am sure it'll take quite a toll
I am thankful I am whole
I am bold
I am labelled
I am Somali
I am jolly
I am a hoodlum
I am Muslim
I am black
I am this
I am that
I am sure of one thing for a fact
I am a human

INITIALLY, ABDULLAHI DIDN'T WORK well with the authorities. Before being charged and assigned legal representation, he lied to the FBI, protecting his codefendants. But gradually, as his lawyers spent more time with him, even the prosecutors could see his worldview changing. "We work with people cooperating with the government all the time—gang leaders, drug leaders," Minnesota's former U.S. attorney Luger told me. "You get to be able to tell if they're doing what they have to do, or if they're really changing. And we all believed he was changing. Some of that can be attributed to the fact that he was spending time with the law, finding out that we're not the bad guys. That happens. But it was more than that."

At trial, on the witness stand, Abdullahi would testify against three of his former friends. This pitted him not just against his codefendants but against many in the Somali American community. "Liar!" yelled a spectator at one point during his testimony.

It wasn't the only such interruption in the highly charged trial, in a city whose Somali community was weary after over a decade of tensions with police and federal agents. After 9/11, wrote Arun Kundnani in *The Muslims Are Coming!*, Minneapolis police officers would drive around to Somali neighborhoods, roughing up kids randomly and insulting Islam. After a number of young men left to join Somalia's terrorist group Al Shabab in 2007, FBI agents targeted malls, schools, and libraries, questioning young people of Somali origin. Much of the surveillance was highly intrusive, wrote Kundnani, a prominent writer and scholar on race, Islamophobia, and political violence. "Somali students reported being approached by FBI agents in campus libraries or receiving phone calls from agents instructing them to leave classes in order to answer questions." As youth in the community felt increasingly branded as terrorist suspects, tensions grew between those who would cooperate with the federal agents and those who wouldn't. Mosques, fearful of being labeled "radical," avoided legitimate forms of political dissent or discussion. The atmosphere slowly choked outlets for young people to challenge discrimination or civil liberties at home, or American foreign policy overseas.

It was against this tense backdrop that Abdullahi and another accused terrorist, Abdirizak Warsame, testified against their codefendants. The morning Warsame took the stand, the mother of another codefendant approached his mother, saying she wanted to kill her. Warsame's mother, Deqa Hussen, is a solid woman of forty-three, with steady eyes in a broad face. She was glad her son told the truth in court, she told me, but her family had paid a heavy price for his testimony. Some in the Somali community accused them of being, as she put it, "a snitch family." Her daughter had been "jumped" at the mosque, and "sometimes people give me a hate face at the mall." Still, Hussen believes that America's rule of law will keep her safe. "If I were anywhere else than here, I would not be walking."

IF HUSSEN TRUSTED THE American legal system and police to protect her, many of her fellow Muslim Americans did not. In the years following 9/11, Muslim communities nationwide felt targeted and stigmatized. Cities embarked on heavy-handed, and in some cases unconstitutional, surveillance of mosques, Islamic societies, and Muslim community centers. The Obama administration later tried a softer counterterrorism approach, retiring the Bush administration term *War on Terror* and funding countering violent extremism (CVE) programs, cast as ways to prevent radicalization in communities. And yet as the Brennan Center for Justice's Faiza Patel and Amrit Singh of the Open Society Justice Initiative point out, many CVE programs were based on the old and largely debunked formula of radicalization: that one could predict that someone was planning to commit violence from outward signs. A Brennan Center analysis noted that CVE programs labeled "broad swaths of political speech and expression as 'pre-criminal,' and have harmed the very communities they purport to support."

With the Muslim travel ban in place and openly Islamophobic officials in the White House, the Trump presidency only added to suspicions that CVE programs targeted Muslims. Under the Obama administration, two groups working to counter far-right extremism had received funding. The Trump administration canceled both grants and savagely cut the budget of the office administering them, an action that chimed with its line that jihadism, not white supremacism, was the major terrorist threat to the United States. And yet the FBI concluded that white supremacism killed more Americans between 2000 and 2016 than any other movement. The Brennan Center reported that 85 percent of Homeland Security's grants to CVE programs explicitly targeted Muslims and other minority groups. During the Trump era, notes a report from the center, CVE programs tended to see diversity itself as "suggestive of a national security threat."

MCKINLEY, WHO'D WORKED WITH Homeland Security in New York after the bombing of the World Trade Center, had witnessed the excesses of the post-9/11 panic over Muslims up close. Yet it rankled that many local Muslims dismissed Heartland Democracy as surveillance by stealth, simply because it received CVE funding: "Everybody thinks I work for the FBI, or some other nefarious deep state," she says. She shares an email she received from a local organization after Heartland Democracy reached out to see whether they'd partner on a federally funded prevention of violent extremism project. "We believe the countering violent extremisms commissioned by the government are very problematic," said the reply. "CVE discriminatorily targets the Muslim and Somali communities, increasing policing and intelligence-gathering under the guise of providing social services."

McKinley thinks the growing suspicions in Minneapolis's Somali community have choked off many conversations about radicalization. "It's just like, 'You're doing CVE, you're working with the FBI, the FBI is bad, they're spying on all the Muslims. End of story.'" Local Muslim groups argue that support for their community should focus on social issues, not radicalization. "They'll say, 'Don't talk to me about terrorist recruitment unless you're going to provide better education and jobs for my community.' But then does that mean, 'Don't talk about drug use, unless you provide better jobs and education for our community?'"

She shrugs and is quiet for a second. Abdullahi would be her first and last terrorism-related case. "I'm moving out of this space," she says. "It's not sustainable, and it's too politicized."

Her decision suggests the collateral damage of a securitized approach, in conversations shut down, targeted communities' suspicions stoked, and silence. Kundnani closes the final chapter of *The Muslims Are Coming!* with a stinging critique of the ways post-9/11 counterterrorism policies helped seal off spaces for young Muslims to voice legitimate dissent. Excessive surveillance meant mosque leaders were afraid to engage with those seen as harboring radical views, he wrote, while "flawed models of the radicalization process have assumed that the best way to stop terrorist violence is to prevent radical ideas from circulating." In his view, quite the opposite is true. "What is needed is less state surveillance and enforced conformity and more critical thinking and political empowerment," he wrote. "Radicalization—in the true political sense of the word—is the solution, not the problem." Allowing a free flow of debate produces fresh and progressive ideas about a society, bubbling up from communities themselves. By fostering a climate for new solutions, a society stanches the need for terrorism, which Kundani notes "is not the product of radical politics but a symptom of political impotence."

As it was, Abdullahi served time for trying to join what Judge Davis, at his sentencing, had called "a terrorist organization that's probably the most dangerous this world has ever seen." His jailhouse conversion, as witnessed by Amin, followed in a long American tradition of radical thought. Those strategizing about protecting American democracy from terror probably didn't anticipate this scene, the essence of American ideals: two first-generation Americans, both Black, sitting in a prison cell, discussing our country's canon of dissent, and debating the meanings of freedom, a meaningful life, and American manhood.

ON THE NOVEMBER DAY in 2017 that Judge Davis was to decide whether Abdullahi could go home, I sat on the thirteenth floor of the federal courthouse in downtown Minneapolis. Small groups waited to file into Judge Davis's courtroom, chatting and laughing in Somali and English. A security guard led a sniffer dog on a leash, checking for bombs. Loved ones shook hands with lawyers. The sky was cobalt blue, and an American flag flapped on the skyscraper outside. *Hamdilallah*—"Praise God!"—said one man, smiling broadly. "It's a happy day." Perhaps it was the bright blue sky, or the flapping American flag on the skyscraper opposite, but it did indeed look like one: sun, Stars and Stripes, loved ones shaking hands with lawyers.

When Judge Davis entered the court, Abdullahi unfolded himself to stand and face the bench, towering over Manny Atwal. Davis listened as the probation officer gave a glowing report. Then he looked hard at the defendant. Transitioning to normal life wouldn't be easy, the judge warned: "You're going to be ostracized by your own community—at least a certain part of it."

Abdullahi agreed it would be tough.

"Are you ready to move back home?" Davis asked.

"Yes, your honor," responded Abdullahi.

It felt damn close to a Hollywood ending, what with the beaming judge, the jubilant parents, the general sense that an individual had triumphed and that justice was served. But for Abdullahi, after all the rancor and suspicion the case had created in his community, the medium term was murkier. And like most Hollywood stories, this one was extraordinary, a one-off.

Seen from a certain perspective, it felt like a work of propaganda. It wasn't that McKinley and Amin had engaged in indoctrination; they'd worked to get Abdullahi to question orthodoxies, both about himself and about the promises America makes.

The propagandistic element lay not in the experiment's content but in its form. It left me uneasy that the deradicalization experiment had been so focused on a single individual—indeed, had been built on America's bedrock creed of individualism. It had framed Abdullahi's mistakes as entirely his own—not as actions linked to larger social or political problems. Much like his redemption, Abdullahi's fall had been his alone.

Earlier, a local journalist had asked Amin why Somali American youth were leaving Minnesota to fight with foreign jihadis.

Amin countered with a question: "What are we doing to make people want to leave us?"

Silence. Raising the possibility of a broader social complicity in the problem produced only a stony reaction in the journalist, who moved swiftly on. Terrorism, it seemed, had nothing to do with American society, only with faraway places and foreign people.

MCKINLEY AND AMIN'S WORK with Abdullahi had clearly been a labor of love, but it had also been an experiment, not to be repeated. Would any country lavish such individual attention, over the long term, on a larger cohort? How would it work?

As I searched for successful deradicalization programs, one city kept coming up: Aarhus, in Denmark, which was famous in counterterrorism circles for the elaborate support it gave people convicted of terrorist offenses. In a scheme that sounded as improbable as a Hans Christian Andersen fairy tale, police and social workers were helping former ISIS fighters find jobs, psychiatrists, and apartments. Critics dismissed it as the "Hug a Terrorist" approach, but the weird thing was, it seemed to get results.

I flew to Copenhagen on a freezing January day, took a train to Aarhus, and went straight to the city's central police station, in search of its famous crime prevention unit. Back in Minneapolis, Mary McKinley and I had giggled at the notion of a "Terrorist Drop-off Center." Aarhus, it seemed, actually had one.

THE "TERRORIST DROP-OFF CENTER"

IF A TOUGH COP were a building, he'd look like the Aarhus police station. A block of brick as dull as dried blood, it has many floors and no windows. But go around the back, and you'll find, opening onto a street of boutiques, a traditional Danish two-story house, painted creamy yellow. Lights glow in the windows. With coffee cups set out for visitors on a pine table, and a wooden dollhouse standing neatly in the children's corner, the city's crime prevention unit looks a little like a cozy room setup in an IKEA.

From this "little yellow house," as Detective Thorleif Link calls it, he and his colleagues try to stop locals from heading toward violent extremism and to rehabilitate those who have. Brawny and middle-aged, in a tight black T-shirt and black jeans, Link greets me warmly. Warm, too, is his greeting for the whippet-thin guy I'd watched pacing in the police station foyer. The detective has been tracking the man's involvement with the extremist group Hizb-ut-Tahrir for two years, and greets him like an old friend. When they set a date to grab a coffee, Link thanks him for making the time, clapping a meaty hand on the man's shoulder.

"A diagnostic sociopath, whose life is heading downhill fast," he tells me cheerily as he ushers me into his office.

Friendly pressure is Link's modus operandi. He's doubtless drunk more coffee with returning ISIS fighters than any other policeman in the West. Starting in 2012, the placid town of Aarhus watched dozens of its Muslim citizens leave for the Syrian conflict. Of the thirty-six who left, twenty had returned by the month I visited, and all of them had made their way to the little yellow house. Most claimed they hadn't fought but had driven trucks, or helped in medical tents, or guarded refugee camps. In 2015 Denmark would make it a crime just to travel to Syria without permission, but in the early days of the conflict, the returnees faced no legal repercussions unless the prosecution proved they had actually fought for a terrorist group. "We couldn't arrest them, but we wanted to get close to them," explains Link.

He shows me a photo of one youth, his shoulder pocked with a bullet wound. The young man's parents had been "worried, scared, and unhappy" during his time in Syria, says Link. Shame kept them from speaking frankly to their neighbors, so they turned to the policeman for support. The day after their son returned, they brought him in to see Link. Gently, the policeman talked to the young man about how he might get his life back on track in Denmark.

Getting up to go, the former fighter asked shyly, "I have a friend who also wants to come talk to you. Can he call you?" Sure, said Link.

The next day the friend called the policeman and arranged to come in.

Later the first guy called again. He had another friend, still in Syria. Could he come by for coffee, too? No problem, replied Link.

The young man flew back from Syria, and showed up at Link's office a few days later.

In his eight years on the job, Link has guided former extremists toward jobs, apartments, psychiatrists, university degrees, and careers. Throwing open his desk drawer, he shows me a bottle of perfume sent him by one former ISIS supporter he helped, a token of her gratitude.

Getting close to the extremists is at the core of the Aarhus counter-radicalization strategy. Steffen Saigusa Nielsen, a social psychologist and one of the Aarhus program's architects, told me, "We're not the ones breaking down the doors. That doesn't play well with building relationships." He recalled sitting at a roundtable at an international conference, where he and other security experts were debating how to handle a particular returning foreign fighter from the Islamic State. The other experts discussed how to secure an arrest warrant, but "I was the only one who was like, 'Who's going to talk to him?' Everybody else was working at the suspect from the outside."

For many officials in the coalition that fought ISIS, outside is precisely where foreign fighters should stay. If French jihadis were to die in Iraq and Syria, declared France's defense minister Florence Parly, "I'd say it's for the best." Obama's appointee as top envoy to the coalition fighting ISIS, Brett McGurk, announced in 2017 that the coalition's aim was to make sure foreign fighters died in Syria: "If they are in Raqqa, they're gonna die in Raqqa." Aarhus takes a cozier approach, trying to draw foreign fighters in rather than simply letting them die or stay overseas. "Aarhus does want these young people to come back," Mayor Jacob Bundsgaard said in 2015. "The longer they are away, the more damaged they are when they return."

By deciding to welcome back these "damaged" citizens, the city was trying to find a practical solution to the problem of youth who felt alienated from Danish society. In marked contrast, the UK and Australia controversially stripped citizenship from a number of ISIS volunteers and supporters after the Islamic State's defeat, leaving many stranded in refugee camps.

The Aarhus approach also bucked a broader national trend in Denmark. In 2015 right-wing populists made a strong showing in elections to the Danish parliament, which set a xenophobic tone to the country's affairs: politicians tightened immigration laws, passed burqa bans, and called for the closure of all Muslim schools. But in Aarhus, the crime prevention staff work alongside social workers, teachers, and community leaders to set up returnees from Syria with lives designed to make jihad look less appealing than participating in Danish society. The program was built on Life Psychology, a theory developed at the department of behavioral sciences at Aarhus University, which posits that everyone wants and deserves a "good enough" life, and that Denmark should arm all citizens with the tools to pursue it. Link likens the crime prevention unit to a public library, designed "to support, enable, and empower a particular community." Naturally, there are limits. "We say, 'You can come to us for help, but if you violate Danish law, we'll also help you to prison.'"

The unit deals both with people convicted of terrorism offenses and with those whom authorities deem to be at risk of radicalization. As police set out to design the program, their first task was to define *radicalization*. At first, they followed the definition they'd seen other officials use: a process leading someone to gradually accept "violence and undemocratic means to further a political or religious agenda."

But after a couple of months, they realized that the definition was too broad and value-laden. Why should the police concern themselves with "undemocratic means"? they wondered. They decided to tackle extremism simply as crime prevention, rather than as a threat to democracy. Once they did so, "everything clicked into place," said Police Superintendent Allan Aarslev. Where politicians or populist rabble-rousers might try to frame violent extremism as an existential threat, these policemen were practical: extremism becomes an issue only when someone breaks the law. Like Mary McKinley in Minneapolis, they refused to be hampered by ideological baggage about civilizational struggles. It's one thing to set aside charged political atmospherics to help one kid, as McKinley had. But the crime prevention unit made the tactic of focusing on actions, not ideologies, into a policy.

LINK SEES FAMILY AS the Swiss army knife for disengaging former fighters. He has handed out tissues to weeping mothers, and has shoved his phone number across his desk to stressed fathers, telling them to call him, no matter what the time. When he talks to radicals themselves, it is family that Link uses to puncture their idea that fighting overseas made them good Muslims. He'd say, "You went to Syria, and you did that for yourself and for your prophet, right?" They'd nod.

While they were off waging war, Link would continue, "I saw the sadness in your brother's eyes. I saw your sister left alone. They felt betrayed, because you left as a thief in the night."

He'd press further. "You didn't take care of these people, after you left, but I did."

Link's approach echoed the fatherly philosopher tone that Ahmed Amin had used with Abdullahi. And his determination to forge relationships echoed Simon Cornwall's "hippieish" approach to being a parole officer. But the crime prevention unit, with its resources, allowed Link to spend an extraordinary amount of time with families and young people—even if they hadn't committed a crime. It was a cuddly, well-funded form of state surveillance, in which Link would act like a social worker or parole officer one day, and a life coach or family therapist the next.

Care is a key weapon in Link's arsenal, just as it is more broadly for Denmark's welfare state. The warm pressure they apply to fighters poses the implicit question: *If the Danish system can be so supportive of you and your family, then why on earth would you turn to violent extremism?*

Link spent seven years showering one man and his family with assistance, "using every tool in the toolbox I possibly could." The man, whom Link referred to as M., was a returnee from Syria, prone to violence. "Like a mad dog, really," he said. During M.'s prison sentence for fraud, Link would visit the man's wife and toddler at home. He even drove M.'s wife for an hour to the prison on visiting days. "I was helpful in every way, and he saw it." Link smiled. "His family began to see me as a real problem-crusher."

Once he arranged for M. to come from prison to the little yellow house for lunch with the offender's family. Driving to Aarhus gave Link "the opportunity to be with him, talk to him, be close to him." He told M., "I know you didn't have a father around you, and now you see history coming round again. It hurts me when I see your little boy, not understanding why his daddy is in prison. You're a grown-up man. You should do something about this."

On M.'s release, Link met weekly with him. On a huge whiteboard, they sketched out strategies for him to pursue the education he wanted. M. got a haircut and trimmed his beard. He confided that he had a passion for Danish design and talked knowledgeably about politics. "What about, if instead of going over there to Syria, you become a journalist?" Link suggested. "Have you ever thought about changing your sword for a pen?" He even found a young journalist to tutor M. for the exams the Danish state requires to work in media, and the two met weekly in the local library.

All seemed to be going well—until a few months in, when M. disappeared.

At the time I visited, Link hadn't heard from him for a couple of months. "We never had the feeling that we really had him," he admitted. "Though I hope one day . . ." His door was still open, should M. want to commit to making a change. But if he did return, "he has to know that we're not a gift shop," said Link. "You can't come in, take everything you want, and walk out again."

I leave the yellow house at dusk. Aarhus streets are whisper-quiet, even at rush hour. To an American like me, the benefits that Aarhus offers its former radicals was a magical tale of Nordic welfare. The system was so well funded and so forgiving that a policeman could spend seven years—a biblical block of time!—courting and supporting one convict. It felt more like parenting than policing, this faith in the state's ability to help change people. The Aarhus model was the darling of deradicalization conferences, and yet I knew it couldn't be replicated easily, reliant as it was on lavish funding and Denmark's unique political DNA.

What's more, something disquieted me about M.'s story, and not just because Link's caring, and then caring some more, seemed to have failed. It was, I decided, the whiff of official paternalism. The local university had come up with a good life theory that explained what made a contented Danish citizen, and the white men in the yellow house had tried to make it work.

I think about the Infohouse—the turbine engine of the Danish de-radicalization strategy. A twice-monthly roundtable of local police, outreach workers, job center, and school authorities, it is a model of cross-agency information sharing—and of how much information these agencies have to share. Everyone brings a laptop, and when the name of a person of concern comes up, they pool the files on them. In the tightly webbed net that is the Danish welfare state, these files often date from birth. If your dad lost his job or your mother got cancer, if your family had disputes with your neighbors on the housing estate, or if you're caught smoking dope or playing hooky from school, it's on some state database. Every municipality in the country has resources earmarked for the prevention regimes, based on idea the that catching troubling behavior early saves on building prisons later. "In Denmark, vulnerable people are very close to society," Link explains. "If you're in the system, then the Infohouse has enough information that we can draw a sharp profile of the person."

So there's the catch, I thought. The welfare state's safety net had to be woven out of something, after all. If it had the taint of paternalism about it, a slightly spooky lurking quality, was that so terrible? When one fell outside social norms, was it so bad to be watched, even cradled, by the state? The interventionism of the Danish state felt alien to me, until I recalled that I too benefited by being sheltered by a welfare state, the year I got cancer in the UK. From my sickbed, I'd shock American friends by telling them about all that the National Health Service provided me, gratis: not just chemotherapy and hospital stays but massages and family therapy, too. And now somewhere, on some national health database, I'd imagine there's a record of the state of my marriage as well as my weight and blood pressure. They took responsibility for me and took notes while they did so.

A COUNTRY'S APPROACH TO deradicalization is often a Rorschach test for its mainstream values, since deradicalizing someone requires defining what makes someone radical and what normal looks like. So it is that the Saudi program encourages young extremists to settle down with wives and embrace Wahhabism, the state-sponsored brand of conservative Islam. Or that France started a short-lived program where suspected extremists sang "La Marseillaise" and attended history lectures on the glories of the French Republic. (Unsurprisingly, an official report deemed the conceit a "total fiasco." The experiment served as a reminder that a prescribed cure often says more about the doctor than the patient.)

In Denmark, I'd seen how the rehabilitation program mirrors the national definition of "the good life," meeting the minimum standards of contentment as defined by state policy makers. In Minnesota, the Heartland Democracy program hinged on Abdullahi finding it as an individual, even if it meant breaking with members of the Somali community. In both cases, state officials worked to replace extremists' revolutionary utopian fervor with secular and practical solutions that met their material needs.

The more I thought about it, the more the Aarhus deradicalization approach bore similarities to another Danish cultural value: *hygge*. A Danish lifestyle promoting the everyday pleasures of coziness and conviviality, *hygge* had recently been in vogue in Britain, with newspaper columnists touting the benefits of simple togetherness and fireside chats. For Danes, to *hygge* is to gather with close friends in a warm house. This soft pressure of togetherness, the friendly insistence on pulling up your chairs in a tight circle around a warm fire, radiated through the Aarhus model. These Danish values were so fluffy and twinkly and well funded, why wouldn't everyone want to embrace them?

Circling around a fireplace can exclude as well as include, so the practice is more than simply a marketing tool or cold climate comfort. Seeking shelter from the storm can read as fearing and mistrusting what lies outside, say *hygge*'s critics. "In spite of its egalitarian features, *hygge* acts as a vehicle for social control," wrote the Danish anthropologist Jeppe Trolle Linnet. It "establishes its own hierarchy of attitudes, and implies a negative stereotyping of social groups who are perceived as unable to *hygge*."

OF THE FIVE HUNDRED people who have been referred to Aarhus's crime protection unit, twenty-nine have been assigned their own personal mentors, chosen from the community and trained by Aarslev's team. The unit plays matchmaker, choosing mentors who act as antidotes to the reasons their charge was drawn to the extremist scene. "If it's a thrill-seeker we're dealing with, who just joined for adventure, then we don't need to match him with someone well versed in religion," Nielsen explained. "If they're someone with a lot of social problems, we'd probably pair them with a social worker who knows how to tackle these issues. If you've got a thinker who has rationalized going to join the caliphate, then you try to find a young, grounded Muslim, so he can have a mix of a role model and a religious sounding-board."

When Link began working with a young man I'll call Bashir, he knew that the youth needed a successful Muslim role model. Bashir was bright, angry, and one of a tight group of Aarhus youth, several of whose members ended up dead on a Syrian battlefield. To prevent him from following them to Syria, Link reckoned, Bashir needed someone who could show him what was possible for Muslims in Denmark.

I meet Bashir in a shared office space for small businesses on the outskirts of town. Slim, with a wispy goatee and a technicolor Adidas sweatshirt, the twenty-eight-year-old has a quiet confidence. He was born in Mogadishu, but having arrived with his family in Aarhus when he was five, he grew up feeling Danish. He had white friends at school and was able to ignore the "Islamophobic trash-talking" he sometimes heard on Danish television. When his friends in the neighborhood would declare that they weren't Danish but were Palestinian or Pakistani, he couldn't fathom what they meant.

By his early teens, though, he began noticing the cultural gear shifts that daily life required of him. At his school, across town from his house, surrounded by white kids and other immigrants' children, "you raise your hand, you answer the question," he says. "You feel totally, one hundred percent Danish." Back in his neighborhood, among Afghans, Palestinians, Iraqis, and other immigrants, an Islamic identity united the neighborhood: the pizza guy was Muslim, as was the grocer. The street's idiom was pan-Islamic: people would greet one another with *salaam*. Back home, Bashir would code-switch for a third time, speaking Somali with his family.

Navigating these three cultures was manageable until Bashir was in his final year of secondary school, when his parents took him to Saudi Arabia on hajj. Inspired by hearing loudspeakers sing out the call to prayer, watching shops shut down during prayer time, and seeing fellow pilgrims from everywhere, he returned home suffused with a sense of his Muslim identity.

At school, not long afterward, there was a debate on Islam. Some of his classmates called it "barbaric, from the Stone Age," he recalled. One girl even invoked the practice of stoning. He thought, *I can't listen to this without defending my religion.* He was a clumsy debater in those days, so "I just threw some cruel words at her: 'You're talking about stoning?' I said. 'You look like somebody who needs to be stoned.'"

Alarmed, his teacher went to the school principal, who in turn called the police. When two officers knocked on his parents' door, asking for Bashir, his father called him, "telling me to come home in a way that in our family is martial law." The police told his father they wanted Bashir down at the police station first thing the next morning.

That night, his father interrogated him: "What did you do?"

"I . . . went to school," said Bashir, genuinely mystified.

"But did you do something?"

"I . . . don't know."

After a night spent sleepless from "stress like never before," Bashir reported to the police station. There an officer told him, "You don't have to talk to me. You have the right to silence. But some of your classmates think you might be dangerous."

Specifically, they were worried Bashir might bomb the school.

Bashir couldn't hear the next question, "because I was hallucinating." His head swam with images of orange jumpsuits, Guantánamo Bay, waterboarding, and secret CIA flights in windowless planes.

When his focus returned, the questions continued. Was it true he had forced a girl in school to wear a scarf? *No.* Was he a Sunni or a Shia? *Sunni.*

At the end of the interrogation, Bashir was asked to sign a warrant allowing police to search his house. "Leave my family out of this," Bashir urged the policeman. He refused to sign.

Fine, said the policeman. That was his choice, of course. But he could be held for twenty-four hours, should the police choose to do so.

If I slept here, my father would kill me, thought Bashir. He signed the warrant.

He still remembers his mother's face when the police arrived to search the family apartment. "I felt anger like never before," he recalled. "I felt they were attacking my family through me."

By the time they left, telling Bashir he'd hear from them in two weeks, he told himself he'd have his revenge one day.

The weeks waiting for the police report coincided with Bashir's final exams at high school, which would determine where he'd go on to college. He wasn't allowed to attend school, which was a moot point, since he was too distracted to focus. He kept thinking, *Am I going to jail? Do I still get to keep my life?*

Finally, the principal phoned him. "You're cleared. The police didn't find anything."

Bashir returned to school, eager to sit his exams. But the resits had already taken place, the principal said. Bashir had a choice: he could redo his final year or go to a new school.

"I'm innocent, and you brought this to the police," argued Bashir. "Why should I have to pay like this?"

But the principal was unyielding. Slowly, Bashir's mindset began to shift from his early belief that he was a Dane like any other. He started thinking, *They're racist, they don't want me, they're our enemy.* Nor was it just the school, or the police, he realized, but "the whole society, the whole country."

When he told his father that he was thinking of dropping out of school, his father urged him against it. "You lost the battle, but not the fight," he counseled. "Start a new school."

Bashir did, reluctantly, but that summer his resentment simmered, then boiled, when his mother died suddenly from a heart attack. Bashir thought her death was hastened by the stress of the police search. That was when he decided: "If they want a terrorist, I'll give them a terrorist. They punished me, I'll punish them back. They took my future, so I'll take theirs."

It wasn't that he wanted to kill innocent people, he says. "I was just angry at the state, and I wanted to do something about it."

One day at the mosque, an old friend approached him. He'd heard about Bashir's mother and offered his condolences. "And what are you up to now?"

Bashir poured out the story of the past few months.

"I understand you," the friend said. "And I'd like to introduce you to a group of friends who feel the same way you do."

There are other people like me? Bashir thought. *I had no idea.*

IT FELT "FANTASTIC," THAT first time Bashir met the group at an apartment near the mosque. The five guys were in their late teens and early twenties, all the children of migrants to Denmark from Palestine, Pakistan, or Somalia. They sat in a circle in the living room, eating dates, sipping tea, and sharing their stories. One guy's sister had been spat on because she was wearing the hijab. Another felt like he had no access to education or a job simply because of his background. "Everybody there," Bashir noted, "felt like the state had ruined their lives."

As the group kept meeting—always in the apartment, so they could speak freely, away from potential "snitches"—their discussions expanded beyond themselves to the Islamophobia they saw in Denmark. They started watching Anwar al-Awlaki on YouTube. Few in the group spoke Arabic or Urdu, so it helped that the American-raised young preacher spoke idiomatic English. Western governments would one day turn on their Muslim citizens, al-Awlaki preached. "He had lived in the West as a Muslim, so he could relate to our problems," explained Bashir.

Within a few months, the group began discussing where they should go. Someone suggested Pakistan, to study Islam. This being 2010, there was no Islamic State to go to, but Bashir has since said that had it existed, he probably would have gone.

One day after school, Bashir got a call from Detective Link, who'd heard about his case at an Infohouse meeting. "I'm from the East Jutland police," Bashir recalls him saying. "And I just wanted to say I'm very sorry about how your case was handled."

"You're sorry that you ruined my life?" Bashir retorted.

"No, just listen to me," persisted Link. "Could you meet me for a cup of coffee to talk about it?"

Like hell I will, thought Bashir. "But he didn't make it easy to put the phone down," he recalled. "He was so insistent and annoying that I gave in."

Bashir went to the police station and found Link to be entirely different from the police he'd met before, "a big guy, but with a nice voice."

Link said to him, "Your case was poorly handled. They should never have investigated you as they did."

"That's your procedure," Bashir said. "They violated my family. Treated us like enemies of the state."

"You're Danish, Bashir, just like I am," said Link.

"Don't say that," said Bashir, wondering what his new friends would make of this weirdly ingratiating cop. "I'm not interested in your blessings. I want to go to Pakistan. And just to remind you, that's not illegal."

Link kept looking at him.

"You can say sorry as many times as you want," continued Bashir. "I'm going."

"But you are a Dane," said Link, implying that Bashir had all the opportunities that Danishness afforded. "You are a part of this society."

Bashir tried to explain to him, "Look what you took away from me, when I missed those exams—you can't undo that."

As he recalls the conversation for me, Bashir pauses for a second and looks down. "I was very cruel to him," he says in a low voice. "I said, 'Fuck you.'"

He got up to leave, but Link stopped him.

"One last thing you can do for me," Link said. "Would you meet a guy, a Muslim, who's a mentor?"

Bashir hesitated.

"Just to talk?" pressed Link.

Reluctantly, the youth agreed, mostly out of curiosity. "I wanted to know, 'Who is this traitor who works with the government?'"

At the apartment, he told his friends his news. "The police have Muslim infiltrators," he told them. "Snitches. We can't be sure they aren't listening to us."

No problem, his friends said. Indeed, this was an opportunity! He should go, talk to the guy, and report back.

Bashir was delighted. By taking the meeting, he could start digging into the Danish intelligence apparatus. He'd be a double agent.

FOR BASHIR'S MENTOR, THE East Jutland police had chosen a young lawyer named Erhan Kelic. A practicing Muslim, the son of immigrants from Turkey, he had been a prominent interfaith volunteer in the community before Link recruited him.

Bashir and Kelic met at a burger and steak joint. The youth liked the fact that Kelic greeted him as a fellow Muslim, with a respectful *salaam-al-leikhum*.

Still, the first thing he did was pat Kelic down to see whether he was wearing a wire.

"Take your time." Kelic shrugged.

"Do you know what they did to me?" Bashir demanded loudly, aggressively.

As he told his story, he noticed that Kelic listened and didn't interrupt. That calmed him, and what began as a rant ended as a monologue.

"What you have been through was cruel," acknowledged Kelic. "It should never have happened."

And yet, the lawyer continued, if Bashir's ultimate goal was to be a good Muslim, he could do that right here in Aarhus. Being observant was simple in a country like Saudi Arabia, he said, where alcohol was banned, and shops were closed by law during prayer time. The Saudi state promoted outward shows of piety. But in Denmark, "you're an individual, and only judged by God," Kelic observed. "You can think about your choices here. In fact, you could say that you are freer to be more Muslim in Denmark because you are doing it on your own, without political pressure."

But what about the tide of Islamophobia? The television images of Muslims as terrorists and outsiders?

That was the flip side of freedom, Kelic explained. Denmark's guarantees of freedom of speech also gave rights to racists and bigots.

"It's your job," the lawyer urged in his soft, steady voice, "not to let them get to you." He said he had experienced racism, too, and over the years, he had searched for his own path to honoring his Turkish background, his Muslim faith, and his Danish citizenship. "The right wing says you have to be assimilated," he told Bashir. "Others might tell you that it's better to be segregated. But the middle way"—the path that the Prophet Muhammad had deemed the best one—"is to be integrated."

Bashir was disturbed: "I felt like he was attacking me on my own domain." But as the debate continued, he had to admit he was intrigued. "This guy was killing it."

Kelic noticed the effect of his words, too. "I felt he would come back," he said. "I could see it in his eyes. He was interested."

FOR THE NEXT TWO years, Kelic and Bashir continued to meet, first three times a week, and later just twice weekly. For Kelic, the time fell into three distinct periods: developing trust, working together, and stabilization. During the trust-building months, the two would debate for hours, disputing their outlooks on Islam, on democracy, Denmark, and belonging. Bashir would regularly report back to the other guys at the apartment, detailing what this "traitor" was saying. They'd arm him with arguments about the hypocrisy of democracy and Denmark's systemic racism. Bashir would then shuttle back to meet Kelic, parroting the group's lines. "For the first six months, I had my fists up every time we met," he recalls.

Changing Bashir's mindset was a fitful affair. One time Bashir, at his friends' urging, changed his phone number and cut off contact for a month. Some days Kelic could see that "he'd gone back in his shell."

About a year into the mentorship, the two met at Café Ziggi, an elegant restaurant in the center of Aarhus. Bashir "was excited, but in an uncomfortable way," recalled Kelic.

"I'm not a downtown guy." Bashir shrugged. "I was more in the ghetto, eating shawarma or kebabs. And here I was in this totally white restaurant." He was unsure even where to hang his coat. At one point, he leaned over and whispered to Kelic, "Have you noticed, we're the only guys here with black skin?"

Still, it was exhilarating, even if he couldn't understand the menu. When the waiter took his order, he mumbled that he'd have what Kelic was having.

That afternoon Bashir's vision of life in Denmark began to shift. "Before, my view was black and white, like 'we stay here, and Danish people go there,'" he later confessed. "But just sitting there, in that restaurant, where the service was tops, and everything was so nice, I was like, 'Not everybody's a douchebag.'"

Kelic knew he had Bashir the day the youth confessed that he saw him as a role model. "How do you do it?" he asked Kelic. "You have a family, you study, you volunteer, you have a house." Bashir had never met a Danish Muslim who owned his own house. He was blunt: "I want to be like you."

The two began to work together on Bashir's goals: finishing school and studying accounting. Bashir got married. He grew calmer. And he started to see his old friends less often. At first, it was simply that he was busy, but gradually he realized that this was just an excuse. When he heard that three guys from his old gang had gone to Syria, and later, that two of them had been killed, his only thought was *That could have been me.*

Today, alongside his accountancy career, Bashir works as a mentor for Thorleif Link. He applied for the job, not for the money, he assured me, "but to give something back to society." The young man he's mentoring these days is very different than he'd been. "I was a talking guy," he said. "This guy is silent."

The two meet most Sundays and talk about three times a week. When Donald Trump announced that he was moving the American embassy in Israel to Jerusalem, the young man called Bashir, furious. "Are they taking Jerusalem back?" he demanded. "Okay, this means war, right?"

Maybe, said Bashir. Maybe not. But it wasn't his struggle, he cautioned. That lay closer to home. "Your job," he told the youth, "is to make your mom proud, and to figure out a way to make yourself a good life."

AARHUS'S PROGRAM MAY BE Denmark's most famous, its outreach and mentoring the most muscular, but other Danish cities have similar strategies, ones that share the philosophy of inclusion and social cohesion. "The Danish model is that we should talk to people—as long as they have not done something criminal," explains Muhammad Ali Hee, who heads up Copenhagen's unit on extremism. Far from writing off radicalized people as bad or mad, Denmark's counterradicalization units work from the assumption that a move toward radical extremism is "a rational choice," says Hee.

The Danish counterterrorism experts I talked to see radicalization as much like other antisocial behaviors, from joining a gang to drug dependency. They felt extremism is best explained as a reaction to failures in a national system, one carefully engineered to give Danish citizens inclusion, education, and decent chances for success. "We want to bring [extremists] back to society, to tap into their frustration, before they become hardened terrorists," Hee explains.

Even if they do become hardened terrorists, the Danish penal system stresses rehabilitation rather than punishment: a life sentence in prison usually amounts to only ten or fifteen years, and inmates receive education or job training while they're doing time. To really rehabilitate people, explains Hee, you need to give them "an alternative that makes sense." The practitioner's job, he said, is to ask someone attracted to a violent extremist group not "What's your problem?" but rather "Well, what *is* your problem? Tell me about it."

Denmark's approach may appear soft-hearted, but in fact it is hardheaded, grounded in the assumption that alienation from mainstream society, not spiritual yearning or political fervor, drives extremism. The Danish bureaucrats want to give people choices that make good sense. But can the offer of a plumbing apprenticeship quicken the pulse like calls to save Muslim children from bombs? For the young people ISIS wants to recruit, can night classes in accountancy truly compete with a rousing summons to build an Islamic utopia?

NOT LONG AFTER I visited Aarhus, Denmark's right-wing coalition government, responding to a wave of xenophobic sentiment, passed its "ghetto plan." It delineated twenty-five "ghettos," neighborhoods whose populations had higher-than-average criminal records, lower-than-average rates of employment and education, and, controversially, a majority of residents from non-Western immigrant backgrounds. In the "ghettos," which were heavily Muslim, criminals can have their sentences doubled. Offenses for which other citizens are simply fined can be punished with imprisonment. From the age of one, children are required to spend at least twenty-five hours taking classes in "Danish values."

The "ghetto plan" showed the rising confidence of populists and anti-immigrant sentiment, of course, but it also spoke to the intolerant side of the strong Danish sense of social responsibility. In Link's crime prevention unit, I saw the benefits of a society with a muscular sense of national norms and handsomely funded state support. In the "ghetto plan," I saw the underbelly of that ethos. Give it a stress test, like an influx of migrants, and it looked a lot like naked prejudice. The impulse to "get close" to your citizens can so easily be repurposed as repression. As critics of the *hygge* lifestyle pointed out, huddling around the fire can warm you, but if you're not free to step back from it, that closed circle can feel awfully stifling.

I'D STARTED MY JOURNEY to find out about rehabilitation in the West, always planning to travel to Muslim-majority countries to see their deradicalization approaches later. But as I began reaching out to people working with former extremists in Asia, I had to wonder: why had I begun so close to home? My trip itinerary reflected an Islamophobic falsehood, one so well dissolved in Western discourse that it's largely overlooked: that the prime targets of jihadist violence were Europe and the United States. In truth, it's the citizens of Muslim-majority countries who are overwhelmingly the casualties of Islamist terrorism. Since white supremacists marched in Charlottesville in 2017, concern had been growing in the United States about homegrown extremism. Countries like Saudi Arabia and Indonesia had decades of experience dealing with their own domestic extremists. The political weaponization of extremist interpretations of Islam in Muslim countries has parallels with the uses of national narratives by white supremacists in the West. In both cases, the prevailing culture offers extremist views a certain amount of camouflage; their proponents can claim these ideas to be purer forms of mainstream culture.

In a Muslim-majority country, what would rehabilitation look like, stripped of the undercurrent of xenophobia developing in the West? How to treat jihadis in a country where not even the most rabid Islamophobe could ever paint Muslims as foreign or Other? Without this particular in group–out group divide, what then? I wanted to go to Indonesia first, having read about how ex-militants were given support to find second acts as upstanding citizens. The country seemed to have a burgeoning cottage industry of small nonprofits with relaxed and creative approaches to helping former combatants.

WHEN I RETURNED FROM Denmark, I read a news story about Noor Huda Ismail, the co-founder of the Indonesian organization Yayasan Prasasti Perdamaian (YPP), or the Institute for International Peace

Building, which works with former jihadis. I reach Huda on WhatsApp, where he promptly tells me his rehabilitation philosophy: "You know that book *How to Train Your Dragon*," he asks, "where the Viking boy is supposed to kill dragons, like his dad, but befriends a dragon and starts to work with him? That's my approach to terrorists." Building an understanding with formers, and treating them with respect rather than judgment, just works better, he argues. "You cannot destroy their energy." He shrugs. "Rather than challenging it, we should be channeling it."

Huda offers me an invitation to a conference for former militants, to be held in a couple weeks in Jakarta. It'll be attended by fifteen ex-jihadis, as well as Islamic scholars and university professors. The hope is that by mixing with a broader section of Indonesian society, the formers will get a chance to break with their old militant networks. There will be workshops on entrepreneurship, filmmaking, and honing a personal narrative for public speaking appearances.

The whole venture sounds so weird that for a second I think I've misheard him. But that night I phone the airlines and change the date of my Indonesia flight so I can make the conference. Online, I change my hotel booking in Jakarta, moving nearer to the venue. I could have booked into the hotel hosting the conference: all the former jihadis will be staying there, Huda tells me, and the hotel still has rooms. But I draw the line at staying down the hall from a bunch of jihadis, reformed or not. Though I am a little ashamed to be so spooked, I opt to stay at the hotel next door.

ON MEETING THE BEHEADER

THE MORNING OF YPP conference for former terrorists in Jakarta, I walked to the venue on a ring road, filled as far as I could see with idling Nissans and Toyotas. Their passengers sat sleeping or staring at their phones, resigned to commuting in the city with the world's worst traffic. There was no sidewalk, so I walked on the curb, hoping to avoid the motorbike taxis that nimbly buzzed their way through the gridlock. Denmark's ordered cycle lanes felt very far away indeed.

So too did its "ghettos." Indonesia is a nation forged from a dizzying array of differences. An archipelago of 17,508 islands, it is populated by six hundred ethnic groups, most of them Muslim but also Christian, Hindu, and Buddhist. With a long history of international trade, Indonesia has somehow managed to be both culturally porous and spiritually unified. It has the world's largest Muslim population, but has worked to create an ideological underpinning for pluralism. Since 1945, Indonesia's citizens have been taught that a nation is built not on a particular faith but rather on agreement about Pancasila, or Five Principles: belief in a single god, justice, unity in diversity, democratic values, and social justice. This history of hyperplurality may have helped Indonesia adopt a more forgiving attitude toward jihadis than many places. "There was an assumption, especially in the pre-ISIS years, that these were fundamentally good young men who'd gone astray," says Sidney Jones, director of the Jakarta-based Institute for Policy Analysis of Conflict. "That they'd joined these organizations out of a warped idealism, or the sense of wanting to help fellow Muslims being persecuted, and they just needed to be brought back to the right path."

The conference venue was a marble-lobbied, multistoried hotel— the sort of place that some participants might once have tried to blow up. When I took the elevator up to the meeting room, I found it set with the requisite props for a conference: movable microphones, a huge flip chart on a stand, bottles of water beside every seat, and bright orange swag bags with pens, pad, and a program. Huda tempered the arid setting by haring around the room in a batik shirt and Nike trainers, making introductions as if he were hosting a neighborhood barbecue. He'd had an interior decorator deck the room with strings of paper butterflies and brightly colored feedback slips. Time spent in a terrorist network can be dour, he explained, so the decorations and the bowls of hard candy were there as reminders that "life should be colorful." Unlike many in the rehabilitation field, Huda didn't set out to "counter" extremism. Rather, the YPP concentrated on giving extremists different narratives for their lives, as formers left their old networks to mix with new people. This three-day conference would focus not on scripture or civics but on polishing the jihadis' communication skills and personal brands. "The media always call me 'The Terrorist Whisperer,'" Huda tells me. "But I prefer the term 'Observer of the Heart.'"

Most counterterrorism efforts, Huda explained, patronize jihadis. Western programs, in which white non-Muslims counsel ex-militants on how to turn their lives around, carry a whiff of the white savior. But even within Muslim societies, with co-religionists counseling militants, it's all too easy to create an oppositional structure. For a terrorist offender, getting lectures from government-sanctioned clerics on how to interpret the Quran can simply perpetuate a sense of alienation. "Too often, it's like, 'We're the moderate, liberal Muslims, and we're trying to fix you,'" said Huda, who is forty-five but looks a decade younger, with a megawatt smile and a full face framed by Clark Kent glasses. "It's like an exercise in othering."

HUDA MIGHT WELL BE skeptical of what he calls the "fixing the barbarous men" tactic, having nearly been a "barbarous man" himself. The son of two civil servants, he grew up in Solo, on the island of Java. At twelve, he was enrolled in the Al Mukmin Pesantren, a hard-line Islamic boarding school once described as the "Ivy League" for recruits to Jemaah Islamiyah, the militant group fighting for sharia law in Southeast Asia. Huda did well, and on graduation, he applied for a scholarship to go study Islam in Pakistan. Luckily, he quips, he was "saved by love." Because he'd taken his teacher's daughter out on a few dates, he was deemed "morally tainted" and thus ineligible for the scholarship.

Since his schooling had taught him to see Islam as the solution to social ills, he followed the path of many of his classmates into militancy. He briefly joined the Islamist group Darul Islam but soon quit, disillusioned by the infighting. In his late twenties, he began working as a special correspondent for *The Washington Post*. A couple of months after the 2002 Bali bombing, which killed 202 people, he was at a police press conference, when they handed out a wanted poster of a bombing suspect. On it was a photo of Hassan, his old boarding school roommate. What, he wondered, would have made a bright young man want to murder innocents?

Huda went on to win a scholarship to study international security at St. Andrews University in Scotland. Inspired by a group in Northern Ireland that was trying to reconcile Catholics and Protestants, he decided to embark on rehabilitation work at home. "Most people thought I was crazy," he concedes. "They were like, 'Why give a second chance to those who betrayed democracy in the first place?'" His own flirtations with militancy had convinced him that in Indonesia most people were drawn to it not by cast-iron beliefs but by their social networks. To free oneself from the lure of militancy, he reasoned, a former jihadi had to find something new to do, and new people to do it with.

THE YPP CONFERENCE WAS billed as a "communication workshop," and Huda had designed it to mix things up. As speakers, he invited not imams or social workers but brand consultants, businessmen, film-makers, entrepreneurs, and even a rep from Facebook, flown in from Singapore. He'd also invited twenty *ustadhs*—Muslim scholars and university professors—and scheduled huge blocks of empty time into the program. His hope was that jihadis and *ustadhs* would spend hours talking together at the hotel café.

To ensure that they mingled, his team assigned each of the former jihadis to share a hotel room with an *ustadh,* and they paired up members of each group into "angels" and "humans," a sort of Secret Santa arrangement. During the conference, angels would do favors for their humans, sending uplifting texts or bringing them food from the restaurant buffet. Tiny things could alter how the ex-jihadis saw others—and indeed themselves, said Huda: "Change can start from a very small act of kindness."

The air of curated jollity reminded me of Davos, the annual talkfest for billionaires and world leaders held in the Alps. As a young journalist covering that event, I loved best the sessions designed to bond participants through whimsy: snow games with teams of CEOs and oligarchs slipping in the snow, or an orchestra conductor coaxing assembled world leaders and tech billionaires to sing "Happy Birthday." That morning in Jakarta I couldn't tell the jihadis from the *ustadhs* or the social media experts, and I had to ask my translator, Eka, to point out the militants to me. When she did, I marveled at how ordinary they looked, with their wispy beards and button-down shirts, neatly pressed. My first impression was bone deep: *They're simply humans.*

Huda's opening speech evoked the cozy-cheery tone of an American talk show. "We have four generations of former terrorists here today!" he announced proudly through his hand-held mike. He pointed out the representative of the first jihadist generation—a graybeard in a khaki military-style vest, who'd joined the U.S.-backed mujahideen in Afghanistan to fight the Soviets in the 1980s. Huda nodded at members of subsequent generations—veterans of the conflict in the Philippines in the 1990s, and of Indonesia's local Muslim-Christian disputes during the 2000s. "And the latest generation is here too," he said, pointing at nineteen-year-old Afifa. Seduced by the Islamic State's online propaganda at sixteen, she had migrated to Syria along with twenty-five other members of her extended family. Radiant in an orange hijab, she waved and beamed like a prom queen.

The day's lineup included a public speaking coach and a founder of TEDxJakarta, who offered a PowerPoint on packaging one's life story. The jihadis in front of me took notes on her storytelling tips. Use vivid anecdotes. Connect with your audience. Find a narrative turning point to drive home the dynamism of your personal journey.

"Now pick a partner," she suggested, "so we can practice storytelling. Let's choose a story that everyone knows. One person should tell the story of Yusuf, from the Quran, to the other, and the listener should pay close attention to how the story is told." Paired up, the workshop participants began to murmur versions of the famous tale. Pious, handsome, and gifted with the ability to read the meaning of dreams, Yusuf, the Bible's Joseph, endures a murder attempt by his brothers and a spell in an Egyptian prison before rising to high office and being reunited with his beloved father.

After a few minutes, the facilitator went around the room. "What kind of an angle did you choose?" she asked. "What lesson did you want your listeners to draw, in just a few words? Remember, short sentences create curiosity!"

"Prison Brings Success!" suggested one man, to knowing laughter and scattered applause.

Throughout the day, Huda worked hard to keep the atmosphere light. One woman, asked what she'd learned in the first sessions, declared that people are born good, but she can see how they can easily edge into violent groups incrementally, "through small things."

"A bomb is not a small thing," Huda mugged, to raucous laughter.

During the afternoon session on entrepreneurship, a branding expert began by telling the crowd he was a self-made man: "I didn't go to college," he said. "Starting out, I didn't have the money to pay anyone, so I did everything myself."

"Just like a terrorist," quipped Huda.

Nods from the crowd.

In its skillful weave of self-deprecation and pride, Huda's jihadist schtick reminded me of the Jewish jokes my mother used to tell. They shared that in-group knowingness of jests that marginal groups make about themselves. Both used humor as armor against mainstream rejection, and quips that worked to bond, cementing a community.

For Huda, jokes are crucial disarmament tools, a start on the road to changing people. He summarized his rehabilitation strategy as "heart, hand, and head." "First you get a former's heart, you win their trust," he said. "Then you give them a skill—hand. Finally, you can get to their head and, in various ways, encourage them to be open to new ideas. At this stage, you can maybe talk to them about their ideology. They'll laugh at their previous mistakes."

HUDA'S RELAXED MANNER CHIMES with Indonesia's political culture. Polls show that the population isn't much worried about terrorism, perhaps one reason that Indonesia has traditionally had a more forgiving view of ex-jihadis than do many Western countries. "Indonesian programs are designed to bring the radicals on a *hijra* (or passage) back from 'jihad world' to the real world," a U.S. political counselor in Jakarta cabled Washington, D.C., in 2007, relaying information gleaned from Indonesia's counterterrorism police.

In the years right after the 2002 Bali bombing by Jemaah Islamiyah, the Indonesian authorities tried to get close to terrorists in prison, in an effort to learn more about their networks. "They would give them VIP treatment," said Cameron Sumpter, an expert on Indonesian terrorist groups. "The prison guards would eat with them, pray with them, take them out of prison." Even after some eight hundred Indonesian citizens tried to join the Islamic State, the country's antiterrorism laws rendered prison sentences for convicted terrorists relatively short compared to those in many Western countries—a matter of a few years. In Indonesia incarcerated terrorists frequently garner a certain amount of prestige among their fellow prisoners and even prison officials, since many see crimes of ideology as less despicable than crimes committed for greed or bloodlust.

By early 2018, two hundred twenty-six recruits to the Islamic State had been repatriated to Indonesia. Most were enrolled in a month-long government rehabilitation program, then sent back to their own communities. In rehab, the former ISIS supporters attended seminars held by clerics and repentant formers, who sought to shift their worldviews back to an embrace of democratic values. Before returnees were released back into the community, they had to sign a statement affirming their commitment to Pancasila. Unsurprisingly, the results were mixed. One former militant, now working as a deradicalization consultant in a prison in Malang, was beaten up by jihadist inmates who considered him a traitor.

Once the former militants are released from prison, the government and many NGOs are eager to put them in the public eye. Indonesian counterterrorism officials have sometimes put ex-jihadis on TV, in the hope that their stories of the pitfalls of jihad would deter others from joining. Weeks before I visited, the National Counter Terrorism Agency (BNPT) had brought 124 convicted terrorists and fifty-one survivors of terrorist violence together in the ballroom of a Jakarta hotel. The BNPT's head billed the gathering as a public reconciliation, a chance for "mutual respect and understanding . . . the first step toward peace." Others were less convinced: some academics wondered whether the event was a mere public relations stunt, and some victims boycotted the event.

Many Indonesian ex-jihadis go on to find respectable lines of work. Nasir Abbas, a former top commander from Jemaah Islamiyah, now sells high-end honey to health-conscious Indonesians, while consulting on counterradicalization. If a former needs financial help, he can get a government stipend to start a business. Huda's YPP is just one of a clutch of nongovernmental organizations willing to help them find their feet. I even heard about one man who runs a rehabilitation organization letting ex-jihadis live in his Jakarta home.

Cynics might dismiss the government funds, the formers conferences, and the public reconciliations between victims and jihadis as clever stagecraft. But they suggest an officially sanctioned sense of responsibility for former jihadis, even though most Indonesian jihadist networks are committed to replacing Indonesia's pluralistic democracy with sharia law, and their key targets are local police and officials.

Former militants are fellow citizens, just with jihadist pasts.

AT HUDA'S YPP CONFERENCE, I'd expected surliness and suspicious silence from the militants, but everyone was unfailingly pleasant. People laughed loudly and posed for selfies. "Photo bomb!" said one former, creeping up behind a group as they snapped away. The militants hugged lots, formed an orderly queue at the lunch buffet, and at breakfast never failed to ask me how I'd slept. "One of the things you learn about people accused of terrorism in Indonesia," the security analyst Sidney Jones told me later by phone, "is that they're all almost uniformly charming."

In Europe, those drawn to violent extremism often cite the racism and Islamophobia they experience as the causes of their disaffection. Western jihadis tend to be more socially marginal, with lower-status backgrounds than those in the Muslim world, who generally have high levels of education. Half of all Germany's recruits to the Islamic State had criminal backgrounds, according to German intelligence. Indeed, ISIS recruitment propaganda hinted that people with shameful pasts were welcome to join. "Sometimes people with the worst pasts have the brightest futures," read one of its recruiting slogans on social media. The demographic was different in Muslim-majority Indonesia. In Jakarta, I met people who told me they'd joined terrorist groups because that was their family's line of work, or because all the other kids at boarding school were joining, so they did too. Far from being angry loner types, the Indonesian militants I met seemed intensely sociable.

"They're fucking normal!" said Huda.

His claim of normalcy for terrorists is a political act in itself, challenging the way many of us cordon off the terrorists among us. Statistically speaking, Huda's right: studies of militants' psychological backgrounds suggest that they are no more afflicted with mental illness than anyone else. "Terrorism would be a trivial problem if only those with some kind of psychopathology could be terrorists," observes the social psychologist Clark McCauley. "Rather, we have to face the fact that normal people can be terrorists, that we are ourselves capable of terrorist acts under some circumstances."

To declare terrorists normal suggests that they are not madmen or Others but are somehow acting in concert with their environments. As I gained a better understanding of the well-paved roads leading into militancy—a yearning for belonging or adventure, for remaking society, for resisting injustices in your home, or your country, or your world—I found myself wondering not why there were so many militants, but why there were so few. I was increasingly inclined to agree with Huda. They were fucking normal.

In American public discourse, the obfuscations of "normalcy" are elaborate, from the blunt denouncements of "evil" foreign terrorists to the double standards surrounding white supremacist violence. The "mental illness" or "lone wolf" excuse is frequently trotted out for neo-Nazis and mass shooters. Not only does this mental illness plea mitigate their responsibility for their actions, it mitigates ours, too, distancing Them from Us, the society that produced them.

After the white supremacist Dylann Roof killed nine worshippers at a black church in Charleston in 2015, some media outlets and government officials pushed the loner-with-mental-illness line. In *The Washington Post*, the University of Pennsylvania's Anthea Butler pointed instead to the context for Roof's hatred: "Where did this man learn to hate black people so much? Did he have an allegiance to the Confederate flag that continues to fly over the South Carolina capitol? Was he influenced by the right-wing media's endless portrayals of black Americans as lazy and violent?"

That the terrorist is "fucking normal" could well be the most terrifying thing about terrorism.

OR RATHER, ONE OF them. That first morning of the YPP conference, midway through a filmmaking workshop, the translator Eka leaned over to me. "See that guy over there?" she whispered, nodding at a beefy man in a blue blazer. "He masterminded the beheading of three Christian schoolgirls."

His name was Hasanuddin. In 2005 his henchmen carried out the crime in Poso, a small town in central Sulawesi, an area plagued by sectarian violence between Christians and Muslims. The girls had been on their way to school. Their murderers put their heads in black plastic bags and attached a note: "Wanted: 100 more Christian heads, teenaged or adult, male or female. Blood shall be answered with blood, soul with soul, head with head." He served eleven years in prison for the 2005 crime. He's now a teacher at a religious seminary in Poso.

YPP's motto, printed on the conference's orange swag-bags, is

"Bridging Without Prejudice." And on the second morning, when Huda went around the room asking each participant to give their impressions of the first day, Hasanuddin took the mike, cleared his throat, and said the blending between formers and *ustadhs* was working beautifully. "I can't tell the formers from the scholars anymore," he said. In the outside world, sadly, it wasn't like that: "Sometimes when the scholars talk on TV, your statements hurt us formers."

"Hopefully, by the end of this workshop, there won't be any more judgment against former combatants," responded Huda. "We've got to try to understand one another. Sometimes we're too caught up in our own worldviews, and we need to be fair on those of others."

With most of the formers I talked to, I managed to do just that. I empathized with Zaki, who wanted to help people, so joined a charity that delivered clothes and medicine to his fellow Muslims—only to find them asking him for armed protection. I could understand how Kharis, whose teachers at an Islamic boarding school had taught him how to make explosives, believed that waging jihad in Afghanistan was the right thing to do.

But with Hasanuddin, I was too horrified to engage, too disgusted to "bridge without prejudice." For the next two days, during lunch and coffee breaks, I avoided him. That I couldn't bring myself to talk to him went against both the spirit of the conference and my job as a journalist, but his atrocities were simply too brutal. I didn't want to "understand." In a session on social media, a quote from American tech theorist Clay Shirky flashed onscreen: "We feel faster than we think." In the case of Hasanuddin, my feelings were fast and visceral, and they didn't recede with time: his crime was too gruesome, his victims too young, and his cause too loathsome.

It was the closest I'd come in this journey to encountering someone I'd describe as evil. My reaction to him echoed the hideousness of his crimes, hatred calling to hate. I could understand the victims' groups who criticized what they saw as Indonesian society's overweening emphasis on rehabilitation of perpetrators, rather than on helping victims.

———

THE VIBE OF THE YPP conference veered wildly. Huda had chosen speakers carefully, picking people whose identities chiseled away at the tunnel vision taught in terrorist networks. The digital branding consultant who came to speak was a Christian. Many of the speakers were high-powered female professionals, members of a demographic that the Pesantren-trained formers might never have seen. Gender parity was built into the program: ten of the twenty *ustadhs* were women, too. On the second day, I got to talking to one of them, Alimatul Qibtiyah, a gender studies professor from a university in Yogyakarta. The night before, she'd been sitting at dinner with a few formers, when the topic of the United States came up. One former said how much he hated the place and everything about it. "I got my master's degree in America," she coolly told them. "Cedar Rapids, Iowa. Are you going to target me?" She did not tell them that she had had to watch the porn film *Deep Throat* for homework in her human sexuality class. Still, she managed to shock the diners when she announced that she and her husband didn't agree on whether Islam required women to wear veils. "They just stared at me," she said.

The virtues of pluralism were woven into the workshop on parliamentary debate. A young woman in culottes and stiletto heels gave a presentation on debating, then took questions.

"How do you defend an argument in which the other guy is not all wrong, but also makes some good points?" asked one former.

"Acknowledge what's right in their argument, then perhaps add alternative ideas of your own," she responded.

Hasanuddin—or "the Beheader," as I had taken to thinking of him—raised his hand for the mike. He said he was more familiar with talk show screaming and name calling. "On television, I notice that people don't debate the way you've described," he told the woman.

"Maybe," Huda remarked from the corner, "it's because our society loves to bully."

Hasanuddin nodded slowly.

SOME OF THE SESSIONS were subtly tailored to appeal to jihadist sensibilities. When Huda announced that a filmmaker would be giving a session, he said it would be a chance for the formers to learn a "new *dawa*," a new way to spread Islamic knowledge.

Other speakers skewed their talks to appeal to adrenaline junkies. Hassan Ahmad, a humanitarian aid worker from Singapore, showed slides from his missions to Afghanistan, Palestine, and Japan. Aid work was not just a chance to help fellow Muslims but a job that offered excitement and danger—common reasons for young men to join militant groups. He paused at a slide of one colleague, killed in a typhoon in the Philippines, his picture marked "gone but not forgotten." "You can die doing this," he said, shaking his head. "If you die, you want to die this kind of death! Praise God!"

Zaki, the former fighter who claimed he was trying to help people by delivering aid but soon began fighting for them, asked Ahmad a question: "How do we deal with people in a conflict area, but avoid getting drawn back into terrorism?"

Ahmad replied that he'd seen how closely entwined jihadist fighting and aid work could be in conflict situations. He'd worked alongside members of Al Qaeda, delivering relief supplies in Afghanistan, and with militants from Jemaah Islamiyah in Pakistan.

"And you weren't tempted to do jihad?" Zaki pressed anxiously.

"I served in both the military and the police before I got into humanitarian aid," Ahmad said. "I never liked having to clean my firearm. So I'd choose aid work over guns any day."

Groups that the U.S. government classifies as "foreign terrorist organizations" frequently do aid work in the societies where they operate, stepping in to provide services that the state doesn't. Hamas offers clinics, soup kitchens, and schools for Palestinians; Hezbollah has been providing Lebanese Shiites social support since the 1960s. The humanitarian wing of the Pakistani group Lashkar-e-Taiba has helped victims of earthquakes and floods. Just recently, when COVID-19 hit, extremist groups in Pakistan and Iraq took advantage of the slow governmental response to provide relief to the poor in lockdown and distributed food.

Zaki's earnest description of starting out as an aid worker and ending up a terrorist threw me. I saw how sturdily I'd framed "terrorist" groups as defined by their violence, even though I was familiar with the other work that all these groups performed. Lazily, I'd cast militants' social services as Machiavellian attempts to burrow into communities and win people to their cause. In short, I'd accepted a narrative of Violence First and Foremost, Soup Kitchens Second, Strategically Deployed.

To be sure, this may be the trajectory for many groups. A decade after 9/11, Al Qaeda was looking to Hamas's social services as a model to help it win hearts and minds in local communities. In the United States, the Ku Klux Klan sponsored baseball teams and junior leagues during the 1920s; a half century later the armed revolutionary Black Panthers ran free breakfast clubs for kids. My point here is not about the historical arc of particular groups, but how I'd been conditioned to frame them as simply purveyors of violence.

Take the name *Hamas,* which still evokes in me a Pavlovian association with *terrorism,* even though it is now officially a political group, having won its first election some fifteen years ago. To a mother of three in Gaza, Hamas might serve not just as a political party but as a food pantry, a bank, her children's school, and the neighborhood watch. But it was just Hamas's status as a designated terrorist group that concerned an American appeals court in 2011, when it upheld the decision to shut down the Holy Land Foundation, a Texas-based organization raising funds for Palestinian social services. Alleging that the donations committees were funneling money to Hamas, a court had deemed the charity a "terrorist organization," and sentenced five of its volunteers to prison. Even funds sent for schools and clinics aided terrorism, read the 2011 ruling, by boosting Hamas's popularity and allowing the group "to concentrate its efforts on violent activity."

The word *terrorism* can obscure the complexities of the beliefs, activities, and support for militant groups. If we focus solely on their violence, we miss understanding the slower, structural damage from a wider political and economic climate—one that often stokes support for these groups in the first place. When Boko Haram first emerged in northeastern Nigeria in 2009, its first targets were police stations, notes the analyst Sarah Chayes, writing on why corruption fuels extremism. When Chayes interviewed them, the locals recalled that they'd seen the group as liberators from a corrupt and abusive police: "People were very happy [with those first attacks]," they told her. "Boko Haram was saying the truth about the violations by government agencies against the people. Finally they could stand up and challenge. They were claiming their rights."

In the past few decades, as Sanam Naraghi-Anderlini, director of the London School of Economics' Centre for Women, Peace and Security, points out, two global trends have boosted the appeal of violent extremism. The first is the well-documented export of hard-line Wahhabi ideology from Saudi Arabia to Muslims around the world. The second trend, boosting not only jihadist groups but white supremacist ones, is what she calls "rampant extreme capitalism." When governments cut back on public services, whether through austerity drives, an ideological commitment to small government, or service on their international debts, vulnerable communities face a vacuum that extremists can easily exploit. "There are some fundamental structural factors that have arisen because of neoliberalism and extreme militarization, and unless we begin to deal with them, these movements will continue to grow because they are actually responding to people's needs," Naraghi-Anderlini notes. "And they're able to talk to [people's] hearts, not their heads."

IF MILITANTS KNOW HOW to win followers by talking to human hearts, so does Facebook, which was the subject of a session on the YPP conference's second day. Gullnaz Baig, the Facebook expert on counter-extremism who was flown in from Singapore, gave a PowerPoint presentation on the company's content-sharing policies. "You all know who this is," she said, clicking on a slide of Mark Zuckerberg. In fact, I wondered if everyone did, given that many of the assembled had spent the decade when Facebook conquered the world deep in the jungles of Southeast Asia.

Afterward, when Baig took questions, Afifa, the teenager recently back from the Islamic State, raised her hand. "ISIS followers used to have many fake accounts, and then Facebook would take them down," she said. "If the account was taken down, people would just say, 'My account has become *shaheed* [a martyr],' and they'd just start another one. One dies, and a thousand grow. How does Facebook respond to this?"

A good question, responded Baig, who explained how the company traced, then deleted, linked accounts that it deemed dangerous.

Later, we listened to an Indonesian entrepreneur talk about personal brands. A brand requires passion and commitment, he told us. He clicked through a PowerPoint of pictures of historical people who'd had strong brands, including Saint George, always identifiable from his dragon, and Napoleon. "Everybody in this room has their own branding!" beamed the businessman. "All they need to do is tailor it."

I assumed his paean to selling the self would fall flat with a crowd of ex-jihadis, many of whom had lived austerely in Philippine jungles or Afghan mountains for years. I was wrong; they seemed rapt. Later, when I asked Huda about it, he wasn't at all surprised. He'd seen—indeed, helped—many formers reinvent themselves as businessmen. "There are a lot of similarities between terrorists and businessmen," he said. "Like businesspeople, terrorists are risk-takers, people persons, storytellers, and in their own way, are often charismatic."

Indeed, Huda's initial work with jihadis had focused on the innate entrepreneurialism that many possessed. He'd offer them seed money and advice to set up their own businesses, on the grounds that keeping them busy was a great way to steer them away from terrorism.

Jihadist networks promise people meaning and belonging, and Huda knew he had to do the same. "The most important thing is to make these guys feel significant," he observed. "I didn't want to give them just any old job, but to make them feel part of something." The first entrepreneurial forays had flopped. He helped one former jihadi set up a one-man car rental business—which ended when the man drove away in the car, never to return. Another man borrowed seed money for a T-shirt printing business and started producing shirts emblazoned with LONG LIVE OSAMA BIN LADEN. Huda helped one ex-jihadi launch a fish-breeding business, but after the tight-knit camaraderie of militant life, the man found it too lonely.

A far more successful arena was the restaurant business, said Huda, where formers could work on teams, serving food to whoever came in.

Among his most successful restaurant entrepreneurs was Machmudi Hariono—who goes by Yusuf—a former militant who'd fought with the Moro Islamic Liberation Front in the southern Philippines. He was arrested in 2003 after being found with explosives in a safe house in Semarang, Indonesia. Yusuf spent his first two years in prison in a darkened room in solitary confinement. Later, when he was allowed to interact with other inmates, they gave him respect, as being a terrorist had a certain amount of cachet. But nobody from his former network reached out to him: "I gave everything for the network, and when I needed them, when I was suffering, it was just my brother and my mom that showed up."

Yusuf served five and a half years of his ten-year sentence, and after he was released, he was determined to build a life outside his old network. Huda got him a job cooking duck in a restaurant and, after two years, set him up in a café in Solo called Dapoer Bistik—Beefsteak Kitchen. When *Time* interviewed Huda and Yusuf in 2010, the magazine reported that Huda was "worried" about Yusuf. "Yusuf shows no repentance for his past life," wrote reporter Hannah Beech. "He recently named his new daughter Armalita, after a favored assault rifle." After his night shift, he would kick back with a book on jihad in the Philippines. The article closed with him saying "I would like to fight again," looking the American female journalist squarely in the eye for the first time. "That is my passion."

WHEN I MEET YUSUF at the YPP conference, he is warm, funny, and far more relaxed than the guy described in *Time* as having a "tight-set jaw and alert eyes." He has an Artful Dodger air, joshing with me about getting a visa to go to England, to see his beloved Manchester City soccer team play. He sends me cheery messages on WhatsApp: a picture of his five-year-old at a gun show, hoisting an AK-47, a shot of Yusuf beside a friend's orange Defender jeep, captioned "007, James Bond," and a short video of him set, somewhat bizarrely, to the theme of *The Pink Panther.*

What happened in those eight years? I asked him.

Beefsteak Kitchen, where he cooked, cleaned, and served others, had much to do with his reformation, said the forty-two-year-old. Restaurant work had forced him to broaden his worldview. "My jihadist networks taught me to hate people who are different from me, but through the café, I learned to meet new people. Even if they're nonbelievers, you have to serve them anyway." Christians came to the café, as did Chinese Indonesians, another minority whom jihadis are taught to revile. One day somebody who identified himself as a victim of a terrorist network walked in. Another time the policemen who had arrested him came in for ribs, said Yusuf, and they ended up sharing a few laughs. Members of his old network dropped by, too, dropping hints that Yusuf should return to the jihad. "If you like fun toys, don't just buy plastic guns," said one veteran warrior, pointedly. "Buy the real ones." But Yusuf was disturbed by the growing trend toward bombing civilians rather than pursuing jihad against other armed groups in a war. When jihadis would ask what he was doing, he'd answer firmly: "I'm cooking now. That's my job."

Yusuf was planning to take a small group of former fighters to spend the night in a friend's high-rise apartment the day the conference ended. "In the past, they would have seen an apartment as too luxurious—something for *kafirs,*" or infidels, Yusuf said. "I want to broaden their view, and maybe, they'll share their story with other formers, and broaden their views, too."

Huda calls Yusuf "my right-hand man," explaining that his charisma and successful transformation have helped bring others into the nonprofit's fold. "It's like multilevel marketing." Huda grins. "Members get members. If you've got one fucking good story—and Yusuf has one—then you can inspire others."

I found Huda's deployment of global brands and business lingo at the meeting slightly discomfiting. At first, I reckoned it was simply my innate snobbishness about phrases like *multilevel marketing* and *personal brand.* Ever the English major, I have an instinctive aversion to the patois of global commerce. But during the entrepreneurship sessions, as I watched the formers listening so intently and scribbling notes, I realized that I should get over myself: that these buzzwords were simply part of the language of storytelling in a globalized world. On a planet shrunk by technology, entities as disparate as global corporations like

McDonald's and Apple and militant groups like Al Qaeda and ISIS were all trying to find ways to connect with their audiences. Business websites were full of advice on "brand storytelling," urging companies that well-told stories were more effective than dry data in winning loyal customers.

ON THE LAST AFTERNOON of the conference, the mood was buoyant, the buzz from this supple, subtle experiment palpable. With a little help from Huda's staff, the jihadis and the *ustadhs* had formed their own WhatsApp group. The formers who were aspiring filmmakers had been promised a multimedia platform where they could upload videos. Zaki had plans to start an aid organization, staffed by former jihadis. Everyone spent the last hour posing for photos and exchanging phone numbers. "Huda," one young participant declared, "is custom-made by God!"

Watching the scrum of people hugging and chatting, I marveled at the curious sense of joy that the conference had generated. More daring than either Minnesota's miniature civics lesson or Denmark's state-sponsored paternalism, it had infused its participants with optimism and a sense that they had a raft of possibilities. Shuffling jihadis' social networks and channeling the drives that had drawn them to militancy into mainstream projects felt radical in the best sense of the word. Huda's program answered their yearning for adventure and belonging with more of the same.

I felt changed, too. A week before, I'd wondered at the wisdom of booking a room in a hotel with jihadis; now I found myself asking a former ISIS supporter whether he would take me to his Quranic study session with his old jihadist buddies. He readily agreed, and for a few minutes there, I seriously contemplated making the seven-hour journey on the back of his motorbike to meet his ISIS pals. A three-day conference can have potent effects.

At the day's end, I was in the elevator, shuffling through the business cards that I'd collected, and wondering if I could find a quick *laksa* for dinner. Just as the elevator doors were closing, Hasanuddin the Beheader got in.

"Are you going down?" he asked, smiling.

I nodded, a knot tightening in my stomach, my knees feeling weirdly liquid.

We rode in silence, until he asked, "Did you enjoy Indonesia?"

"Yes," I squeaked. "Very much."

If I'd been thinking like a journalist, I would have engaged him. By the rules of my own quest, I should have at least asked him for a cup of coffee, should have asked him why he'd done what he did. Like the other jihadis, he must have had a mother and a context for what he'd become. His backstory might help explain what I could only think of as evil. Indeed, if he had truly renounced violence, then his reformation was rather more spectacular than that of someone who'd merely picked up a gun and joined a group like other guys in the neighborhood. Surely I should try to explore it.

I didn't. My experiment in understanding had reached its limits. Hitting this bedrock was unsatisfying and inconsistent. Even now, I still don't fully understand why I could not chip away, even just a bit, at this man's monstrousness. Was it because his victims were teenage girls? Or because his act was so gruesome, it beggared the imagination? Or because it was planned so meticulously? I couldn't bring myself to examine his motives, and I didn't care to learn what might have led him to be a murderer. My will to understand sputtered out, doused in revulsion. And my refusal to humanize Hasanuddin, I felt, undermined aspects of my own humanity: it blocked off my capacity to be curious, to listen, to search for a defense of the indefensible.

The elevator doors opened. Heart pounding, damp-palmed, I stammered goodbye and walked quickly away. Huda had faith in a "fucking good story" to change people's minds, but I couldn't believe the Beheader would have a good enough one to change mine. And so he remained as he'd been when I first saw him: a monster.

LOSS OF FAITH

HUDA KNEW WELL THE power of stories, not least because ISIS was so good at using them to lure recruits. Among those who believed the Islamic State's promises of a utopian future was Afifa, the Indonesian teenager I'd met at Huda's conference. (Fearing retribution from ISIS followers, she asked that I use pseudonyms for her and her family.) As a recent returnee from Raqqa, she'd had a certain amount of celebrity among the former militants who attended. Funny and outspoken during the workshop sessions, darting around for selfies and introductions during breaks, she possessed preternatural confidence and charisma.

More proof of her force of personality: at just sixteen, she had helped convince twenty-six members of her extended family to leave Indonesia and emigrate to the Islamic State. Afifa's family was prosperous and successful. None took issue with democracy or the Indonesian state. Indeed, her father was a top civil servant. Yet somehow, through ISIS's propaganda and a contagious strain of groupthink, the family convinced itself that it needed to go. Their privilege, the size of their group, and the fact that a teenage girl had convinced them to go made

their example extraordinary. Yet their seduction by the Islamic State—
and their disillusionment from it—followed some common patterns.

ONE NIGHT AFTER THE YPP conference had finished for the day, I
watched Afifa and her sister hunch over a portable printer, photocopying the deeds to a family house. Nineteen-year-old Afifa, vibrant in a
bright orange hijab, and twenty-one-year-old Putri, solemn in a black
one, watched as the printer spat out pages; then they stacked them resignedly. The house had been in their family for decades, but because
they needed the money, the girls' mother, Zahra, had decided to sell it.
Just three years ago they had been wealthy, with several houses and a
good salary from the girls' father, Muhammad. But that week Muhammad had gone on trial in a Jakarta courtroom, charged with training
with ISIS and funding a terrorist group.

What would possess a wealthy, educated family to jettison their
lives in Indonesia to join ISIS? Zahra had attended the YPP conference
with her daughters, and over and over I would ask her why a family like
theirs would ever join the Islamic State. And over and over Zahra
would say, "It's because Afifa ran away."

EVEN AS A FIFTY-ONE-YEAR-OLD mother of three lately returned from
war-torn Raqqa, Zahra retains a placid beauty and preternatural calm.
After graduating from university with a degree in biology, she met her
future husband, Muhammad, at a charity event, while they were wrap-
ping parcels for Eid al-Fitr. Neither had been raised in a particularly
religious family; she'd never worn a hijab till after she married, and
he'd never prayed much till he met her. As Zahra stayed home to raise
their three girls, Muhammad threw himself into his work, eventually
rising to the top tier of the civil service in Sumatra. "He rarely spent a
lot of time in the house," said Zahra, her voice low, her face swathed
in a dove-gray hijab.

Looking back, she realizes that her life might have been a bit lonely,
perhaps a little empty. But they were basically happy, making trips
to the mall to play in the arcade's ball pit when the girls were small,

taking them to swim and play badminton as they grew. Mother and daughters would gather to recite the Quran together, "but just like usual Muslims," said Afifa, "not fanatics."

Afifa was a determined and precocious child who began walking and talking early. Zahra remembers having to go to kindergarten with her for about four months, so loudly did Afifa howl when her mother tried to leave. Bright and strong-willed, Afifa was the queen bee of her middle-school clique, a champion swimmer and a top student. "I was smart." She nods, her glasses and hijab doing little to obscure her shining eyes and wide smile. "I was a bully." She can't remember why now, but "I used to bully my friend until she'd start crying."

In high school, she grew increasingly interested in Islam. Her father was too busy at work to talk about it with her, so she set out to teach herself, mostly online. Deciding that her hijab had been too short in junior high, she took to wearing a longer one. Assigned to do a history project on early Islam, she became captivated by descriptions of life in seventh-century Medina. *Wow—this life!* she recalled thinking. *I have to live in a place like the Prophet Muhammad's era! There was so much justice and peace, and people were so happy!*

In 2014 one of Zahra's brothers, a Jakarta businessman, told the family that a new Islamic caliphate had been declared in Syria. "We were like, 'Is this real or not?'" recalled Afifa. Initially, she wasn't terribly interested. But as she researched the self-styled caliphate on social media, she fast became enraptured by the promises its websites made. All the testimonies from jihadis were rhapsodic. Mimicking the online posts, she rolled her eyes and put on a falsetto voice. "Oh, I feel so very happy here, with so many sisters and brothers!" "It's just like the Prophet's era. We should all do *hijra* [emigrate]." The website made it sound as though a migrant would gain both "paradise on this earth, and paradise in the hereafter," she said. Most moving were the Quranic verses the recruiters used: "He who emigrates [from his home] in the Cause of Allah," said one, "will find on earth many dwelling places and plenty to live by." Everything—housing, electricity, and medical care—was free for anyone who came, the websites promised.

Poring over the Tumblr accounts of women who had migrated—like *Diary of a Muhajirah*, a propaganda site written by an ISIS recruit with the moniker "Bird of Jannah"—Afifa found breathless accounts of daily life in the Islamic State. Later, when I saw screenshots of the blog, it was easy to see how captivating a bored teenage girl might find the descriptions of manly warriors living a life of stripped-down religious vigor:

> These man, they are not from illiterate backgrounds. Many of them came from a wealthy family and lived like a king/prince back where they came from.

> These man too has desires and wishes. They too wants to live in the comfortable zone with their loved ones, and to have a "normal" life like everyone else.

> But for the sake of Allāh they left everything behind. Family, wealth, youth, desires, likes and they have choose to be the shield of this Ummah, to answer the call and cries of their oppressed brothers and sisters.

> You see, these man are sleeping in trenches, left their comfortable beds. Eating dry bread and drinking warm tea, perhaps they have forgotten how does their mom's cook taste like.

> You saw the fierce side of them. Have you wonder the other side of them that we hardly bother—the soft side?

The heady mix of rugged pioneer life, vigorous piety, and erotic promise was perfectly pitched to capture the imagination of a metropolitan teen like Afifa. Scott Atran, an anthropologist who has studied why young people join extremist groups, believes that many joined ISIS not because of its violence but because the idea of building a new caliphate felt intrinsically energetic and optimistic. Far from wanting to destroy civilization, he noted in a 2018 interview, "they want to build a perfect utopian society." ISIS appealed to young people by selling itself as "a glorious, equal opportunity, youthful, dynamic adventurous movement," he said.

Then Afifa started to hear about the Islamic State's beheadings, lashings, and immolations. But the recruiters assured her it was fake news. "This is not from ISIS, but another group that hates ISIS," she recalled them reassuring her. Desperate to believe in this brave new world, she didn't think to question them. Trusting the people she'd met on Tumblr, people who were already in the "Blessed Land," she found their arguments convincing.

For teenage Afifa, news of this utopia appeared just at the moment when her brain was primed to embrace it. Her prefrontal cortex, which deals with decision making and risk assessment, among other things, was about a decade off from being fully developed. Neuroscientific studies—echoed by stressed parents of teenagers—attest that adolescents tend to see a scenario's best outcomes far more readily than its worst ones, no matter the reality.

At home, Afifa embarked on a campaign to persuade her parents to emigrate. Nights, in the bedroom she shared with her eleven-year-old sister, she'd play clips of kids in the Islamic State on swings in playgrounds and studying in neat classrooms. Her older sister Putri was away at university, but on her visits home, Afifa would stress the opportunities for further education that ISIS offered. The Islamic State needed doctors, Afifa told her. They could go to medical school if they wanted, or even to agricultural college.

Putri is quieter and paler than her sister, with a pinched and wary look. When Afifa enthused about Syria, Putri responded cautiously, "It's good that there's a caliphate, but it doesn't mean I want to go there," she recalled saying. "Besides, if it really is the true caliphate, it will spread to other countries in two or three years' time."

Afifa didn't want to wait. With her father Muhammad in mind, she noted a website that listed ten jobs that men could do in Syria if they didn't want to fight on the front line—that is, if they wanted to work at all. "They said, 'Anyone can do anything. But if you don't want to do anything, you can live there freely, and ISIS will give you money.'" When Afifa asked a recruiter on Tumblr what her father could do in the Islamic State, he assured her that "money's not a problem. If he wants to have a job like he did in Indonesia, he'll have a bigger salary in Syria."

Over several months, Afifa kept wheedling to her family. She spoke of the justice enforced by the caliphate's sharia courts. There was no corruption or poverty in Raqqa, in contrast to Indonesia. Muslims drawn from around the world felt camaraderie there, building a dream together. The family would be able to spend more time together, she told her parents, what with its better work-life balance. No longer would her father have to work the long hours at his desk, as he did in Indonesia.

When Afifa tells me that she'd hoped to see her father more, I'm reminded of Nicola and her suspicion that Rasheed was lured in part by his nostalgia for the Benyahia family's days on the beach in Yemen. For some, the Never-Never Land of the Islamic State promised an escape from the rat race. "Think about it, don't we all aspire to not having to work nine to five?" Nicola had asked me. "Don't we all want better work-family-life balance? If you take away the ideology, what's the difference between the pitches from these groups and the television programs telling you to move to the South of France?" Quitting the rat race to enjoy the pleasures of paradise promised in the Quran? Online, the Islamic State promised the best of all worlds: a trip back to the future, mixing nostalgia for simpler days with the promise of paradise.

There are many examples of this millennial nostalgia, this glance backward to a golden age and the forward-looking vision of replicating it. President Trump vowed to "make America great again." In the UK, the pro-Brexit crowd demanded Britons "take back control." If these slogans hinged on nostalgia, ISIS propaganda promised even more: a return to the Islamic world's earlier glories—as well as the allure of building a brave new world. The chance to create a new society was a pillar of ISIS's propaganda strategy, wrote the security analyst Charlie Winter in a 2015 report: "Joining the 'caliphate' is not simply an exploit for those wanting to shoot a gun—recruitment to the Islamic State cause is sold as a means of participating in God's project on Earth. There is a frontier-like allure to it, as uncommitted supporters are convinced to migrate and engage by the promise of being a 'founding father or mother' of this utopia." ISIS propagandists echoed nineteenth-century proponents of Manifest Destiny, who said God and Providence were behind America's westward move to conquer a continent.

———

LISTENING TO AFIFA, WHO clearly dreamed of new frontiers, I wondered why I was interested in stories of "lifestyle" factors pulling people to the caliphate. Did my focus on individuals' personal reasons for joining a militant group undercut the importance of genuine political grievances? Now that I thought about it, my focus on the youth of recruits seemed similarly problematic. To be sure, terrorism is a young person's calling, with most fighters in their twenties and thirties, and most leaders in their thirties or forties. But I'd started out looking at ISIS recruits as adolescents, as mothers' children. Did a focus on young followers rather than on committed leaders oh-so-gently strip them of political gravitas or pious beliefs?

I'd begun by writing about the recruits' youth and naïveté because it rehumanized people who were too often dismissed as monsters. But by doing so, I'd accepted another dominant narrative, in which militant groups were powered by emotion, not by legitimate dissent. After CNN reported the Islamic State was attracting young women, over social media, with pictures of jars of Nutella and kittens, commentators rightly pointed out the tones of sexism and cultural condescension in the news report's assumptions. *Becoming Mulan?*, a study about women recruits to ISIS, reports three main reasons that women gave for why they joined: They felt the *ummah*, or worldwide Muslim community, was under attack. They wanted to build a caliphate. And they believed it was their duty as Muslims to do so.

What does it mean to refuse to take recruits' words at face value? Did a search for root causes undermine not just people's political and religious beliefs, but their agency? By focusing on the human frailties that may have pushed people toward violent groups, I was subtly echoing that well-worn assertion about terrorism being "the weapon of the weak." As Cihan Aksan and Jon Bailes argued in *Weapon of the Strong: Conversations on US State Terrorism,* framing terrorists as "sub-state *desperadoes* with limited power and resources who resort to such indiscriminate and horrific violence" allows powerful actors to avoid scrutiny: "So if you happen to have political legitimacy, command a large and well-equipped military, and influence international affairs, you cannot be called a terrorist."

ALL THE TIME AFIFA spent surfing ISIS propaganda sites took its toll on her schoolwork. Before, she'd ranked second in her class, but now she was having to take remedial courses. Her friends marked the change. "What's wrong with Afifa?" they'd ask. "She's suddenly so lazy." But school felt trifling, and daily routines boring, next to the glories of Syria.

Desperate to fund the trip, Afifa entered a photography contest for the prize money. She didn't win, but when she read about British and French girls her age going alone, she decided she wouldn't wait for either her family or the funds. She wasn't sure how she'd do it, since her mother refused to hand over her passport, but one day she came home from school, filled a backpack, and ran away from home. In a note for her parents left by the front door, she wrote, "We must go to Syria. We must do *hijra*," recalled Zahra. "Please handle all the formalities for me to leave school. I'll only come home if you can show me the letters saying you've done so."

It worked: the next day Zahra signed the papers for Afifa to drop out of school. When friends asked her why, Zahra said it was because Afifa wanted to be an entrepreneur, a career that didn't require a high school diploma. She told the school officials that her daughter would now be home-schooled.

AS I LISTEN TO this story, I begin to see why some experts have questioned government counterextremism tactics employing reason, curated messages, and theological debate. Countering the pull of extremist groups with "moderate" arguments, whether by kindly government-vetted imams or by online countermessaging, doesn't work with those seeking adventure or more meaningful lives.

Nicola's skepticism about reasoning with radicalized people is corroborated by the work of Nafees Hamid, a cognitive scientist who studies the neuroscience of extremist thought patterns. At the Autonomous University of Barcelona, Hamid ran two experiments measuring "sacred values"—those someone holds so dear that she is impervious to material gain. He gathered a group of Pakistani immigrants in the city who supported Lashkar-e-Taiba, an Al Qaeda affili-ate. They qualified after filling out surveys in which they said they approved of armed jihad as well as violence against civilians, and that they'd be willing to personally carry out a violent action in support of their values.

Having mapped out which values each participant considered sa-cred, Hamid then put them in a brain scanner and gave them an fMRI, which measures blood flow to certain regions in the brain. Above their heads, in the scanner, flashed a series of statements, such as "Strict Sharia should be implemented in Muslim countries" and "All Muslim countries must be replaced by a single Caliphate." Participants were given a joystick and asked to score their reaction to each statement, on a scale from one, which meant they were impervious to it, to seven, which meant they were willing to die for it. Then, he examined which areas of the brain had the most activity by measuring the blood flow to them. For nonsacred values, he found that both the limbic or emo-tional parts of the brain, and the parts that control reflective thinking, self-control, and abstract reasoning, lit up. But when the value was sacred—something the participant would fight and die for—only the emotional parts were active. No blood flowed to the parts handling logic and reason.

When someone holds a particular value as sacred, argues Hamid, it's a waste of time to try to reason with them with peaceful readings of a Quranic verse or to point to the suspect motives of a pop-up ca-liphate. To do so is to be like a boxer "trying to punch someone's shadow, hoping to hurt them," he elaborates. "You're not going to land a punch. By trying to use reason or logic, you're not even activating the parts of the brain that are involved. Those parts of the brain that pro-cess that kind of information aren't even online."

FOR EVERY FAMILY ISSUE Afifa mentioned to ISIS recruiters on social media, they offered a solution.

Zahra's brother's business had debts. ISIS could repay them.

An aunt had a growth on her neck that she couldn't afford to have fixed in Indonesia. ISIS would give her free treatments.

The aunt's son had severe autism and couldn't walk. ISIS would provide him free medical care.

Week by week, relatives began finding compelling reasons to emigrate. Afifa's grandmother began championing doing *hijra*. She was near the end of her life, she said, and wanted to be in "Blessed Shaam," as the Quran calls the Levant, surrounded by her family. "Besides," Zahra recalled her saying, "who will take care of me if all my children are going to Syria?"

The granny longing to die surrounded by family, the mother looking for help with her son with special needs, the daughter looking for her dad's attention—these were ordinary needs, affixed to the extraordinary plan of joining the Islamic State. This family of middle class professionals had found practical reasons to justify their *hijra*. It was a reminder that, as radicalization expert John Horgan had observed, not all radicals will get involved in terrorism, and not all supporters of terror groups will hold radical beliefs.

Zahra and Muhammad finally relented. Afifa called her sister Putri with the news that the family was going. Putri got the call on the day of her English test—her last exam of the semester. She didn't want to go but feared faring for herself if she didn't. "I was still a spoiled child," she said softly. "I didn't know how to get a job. I still depended on my mom and dad for money and everything. If they left me there, I'd be alone."

Zahra and Muhammad sold their house, and the family spent a few days shopping for the trip. "We bought new shoes," said Afifa cheerfully, waggling her feet in her Technicolor sneakers. "New clothes! New backpacks!"

She described the preparations, as bubbly as any teen recounting her shopping spree before a summer vacation.

DESPITE THE HOURS I spent talking with the various family members, I still couldn't understand why Zahra and Muhammad had finally capitulated. How could two parents allow themselves to be convinced by their sixteen-year-old to chase a dream she'd found online? I could have understood it if they'd been poor or desperate or uneducated. I could even have understood if they'd been wildly unhappy. But they were none of those. At most, as far as I could tell, they nursed the mild ennui of the metropolitan upper middle class.

Several times I tried appealing to Zahra, mother to mother. "I know what it's like to face the arguments of a strong-willed teenager," I said. "My daughter Nic's the youngest in our family, but she's easily the most determined. My husband and I, and her elder sister, are pretty easygoing on the small stuff. So when, say, we're deciding whether to go out for pizza or Indian food, Nic often gets just what she wants . . ."

I trailed off, not adding what I was thinking: . . . *but when it comes to big issues, the grown-ups are in charge. Selling the house and joining the Islamic State? What the hell were you thinking?*

"I was worried about Afifa running away again," Zahra said simply. "I couldn't go through that again." I wondered if it was guilt, depression, or simply a gap between my culture and hers that gave Zahra such a muted air, as though she were watching the world from behind a thick plate of glass. When talking about her youth, or Afifa's childhood, she grew animated, clinging to the details as though it were only those times that were real. When she spoke about Raqqa, it's as though it was just a footnote to her life, something she happened to do, for a brief time, once.

IF YOU'RE SCARED ENOUGH that you'll lose your kid, I suppose you'll do pretty much anything. And in this case, other powerful forces were pressing Zahra and her husband to go: over time, the extended family had started telling themselves stories justifying *hijra*. When I think about it, this family's decision to leave was not all that different from that of many other groups joining ISIS, insofar as they've been victims of groupthink. Radicalization often occurs through small circles of like-minded people convincing one another of a manufactured truth, making the extreme seem, in the last resort, only sensible.

The "bunch of guys" theory, postulated by the psychiatrist and counterterrorism specialist Marc Sageman, holds that friendship and kinship circles are key to a mutual radicalization process, where the self-sufficiency of a small group spurs groupthink among its members. And of course, adolescents are particularly prone to egging one another on toward ever more intensity. Christianne's son Damian in Calgary, like Abdullahi Yusuf in Minneapolis, had been convinced to go to Syria after joining tight circles of young men, whether playing basketball or studying the Quran. They goaded one another toward buying those plane tickets to take them to battlefield glory. In tight groups, reality and logic can be remade, note Clark McCauley and Sophia Moskalenko in *Friction: How Radicalization Happens to Them and Us,* their seminal study on radicalization. Where group consensus is strong enough, it can "make a value judgment seem as objective as the consensus about which tree is tallest."

Afifa's story was a reminder that families are often little worlds unto themselves, their mutually reinforcing certainties tightly knotted together. They build their own internal mores and logic over years of codependence. This family was blinded not by ideology, anger, or testosterone but by wide-eyed idealism. But it still nurtured its own set of reinforcing truths. "We invited each other," Afifa says. "First my uncle, to his family, then to mine, then to my grandmother. Another cousin invited her uncle. . . ." The chain was forged by blood, belief, and love.

"Afifa always wanted everything done together," Zahra observed. "Family togetherness was very important to her."

In August 2015 Afifa, her sisters, her parents, and other relatives left Jakarta for the Islamic State. The group of twenty-six ranged in age from Afifa's one-year-old cousin to her seventy-eight-year-old grandmother. Flying first to Istanbul, they took in the Blue Mosque, then traveled to Kilis, on the Syrian border. Their Tumblr contact had given them the cellphone number of a smuggler, who advised that since there were so many of them, they'd be less conspicuous if they split into a few groups. One of Afifa's uncles and his family went first. Unbeknownst to the rest of the group, Turkish police caught them and flew them back to Jakarta.

Afifa's group left next, taking a taxi to the Syrian border by night. They walked for three hours in the pitch black, stumbling through a watermelon patch and farmers' fields, their feet sinking in the soft soil. Zahra fell a few times; Afifa's grandmother ripped her foot on a barbed-wire fence.

At around three A.M., the smuggler told them they were in ISIS territory, whereupon Afifa sank to the ground and kissed it. A few men from ISIS picked the group up and took them to a safe house. The family napped and prayed, while the officials checked their bags, took their ID cards and passports, and gave them suitable clothing.

"It was the first time I wore niqab," giggled Afifa. "It was like, 'Whoa!'"

The Islamic State guards took the women to a dorm and took the men someplace for what they called "Islamic education." The women wouldn't see their male relatives again for four months.

DISILLUSIONMENT WITH THE REALITY of militant life might be relatively common, but like so much in the deradicalization sphere, it varies greatly from person to person. Having your illusions shattered doesn't necessarily mean that you've abandoned violent or radical beliefs, notes radicalization expert Horgan. "You can be a returning foreign fighter who might be disillusioned because you wanted to be a suicide bomber, but in fact you're cleaning boots." In *Why Terrorists Quit: The Disengagement of Indonesian Jihadists,* Julie Chernov Hwang explains that ex-jihadis consistently cited disillusionment with the group's tactics and leadership. Afifa and her family joined as followers of the Islamic State, not as fighters for it. But even for a group's followers, witnessing hypocrisy in the leaders can sow doubt, triggering the questioning and reevaluation that is so crucial to leaving a group.

Horgan cites an anecdote about Patrizio Peci, a member of the Red Brigades, the far-left Italian militant organization active in the 1970s. His disengagement began when he went to meet a new group leader—only to find him using a bread knife to pick the dirt from his toenails. "These are just little things, nothing," Peci said. "But I was worried. I thought, 'If everybody behaves like this, how will I be able to live among them?'" I had heard a similar sentiment from Kharis, a onetime Indonesian radical, whose yearning to do jihad was blunted by the filthy personal habits of the jihadis. "The mosque and our rooms were disgusting," the twenty-two-year-old recalled. "Our clothes were very dirty, and we were really smelly." Even more disturbing than the poor personal hygiene was the fact that "we were never nice to other people," he told me. "We'd never say *salaam*."

Reality can bite deep and work as a powerful antidote to propaganda. This is one reason governments and rehabilitation groups are often eager for repentant formers to tell their stories. Conversely, attempting to join a militant group but failing to do so can leave people's idealism dangerously intact, notes New York lawyer Steve Zissou, a veteran of numerous terrorist cases: "Wannabe jihadis don't get disillusioned."

AFIFA AND HER FAMILY'S disenchantment started with their slow realization that Raqqa was nothing like the paradise pictured on Tumblr. The women's dorm was filthy, particularly the bathroom. The family had employed servants back in Indonesia, but here Afifa had to get used to the daily cooking and cleaning. She'd expected to be part of a pious sisterhood, but that didn't exist: the women in the dorm were waspish, gossipy, and quarrelsome. One of them was a thief. Instead of talking softly and with dignity, as Islamic etiquette dictates, the dorm residents seemed to yell all the time. Once Afifa walked into the living room to find two women screaming and fighting with knives, "as though they were trying to kill animals!" As Putri put it with characteristic understatement, "They had anger management issues." Other locations in Raqqa were hardly more humane: Afifa's grandmother went to the hospital to get stitches in the foot she cut on a fence near the Turkish border, but the nurse was rough with her, neglecting to wait for the anesthetic to take effect before stitching her wound. Zahra had to hold her mother as the old woman sobbed in pain.

Many of the online promises that had so captivated Afifa turned out to be bogus. The regime's much-touted "justice" had two tracks, one for ISIS fighters and one for locals and those who weren't active members; the latter had to pay more for services. There were courses in computer studies, as Putri had hoped, but they were available only to men.

Instead of free education, the sisters received marriage proposals. The dorm's "house mother," the wife of an ISIS fighter, fielded requests from jihadis to arrange marriages with the sisters. "She came to me and said, 'This man wants to marry you,'" said Afifa. "I was shocked. I didn't know anything about the guy—just his name and his country!" She and her sisters had many proposals. Fighters even asked her father to let them know when his eleven-year-old daughter got her first menstrual period. Once she did, she'd be marriageable. Afifa and her family rejected them all.

The other women in the dorm kept asking Afifa why, at seventeen, she wasn't married. By staying single, they said, she was shirking her duty to the Islamic State. "Where is your jihad?" they demanded.

"My jihad," Afifa would reply, "is not just about marriage."

THE BAD MANNERS THAT the family found in Raqqa raised their doubts that the Islamic State was truly Islamic. When Afifa, who wears glasses, would flip back her top veil in order to see in the market, the religious police would shout at her to put it back. "Really loud, too!" she said. "'Fear Allah, sister! Fear Allah!' Like we did a big sin!"

When U.S. airstrikes hit the town of Al Tabqa and caused an influx of ISIS refugees to Raqqa, many fighters were taking over apartments and houses. ISIS soldiers simply banged on a door, and if there was no answer, they'd break it down. So Zahra and her daughters put a letter on their door, explaining what the Prophet said was the correct way to enter the house, and quoting the Quran, on how to get permission to enter. No sooner had they put it up than someone ripped it down and barged in, looking for a place to stay.

One day the religious police arrested Afifa's aunt Karimah for not wearing a second veil over her niqab. At the police station, she was told to buy what the Islamic State called "sharia clothes." Karimah retorted she wouldn't spend a cent on them, since the Quran said caliphate leaders need to provide their citizens with all that they needed to live Islamically proper lives. The police were rude, but they let Karimah go.

Though Karimah was angry, she immediately decided to do *dawa*, or Islamic education, guiding the ISIS police to the right way of doing things. "We all thought it would be easy to advise one another under the Islamic State," explained Afifa. In the land of true brothers and sisters, the family thought, *It won't be hard, they'll accept our advice.*

Her aunt went back to the police station, Quran in hand. "You are the authority, the government," she explained to the policemen. "Under a true caliphate, you have to give these clothes for free. You can't sell them."

The men gawped at her.

"What's more," she continued, "you should think about your manner when you tell people how to behave. You have to do it kindly, speaking gently. Think of the Prophet Moses, how gently he advised the Pharoah, a man who had been so cruel to his people! It's your obligation to follow Moses." The Prophet Muhammad and his followers never cashed in on the needs of others, she chided them, but gave freely. What about all those ISIS videos she'd seen back in Indonesia, promising that everything from houses to clothes would be free in the new caliphate?

Her advice didn't sit well with the religious police, and not long afterward, three of them showed up at the family's house, their tones far from Moses-like. "What have you ever done for ISIS?" they demanded. "You just want free stuff, and you advise us like this?" They were, Afifa tutted, "very arrogant."

The stories the family had told itself seemed increasingly hollow. Afifa was realizing, "Wow, this is not the real caliphate." When the family's men returned from their four-month stint in "Islamic education," she grew even more certain. Refusing to go to the front line to fight, they'd been put in jail. Afifa, who'd convinced her father that he could choose a desk job, was shocked. She even went to the officials to remind them of the promises she'd read about online.

"Your men are hypocrites, to come here and not help fight," they told her. "What has your family done for ISIS? You ask for this and that, but you haven't given us anything."

The family rented a separate house to hide the menfolk, so they wouldn't be forced to go to the front. Afifa's father and uncle rarely went outside, but when they did, they covered their faces with shawls so as not to be detected. Once Afifa's uncle passed a knot of people after a beheading, looking on as children pelted the corpse with stones.

AFTER SIX MONTHS IN Raqqa, the family realized they had to escape and set about looking for someone to smuggle them out. The sisters giggled as they told me their escape story, tripping over one another's words, breaking in to add or correct details, as families do when re-counting a shared adventure. "It wasn't an easy thing to plan to escape, because there were so many spies in Raqqa," began Afifa. "ISIS spies pretend to be civilians, and vice versa." It took them a year to find a smuggler. He promised to get them out, but instead stole their phones, backpacks, and thousands of dollars.

The second smuggler was a woman. She kept saying the border was closed and they had to wait. She eventually ran away. Said Afifa, "We hadn't paid her, but it hurt."

The third smuggler was older, a grandfather who ran a market stall selling pesticides. They'd need a sponsor in the Kurdish area to take refuge in the camp there, he claimed. He had a friend who might help them. All he needed was $4,000 in cash.

He'd warned them that the route out would be dangerous, and it was. ISIS had sown the ground with land mines, and the area was rife with spies and snipers. When the family reached the Euphrates River and tried to cross it, they found that many fishing boats had been bombed, so the fishermen they'd hoped to pay to row them across were too frightened to do so. They tried to cross by the bridge, but it too had been bombed. After a night in the smuggler's house, they fi-nally crossed the Euphrates, this time on their own, in four boats. "My boat leaked," said Putri. "It was carrying six big adults and one kid, and I'm just thinking, *Oh my God*."

A fourth smuggler, Habib, arrived in a pickup truck to drive them to the checkpoint run by the Syrian Democratic Forces (SDF), an alli-ance of Kurds, Arabs, Assyrians, and other ethnic groups fighting ISIS. To signal that they came in peace, Afifa had bought some white cloth in the Raqqa marketplace to wave out the window. "You can never forget your white flag!" she said.

As the car approached the checkpoint, she saw billowing smoke. A ping of bullets hit the car; a puff of dust rose from the ground. "My cousin raised the white flag, but maybe the sniper didn't see it," said Afifa. The group had to retreat to Habib's house and planned to try again later, even though crossing by night would make SDF soldiers suspicious that the families were spies.

Habib said everyone should leave their phones at his house, claiming the SDF would kill anyone with a phone on arrival. "It was a bit ridiculous," Putri observed dryly. "But we were so scared that we did whatever he said."

They tried to cross out of ISIS territory that night but again had to retreat under sniper fire. "You guys are harder to get across than other people," Habib grumbled.

The next morning the family tried a third time, and finally made it to the SDF checkpoint. "We raised the white flag!" said Afifa. "It was like a surrender in a film!"

Afifa thanked God, just as she had when she'd arrived in ISIS territory a year and ten months before. The family was searched again, only this time by Kurds, and the family's women were separated from the men. The women went to a refugee camp, where they had to brave the hatred of Syrian refugees who hadn't joined ISIS. The men were put in jail for two months. Working with the Indonesian foreign ministry, Huda flew out to negotiate the family's release, arranging new passports and a plane trip back to Jakarta.

ONE AFTERNOON WHILE I am in Jakarta, Afifa's family takes me to the house they are renting. After an hour and a half in the car, we reach one of the distant, hastily built outer suburbs. Security is a worry, they tell me, since defectors risk retaliation from ISIS supporters. The taxi drops us off a half mile from their house, in case someone has followed us. As we walk the dusty path in the dusk, I ask Afifa how she feels about what has happened.

For a second, her inner wattage dims. It's the only time in four days that I see her anything less than supremely confident. "Guilty," she says. "Very, very guilty." That's all she says, all she is willing to say, having sealed up her own sense of agency in the affair, even during a week that her father sits in prison. She seems to have an uncanny ability to slide past the issue of her own responsibility, putting it instead on the Islamic State.

So does her mother Zahra. "I'm angry," Zahra told me when I pressed her, once again, about how she felt about her situation. "ISIS lied to me. They don't act anything like their propaganda. They gave Islam a bad image."

Later Dete Aliah, a longtime YPP executive, will tell me that Afifa feels very guilty indeed—so much so that she offered to go to prison in place of her father. It was her fault they left, the girl pleaded, and so she should be serving time. The judge would have none of it, and nor would her father, who was sentenced to three and a half years in prison.

IN THE CINDER BLOCK house they're renting, we sit in the tiny front room, sipping tea and eating coconut biscuits. Afifa shows me the sewing machine that the family bought with 5 million rupiah in seed funding from the government's deradicalization program. Neither she nor Putri is going back to school, as they've decided instead to concentrate on becoming entrepreneurs. Afifa has toyed with a range of business ideas, from making brownies to selling cosmetics, but for now she's sewing tiny cloth purses patterned with flowers or characters from *Peanuts* and promoting them on social media.

Suddenly Yusuf, the jihadi-turned-chef who became Huda's right-hand man, pokes his head through the front door. Huda assigned him to help the family reintegrate after their return from Raqqa. He visits them so regularly he doesn't stand on ceremony today, plunking himself down on the oilcloth spread on the floor, popping a cookie into his mouth, and declaring himself "the handsomest one in the room!"—an undeniable statement, since he's in an all-female household. Later, he tells me he worries about Afifa's spirits and her faith. "Sometimes she seems to reach the point where she wants to give up," he said. He is concerned she no longer does her sunset and nighttime prayers.

When the judge sentencing Afifa's uncle called her to testify on the stand, Yusuf helped her prepare. "I comforted her, using my own experience as a former jihadi," he told me. "After all, I testified in my own trial." The right thing to do, he told her, was to tell the truth. "If you think he is guilty, say so. If you think he's not, say so." He'd even gone with her to visit her father in prison and had suggested that he get in touch with one of his old buddies from his days as a militant. "I told him, 'If you have time, please look up my friend Ali Imran. I know him really well from jail,'" Yusuf said. "He's a Bali bomber, but a repentant one."

ONLY GOD KNOWS
THE HUMAN HEART

THE HEART IS A red box. Airplane black boxes contain hard data, easily read, but not so the human heart. The Prophet Muhammad understood how hard it was to be certain of what lay inside. In an oft-told anecdote from the Prophet's life, a non-Muslim fighter embraced Islam on the battlefield. One of the Muslim fighters thought the man's deathbed conversion was insincere, so he ran him through with his sword, killing him. The Prophet admonished the Muslim for doubting the convert, asking, "Did you split open his heart?" Only God, Muhammad said, knew what lay inside.

I thought about that anecdote in Indonesia, where I was alternately impressed and unnerved by the ex-jihadis I'd met. Their stories underscored the uncertainties of the human heart—and of rehabilitation. Around the world, judges, parole officers, and security services wrestle with what lies in the hearts of former offenders. How can they balance the safety of the public against the risk of reoffending? The direness of a crime against repentance? If someone leaves a violent group, has their worldview truly changed? If their worldview hasn't changed, but if they serve their time and leave violence behind, is that, in fact, anybody's business but their own?

In Indonesia, I met men who had sworn off their youthful involvements with terrorists while in prison—but who hadn't entirely renounced their groups' beliefs. In the parlance of the counterterrorism community, they were disengaged, because they had left their groups and stopped fomenting violence. But they weren't deradicalized—they hadn't entirely changed the worldviews they'd cultivated while involved with violent extremists.

Theirs weren't neat redemption tales, straying as they did from the tidy paths recounted in TED Talks. Their messiness tested my belief in pluralism, as well as my desire for what Huda called "one fucking good story."

AMIR ABDILLAH WAS CONVICTED of helping bomb Jakarta's JW Marriott Hotel in 2009, in an attack that killed nine people and wounded scores more. The following year, asked whether he had sworn off jihad, his response was noncommittal: "Who knows what the heart will decide? Everything is determined by Allah."

Eight years later, when I visited Amir, he was out of prison, living in the same working-class neighborhood in Jakarta where he grew up. A tidy but humble warren of low houses and hole-in-the-wall shops, it's a place where lots of life is lived outdoors. Motorcycles hog the narrow lanes, neighbors shout through open windows, and kids in flip-flops and shorts kick half-flat soccer balls against walls.

When I meet Amir, I ask him what he thinks about a recent government event, when ex-jihadis met their victims for reconciliation. "It was a good idea," he says cautiously. "But it remains to be seen whether the program really touches the participants' hearts." Some of the formers might have attended just for the travel stipends they were paid, he said. "We cannot guarantee their participation was really coming from the inside."

Amir has the physique of the military man he's always longed to be. He's bulky and meets my translator Eka and me wearing a T-shirt with a print of a Colt .45 revolver on it over green-gray camouflage pants. Well-practiced at speaking to foreign journalists and researchers, he has set out bottles of water and paper straws, and he politely motions for us to sit. The walls of the living room are bare, except for

a framed sura from the Quran and a free calendar from a local airline.

Amir sags into a chair across from us, splays his legs as though resigned to an interrogation, and begins to talk in a flat voice. Fighting is
a family tradition, he tells us. Along with other males in his family, his
father fought with a paramilitary group and later with the Indonesian
army, in the 1940s colonial struggle against the Dutch. As a child, Amir
would doodle guns and army insignias in the margins of his school-
books, dreaming of being like his father.

He tried to join the army but was turned down twice, failing the
physical fitness test the first time and the basic education test the next.
He ended up working in a hotel kitchen and playing soccer with guys
from the neighborhood. A friend invited him to join a *halaqa,* or Quran
study circle, where talk often turned to war and jihad, and he began
wondering whether the army was the only way to see battle action. Al
Qaeda's 2001 attack on the World Trade Center proved that jihadis
could stage high-level military adventures. He wasn't interested in
joining the civil strife between Muslims and Christians in Poso and
Ambon, because the fighters there just used machetes. "What really
interested me," he says, "was guns."

His brother-in-law introduced him to a guy who was looking for
recruits for Jemaah Islamiyah. Amir joined, thrilled by the sense of belonging to a military-style group, and what was more, one with links
to Al Qaeda, whose success on 9/11 burnished it with prestige in jihadist circles. He still remembers the day he met the group's ringleader,
Noordin Top. "I was proud of being part of this network," he says,
"because Noordin's name always appeared whenever there was a
bombing incident in Indonesia." He also met Aji, who taught him to
make bombs with potassium, sulfur, and aluminum powder. "When
you're at the store buying these chemicals," the bombmaker advised,
"if anyone asks you about what you're doing, just say you're putting
together a radio."

Amir's eyes light up as he recalls the day Noordin gave him half a
million rupiah to buy bomb ingredients. Leaning forward, elbows on
knees, he mimes how he made a small bomb: he ground up the heads
of matches and mixed the chemicals to make an explosive, then stuffed

it inside the tube of a ballpoint pen. With the pride of a craftsman, he uses a fingertip to show how delicate the crushed matchsticks had to be, and how careful one had to be putting the mixture inside the pen. He enjoyed going to a desolate field with another member of the network to test it out, and loved the rush of knowing it worked on hearing the explosion.

He swigs from his plastic water bottle and sits back. A gecko scrambles halfway up the wall, then freezes. I realize that his excitement in telling the story is matched by my excitement at hearing it. We're enacting, in miniature, the ritual of militant-media symbiosis, perfected in the post-9/11 era. Terrorists create spectacular events—or tell of them—to members of the press, who in turn publish them, garnering infamy for the terrorists groups, who then gain more recruits wanting in on the next spectacular events, and so on.

In July 2009, Amir booked a room in the Jakarta Marriott hotel. A few days later, his group sent an eighteen-year-old suicide bomber to check in there, and another bomber to the city's Ritz-Carlton. In near-simultaneous blasts, the two terrorists detonated bombs, killing seven hotel guests and themselves. Amir stood outside the Marriott, recording it with a camcorder, so they could send a video through their networks to Al Qaeda headquarters. The bomb explosion brought mixed feelings. He was happy it went off, and that they had finally succeeded. Watching through his camcorder lens, he saw the people stumbling out of the hotel, heard the screaming, smelled the acrid smoke. He ran away, feeling nothing. "No feelings." He shrugs. "Flat."

The bombers met back at a safe house in Jatiasih, on the outskirts of Jakarta. They wanted to celebrate their success with a lunch of lamb, but they realized that buying a feast at the market might draw attention to them. So they dined instead on chicken, rice, and vegetables, washed down with water. As they ate, they started planning their next plot: killing the Indonesian president.

The thrill of a successful mission executed by a tight band of brothers wore off after a couple of weeks. Amir had carelessly thrown away the credit card receipt for the suicide bomber's room at the Marriott in a public trashcan. When the police found it, he was soon named as a suspect. On hearing his name mentioned on television, he thought immediately not of his family but of his network: "If I got arrested, what would happen to my group?" And yet during the weeks he was hiding from the police, he began wondering about what made jihad lawful. By Islamic tradition, a legitimate armed struggle had to be a widespread movement, endorsed not just by a vanguard of militants but by the population at large. "A jihad ought to be supported by the *ummah,* or the Muslim community," he explains to me. "But when I was trying to hide from the police, I realized that I was an outcast. If I went to people's houses for help, or to hide, they were afraid."

This feeling of isolation persisted, and he began to wonder why he had decided to wage jihad in Indonesia, a peaceful, majority-Muslim country. If the country was already safe, if they were free as Muslims to practice their religion, why disturb the peace?

From the alley outside came the shouts and giggles of neighborhood children.

Amir shifts in his chair, cracks his neck, and continues his story. On the day of his arrest, he'd left home and gone to the safe house. It was empty, his comrades dispersed. Unbeknownst to him, the Indonesian police's counterterrorism squad had followed him there. He was arrested, and after a trial, he was sentenced to eight years in Cipinang prison. He served only five, but during them, his worldview shifted. He'd always assumed that other Indonesian militants would approve of Jemaah Islamiyah's actions, but upon meeting other convicted terrorists, he found that many disapproved of the Marriott bombing for targeting civilians. What's more, during his years with Jemaah Islamiyah, he'd been taught to loathe anyone involved with the state, to call them *kafirs,* or infidels. But while chatting with the prison guards and even praying alongside them, he began to see them as fellow Muslims. "They were often confused as to why former combatants hated them," he recalled. "They'd tell me, 'I just work here to support my family.' I saw they were the same as us."

SIMILAR EPIPHANIES APPEAR IN the stories of other reformed extremists. Again and again, formers describe the moment a crack appeared in their fanaticism, thanks to some act of humanity by someone they'd once vilified as the Other. Frank Meeink, a former white supremacist raised in Philadelphia, speaks of how his anti-Semitic beliefs were undercut by the kindness of a Jewish furniture shop owner. The man gave Meeink a job when he left prison—despite the swastika tattoo on the young man's neck and the charge of aggravated kidnapping on his record. The former jihadi recruiter Jesse Morton recounts how the kindness of a prison guard chipped away at his hatred of American institutions. Every shift the guard was on, she took him to the local library in Alexandria, Virginia, where he could read Locke, Rousseau, and other Enlightenment philosophers. Studying these proponents of humanism made him look beyond the sloganeering to his faith's humane core.

Julia Reinelt of the Berlin-based Violence Prevention Network, who has worked on deradicalizing neo-Nazis, describes these personal acts of kindness by authorities—or indeed of betrayal by one's fellow extremists—as "irritations" that scratch the old certainties about an extremist's beliefs. "They're little things that crop up, because life is too complex for the black and white pictures extremists draw," says Reinelt. "Sooner or later they come across something that doesn't fit their scheme of things."

For Amir, prison provided a chance for such productive irritations, as he spent time with fellow inmates who were Muslim religious scholars. Some supported Al Qaeda, while others followed ISIS. He chose to engage with the Al Qaeda clerics, he says matter-of-factly, since he found the ISIS followers harsh and hypocritical: "They label people as *kafirs* too easily." In his cell, he reflected on the Quran verses against bloodshed and against targeting fellow Muslims.

But most influential of all, he says, was reading the letters of Osama bin Laden, who in his later years was concerned that the indiscriminate violence of groups like Al Qaeda in Iraq and the Taliban in Afghanistan was alienating fellow Muslims from the cause. "Bin Laden said we have caused bloodshed for Muslims," he tells me.

For a minute or two, the only sound is a street musician in the alley outside, warbling a local pop song.

I ask my translator Eka to ask him again whether what I'd heard was right.

It was. "After Bin Laden's death, there's not been any leader who could compete with him," he says. "Osama understood the jihad clearly. We are nothing compared to Osama."

I feel like I've run through a room toward a sunny patio outside—and smashed straight into a plate glass window. Before the meeting that day, Eka had assured me that Amir was rehabilitated, and in the eyes of the Indonesian state, he was: he had served his time in prison, and he had renounced violence.

And yet nine people had died in the bombings that day, and over fifty were injured. After the Indonesian government's reconciliation meeting between victims and terrorist offenders, staged a couple weeks earlier, the AP had interviewed a victim of a 2003 Jakarta bombing. The man had burns over 45 percent of his body. In my notebook, I scrawled a note in the margin: "Despicable? Should I sit here? Give voice to him?"

On leaving prison, Amir knew the terrorist label would follow him. He set out to overcome it by returning to his local soccer game on weekends. The first Friday was awkward, he says. "I was afraid they would snub me." He didn't bring up his terrorist past, and for the first year or so, neither did any of the other guys. But when he'd quietly settled back into ordinary life, the neighbors started to ask him, tentatively, why he had been involved in the bombing. "I told them about the case," he explains. "I told them that though some people had invited me to do violent actions again, I promised I wouldn't."

A few friends from his youth, like his former colleagues from the hotel kitchen, still won't meet with him. That said, his neighbors and soccer mates no longer avoid him. For a while, he drove a cab but found it dull and hated the air conditioning. He's now set his sights on becoming a motorcycle messenger, and is saving up for a bike.

His mother still frets that he might fall in with his former jihadist network. Whenever there's another bombing, she has Amir's brother call his cellphone right away, to make sure he's not involved. She's old, says Amir, and he doesn't want to do anything to disappoint her anymore. "Being good to parents is a good thing to do," he observes. "Even though sometimes I think what I did was right, there's no point in it if my mom disagreed with it. You don't get blessed by disobeying your mother."

He hasn't met any of the victims of his attack, though he did meet some from other bombings. He's ready now to meet with the Marriott bombing victims, and wants to ask for forgiveness. He doesn't miss his former Jemaah Islamiyah friends much. Most of them have been killed, anyway, during operations. When he sees the few who are still living, he'll still say hello, "so that they don't think I'm a snob."

He's learning, he says, how to appreciate difference and to move beyond the absolutes he'd embraced during his time as a terrorist. The people at the mosque near his new house offer their five-daily prayers in a slightly different way than he does, but he's getting used to it.

He still loves the military and says he would join if only he could. For now, he doesn't want to do jihad, though he won't rule it out in the future. "If one day, a lot of people began to join radical groups, perhaps," he says. "But we need to preserve the good image of our religion. By doing something bad, we don't just hurt ourselves, but also the faith."

On leaving, I chuck Amir's toddler niece under the chin. I wish Amir luck in saving up for his motorcycle Both actions are sincerely meant: the kid is cute, stumbling around giggling and brandishing a toy pistol. I want Amir's life to go well—not least because I know that if it does, he's less likely to turn back to his old network. But I wonder about the morality of my feelings. He'd helped kill innocents, calmly watching from across the street as they were blown up. He seems, for now at least, a relatively harmless guy, albeit with a bad past and odious political beliefs. His support of Al Qaeda unnerves me, as does his admission that it was partly out of respect for his mother that he distanced himself from his early acts. Still, the bored man who professes it appears to have moved past violence. He's done his time in prison, and in the eyes of the Indonesian government, has earned his freedom.

Eka and I make our way to the main road and a taxi. I'm slightly deflated, since Amir's story didn't deliver the neat satisfaction of catharsis. The journalist in me instinctively craves a happy denouement. But on reflection, I wonder whether there is more value in our slightly less conclusive, more honest encounter.

———

PERHAPS IT WAS THE curious stares from the neighborhood kids, or the ungainliness of my backpack in the narrow alleyways. Perhaps it was the slightly infantilizing feeling of needing Eka to translate most of my interviews here. In any case, a wave of self-consciousness about my American-ness washed over me. That was to the good: done right, all travel should trigger self-scrutiny. At some point, the traveler should swing around the binoculars and train the gaze on her own culture.

My visit to Jakarta, as my first foray out of the West reporting this book, focused me on the possibility that to those I met, I was a living, breathing embodiment of Brand America. Perhaps to Amir, or the other formers, I was a reminder of all the state-sponsored terrorism the United States condoned, even supported, in Iraq and Egypt, in Saudi Arabia, and even in Southeast Asia, where the U.S.-backed repression in East Timor had killed an estimated one-quarter of its population. "I used to see Americans and hate them," one Indonesian militant at the YPP conference told me. "But now I know how to differentiate between the actions of the government and the people."

To be fair, aspects of my identity can also bestow on-the-job advantages. The white privilege that had eased my paths into a Minnesota courtroom and a Danish police station might only be amplified here. Perhaps I came across as an exotic emissary of the land of Harley-Davidsons and iPhones.

Neither image boded well. If I'm just a figure dragging America's baggage behind me, the prospects for mutual understanding seemed pretty bleak. That's the logic of the militant who targets an American: the terrorist takes aim at their political baggage, not at them. How much more productive, surely, to meet with militants unburdened. Since I wasn't worried that Amir was a danger to anyone anymore, the most humane approach was to focus not on the biggest mistakes of his life but on the person in front of me: a melancholy man unsure of his next job, saving up to buy a motorcycle. While he was meeting neighbors as a weekend soccer player, a fellow worshipper at the mosque had helped him find his way back into society. Should not a foreign visitor afford him the dignity of being present in the moment rather than the past?

——

OUTRAGE IS MORE BRACING than discomfort. A few months before my visit to Jakarta, *The New York Times* had run a profile of Tony Hovater, an Ohio white supremacist and Nazi sympathizer who had marched in the 2017 Charlottesville rally. The piece painted a portrait of the man's unremarkable days, describing him as "the Nazi sympathizer next door . . . whose Midwestern manners would please anyone's mother." Many *Times* readers were incensed, offended at what they saw as an attempt to normalize white supremacy. The Anti-Defamation League's CEO Jonathan Greenblatt criticized the *Times* for "treating the abnormal as normal," and for "humanizing the inhumane." Online, the pain of those who had personally suffered from Nazi acts was palpable: "You know who had nice manners?" responded one Twitter commentator. "The Nazi who shaved my uncle Willie's head before escorting him into a cement chamber where he locked eyes with children as their lungs filled with poison and they suffocated to death in agony. Too much? Exactly. That's how you write about Nazis."

Had I lost family to Nazism or any other form of violent extremism, my reaction might be the same. I'd like to think not. But as it is, I disagree. To write about Nazis, you can't start at the gas chamber door, but must start farther back, so as to see the paths that led to it. As Hannah Arendt famously showed, the truly terrifying thing about the guards and barbers at Auschwitz was that they were not monsters but ordinary Germans. If we continue to view Nazis only as Nazis, rather than interrogating why and how they became Nazis, we miss a chance at understanding. To avoid evil acts in the future, we need to complicate our understanding of what forces help drive people to commit them.

But how far from the gas chamber door should we stand, in fact? 1939? 1933? The Treaty of Versailles? Or should one pan outward, looking away from the Nazi himself to actions in the background, like the toxic anti-Semitism that has bubbled away in Europe for centuries? What's the best framing for Uncle Willie's murder? Frame it too broadly, and you deprive the Nazi guard of agency and responsibility—of what makes him human. Frame it too narrowly, and he's dehumanized as a monster. Moreover, you're left, seventy-five years on, at the door of the gas chamber, the poison within still potent.

I don't know what a just balance between rage at an individual's act and an analysis of the paths leading to it would be. I do know, however, that we need to dig deep into the lives of people society deems monsters, looking hard not just at what made them different but at what connects them to the rest of us. Not immediately after an atrocity, when the focus should be on the victims and the violence perpetrated on them. The day after a right-wing attack on New Zealand mosques, the *Daily Mail*'s headline described the terrorist as an ANGELIC BOY WHO GREW TO BE AN EVIL FAR-RIGHT MASS KILLER. That was a whitewash and insulting. (The paper later substituted LITTLE for ANGELIC.) Timing is crucial in excavations for humanity: if you do it too soon, too publicly, or in a manner too politicized, it becomes propaganda. But eventually, one must start hunting. Finding traces of the person's broader culture, interests, and community connections is a basic tool for exit programs around the world.

The task of seeing violent extremists as complex characters becomes all the more important because many of their views sit on a cultural continuum. In societies where hate has bled into the mainstream, extremist groups gain strength and protection from the mainstream views around them. As journalist Shane Bauer tweeted in response to the *Times* article: "People mad about this article want to believe that Nazis are monsters we cannot relate to. White supremacists are normal ass white people and it's been that way in America since 1776. We will continue to be in trouble till we understand that."

Casting Nazis or the Beheader as monsters creates an illusion of safety and certainty. But this sort of security comes at a cost: it shuts down the chance for us to investigate where the monstrousness came from, and where else it might lurk.

"SO, DID YOU ENJOY being a jihadi?" I ask, as Zaki—the anxious would-be humanitarian I'd met at the YPP conference—sat finishing up his dessert in the hotel restaurant with his friend Yudi. A local band mangles "The Devil Went Down to Georgia" a few feet away, so I had to bellow the question twice to be heard.

Zaki nods and smiles, revealing a slightly blackened front tooth.

Back in the late 2000s, he and Yudi had been in the same network in Aceh, fighting for an Islamic State. He'd deliver the arms, and Yudi would distribute them to fighters. Looking at the two of them now, it was hard to imagine anything but jihad drawing them together; they were a casting director's dream of a buddy movie odd couple. Yudi Zulfahri, leading-man handsome, is tall and broad-shouldered, with high cheekbones and hair shaved into a fashionable fade. Zaki Muttaqien is moon-faced and short, with a sweet smile and a shaggy mullet. He has the air of a perennial kid brother, even though he's forty-two and a former terrorist. The first day of the YPP conference, my translator had pointed Zaki out to me as a former ISIS supporter. When Huda asked everyone to talk about the goals for the conference, what struck me was Zaki's eagerness to connect with others. "I'm hoping what we're learning here will not be just a dream for us," he said. "I'm hoping we'll all get blessings from God. By learning about social media, I hope not only to get more money, but more friends."

Yudi and Zaki's paths into and out of terrorist networks were equally distinctive. Yudi, the son of two high school teachers, grew up playing soccer and listening to Guns N' Roses and the Red Hot Chili Peppers. In his final year of college, studying politics, he was invited by a friend to a Quran study circle, held on campus by a Salafi group. His parents hadn't been particularly interested in religion, so Yudi's understanding of Islam was pretty basic. But he was intrigued by the idea of a lean faith, purged of the influences from Hinduism, Buddhism, and animism, which are frequently mixed into Indonesian Muslim practices.

After graduation, Yudi worked as a civil servant by day, and after work, played soccer and pursued the "purest Islam" he could find. At twenty-three, he found it in a tight-knit group of followers of the militant cleric Aman Abdurrahman. Because the group deemed anyone working for the government a *kafir,* Yudi quit his job. He stopped listening to pop music and even stopped watching soccer. "For the jihadi, there is only one truth," he tells me sternly. "They don't tolerate any differences."

He joined a group of Jemaah Islamiyah supporters headed by one of the planners of the 2002 Bali bombings and began military training.

"I went from Salafi to jihadi in just one year," he said, as though recit-
ing the slogan of some macho fitness program. He remembers watching footage of the destruction of the Twin Towers after 9/11 and
smiling. "Al Qaeda was our ideal among terrorist groups," he says.

IN 2010, THE POLICE arrested many members of Yudi and Zaki's network, and each man was sentenced to five years. Toward the end of
Yudi's prison stay, he began hearing about a new group named ISIS. At
first, he toyed with the idea of professing support, as other inmates
were doing. But then he watched the competitive dynamic between
the prison's ISIS supporters and its Al Qaeda supporters. The ISIS supporters were harsher. They labeled anyone who cooperated with
prison officers in any way as *kafirs,* even if they were simply negotiat-
ing for parole or asking to use the Room for Biological Needs for con-
jugal visits with their wives. They kept their cells as dirty as possible,
says Yudi, so that the guards refused to enter. Keeping prison staff out,
they believed, kept their cells—no matter how filthy—"pure" of infidels. Ever the civil servant, Yudi proposed to the prison officers a rota-
tion for cell cleaning, with the result that the ISIS supporters labeled
him a *kafir. Okay, this is too much,* Yudi thought.

In 2014, when the Islamic State declared itself a caliphate, great
confusion arose among the jihadist inmates. Could it be that this was
an Islamic State they could support? Watching ISIS on his phone, Yudi
decided that it was simply "savagery" disguised with a thin veneer of
pseudo-piety. "They were beheading people," he recalls. "Drowning
people. Burning people. Their level of violence wasn't just violence—it
was barbaric."

Yudi proved a cooperative prisoner, even joining the government's
official deradicalization programs. When I ask whether they had succeeded in changing his views, he smiles. "The Indonesian government
doesn't have a clear concept of deradicalization," he said.

I nod, assuming that he was then going to tell me how reflection on
the teachings of the Quran in prison had changed his worldview.

"What really changed me," he continues, "was Al Qaeda's writ-
ings."

They were easy to get, even inside prison, Yudi says, holding up his Samsung phone. His prison sentence coincided with Al Qaeda's attempt to position itself as less violent than its new competitor ISIS. Faced with the slick and successful campaign of the Islamic State, Al Qaeda changed. It tried to graft its brand onto local groups even more than before, attempted to win hearts and minds by starting social programs, and counseled its affiliates against killing fellow Muslims. To Yudi, Al Qaeda's new approach seemed far more reasonable and flexible than that of ISIS. It was willing to accept differences between the four major Islamic schools of law, and it criticized the extreme violence of ISIS as only tarnishing Islam's image. "When I was interested in following ISIS, I was so narrow-minded," he observes. "Al Qaeda broadened my mind. I felt freer."

Tell that to an Iraqi Shiite, I thought. *Or other targets of Al Qaeda's campaigns. A Brooklyn family who lost someone on 9/11. The staff of* Charlie Hebdo, *the French magazine. Or the Yemenis, Algerians, Malians, and Pakistanis killed in attacks by Al Qaeda affiliates.*

Yudi's concept of "deradicalization" certainly diverged from mine. But it did echo what I'd read about prison giving violent extremists time and space to rethink the world. Jail time can either draw people back into the mainstream or push them further from it. Abdullahi Yusuf, the Minneapolis teenager I wrote about in the chapter "By the Book," had his worldview widened in jail by playing chess with a white supremacist. While serving time in an Illinois prison for assault and kidnapping, the former white supremacist Frank Meeink found that his Black teammates on the prison football team helped undercut his racism. But prison can also work the other way. Get the wrong cellmate, or get befriended by a charismatic recruiter who reminds you of the glories of the battlefield, and you can find yourself drawn into violent extremism all over again.

In Yudi's case, prison allowed him to refine his thinking about jihad. He abandoned aspirations of being on the front lines, but he didn't abandon his intellectual allegiance to terrorist groups and ideologies. After he left prison, he enrolled for a master's degree in politics at the University of Indonesia, a course of study that added nuance to his views of the Indonesian government. "Some people see jihadis only as terrorists, or see the Indonesian government only as a criminal," he observes. "In prison, I could only really think that government was bad, jihadis were good. But when I got out, I decided that I wanted to think objectively—to acknowledge that jihadis make mistakes, and the Indonesian government has done some good things."

He insists it wasn't graduate studies alone that helped his critical thinking skills. "Al Qaeda gave me the foundation to go from thinking in a narrow-minded way," he says. "Before, if you thought like the group, you always felt you were right, and you only referred to one source. But Al Qaeda told us to review our actions critically, and to learn from many people." His days of blind obedience were over.

"I was clearly quite a fanatic while I was in the jihadist groups," he says calmly. "Whatever the group said to do, I'd do. I was a fanatical follower of Al Qaeda in prison. Now I still have the idea of war in my head, but I prefer to be careful anytime I get invited to participate in jihad. I really have to think about it hard, and ask, 'What's the war about? Who are they fighting for? What's the reason for it, and is it just?'" He still believes in the ultimate goal of establishing a state governed by sharia law. Nonetheless, his political science classes taught him how difficult that might be. "Establishing a state isn't easy," he's realized. "It's not just about an ideal, but about implementation. The Islamic State may have secured a territory, but they didn't know how to handle the people. They didn't know about public policy."

Yudi tells me he has political ambitions. Smart and slick, he'll be successful, I imagine. Power clearly interests him, as I found in our conversation about movies earlier that day. Yudi's favorite film is *The Godfather*—"*Godfather* 1 and 2—not 3," he specifies. Without the Marlon Brando character to leaven the brutality with his charisma, the trilogy loses its luster. Don Vito Corleone "is cruel, but he cares about poor people," Yudi explains. "He's an honest man, violent only if someone hurts him, but not pure evil." He's not like *Scarface*, Yudi adds, in which Al Pacino's character is "pure gangster, pure criminal. In *The Godfather*, there is morality and humanity."

"A little bit like the divisions you found between ISIS and Al Qaeda?" I ask.

"Yes, I know." He nods. "Yes."

Morality and humanity my ass, I think. Sure, Al Qaeda might have spent a few years on a charm offensive, attempting to rebrand themselves as stately graybeards, a kinder, gentler alternative to the wild men of ISIS. But the analysts I'd read characterized this as a change of rhetoric rather than a change of heart.

The counterterrorism field has a number of thinkers who argued that jihadis are too conservative and intellectually hidebound to re-evaluate their basic principles and policy assumptions. When I thought about it, such assertions echoed the stock Orientalist narratives about a timeless, unchanging Muslim world. Perhaps this analysis underestimated the group's dynamism. A paper by two German analysts pointed out that in 2010, Osama bin Laden called for a "brainstorm" from followers, welcoming "constructive criticism" about the workings of the global network.

Yudi wasn't arguing that Al Qaeda had revamped itself into the Rotary Club. I didn't believe for a second that it had stopped stoking sectarian division, anti-Western sentiment, and even violence. What drew me up short was my own certainty: how automatically defensive I was on hearing the words *Al Qaeda,* how quickly I dismissed the possibility of any evolution in the group's stance. Was Yudi perhaps displaying a flexibility and nuance that I was slow to summon?

IF YUDI JOINED A jihadist group because of his quest for purity, Zaki stumbled into one because he wanted to help people.

Zaki's parents ran a small market stall in Banten, Java, but impressively he'd still managed to attend college. In 2000, after an earthquake in central Sulawesi, he got his parents' permission to join a local NGO, collecting medicine, food, and clothes and distributing them to affected Muslims. As the months wore on, more and more people he'd visited with aid parcels would ask him to help protect them from the violent fallout of tensions between local Christians and Muslims.

It seemed a fairly short step from providing one sort of aid to another, so he joined a local militia, and over the next decade, he belonged to a series of terrorist groups, including Jemaah Islamiyah and Al Qaeda. He set up a military camp in the Philippines, training soldiers to rebel against the Indonesian government. He handled an AK-47, an AR-15, and a Beretta—but he drew the line at bombs, as they caused too many innocent victims.

On his arrest in 2010, he was sentenced to five years in prison. While inside, he read the Quran and contemplated what a just jihad means, which he decided was defending threatened Muslims. News of the rise of the Islamic State fired his imagination. Finally, there'd be a nation dedicated to promoting and protecting Muslims! He phoned a friend, asking him to tap their networks to find recruits for ISIS. The friend obliged, managing to persuade several young men to go to Syria.

After Zaki was released from prison, nobody would hire him. For a time, he tried helping his wife, who made a living by sewing modest Muslim fashions, but it was a tiny operation, and he felt fairly superfluous. Living in an anonymous housing complex, in a town where he knew nobody, was probably safer than hanging out with his old social network back in Banten, but he was lonely and desperate for work. When I asked him whether he was tempted to go back to a jihadist group, he smiled ruefully: "Hungry people cannot think."

His guilt at having recruited people for ISIS kept gnawing at him. He went to Dete, a onetime manager of the YPP who'd started her own NGO helping former jihadis, and proposed that he go back to his old circle of militants, in order to set them right. "I feel guilty," he told her. "In my hometown, there are now lots of ISIS supporters, and I was someone who helped facilitate that. I want to pay for my mistake."

He wanted to go back to his old *halaqa,* or study circle, and go over the scriptural passages the group had focused on, but this time he would teach them "what is actually the real hadith and Quran," he told Dete. He proposed he go twice a month.

"What do you need in order to do that?" Dete asked.

"Transportation, accommodation, food, and reading materials."

Dete tentatively agreed and somehow found the funds.

He takes a soft approach to steering them away from their ISIS-influenced worldview: "I go in and just say, 'How are you? We haven't met for a long time.'"

Then he'll start talking about how the Quran emphasizes mercy and kindness. If they're still listening, he cites verses. They all share the dream of an Islamic state with sharia law, he'll tell them, but they have to be practical about it: "If you do it in a harsh way, will people accept you?"

Trying to change people's minds is a delicate process, he says, requiring patience. "You've got to show a good attitude. If they refuse, you've got to leave them in a friendly manner." Some are receptive, others hostile. "ISIS has divided my friends into two," he says. "The extreme ones are ISIS supporters, and the non-extreme ones join us."

The work is potentially dangerous, both he and Dete tell me, since he might be viewed as a traitor. As he sees it, returning to the *halaqa* is penance for having recruited people for ISIS. "I felt guilty that I exposed my friends to radical views, and that some went to Syria and died," he says. "So I need to correct their extremism. It's my duty."

A terrorist is often presented as someone whose ability to feel has been dulled. But Zaki reminded me that it's often an excess of emotion, not a lack thereof, that draws people toward violent extremism. He embodied what various social scientists have observed: that the empathy of a violent extremist is off-the-charts high but is reserved just for those in their in-group.

A few months later Dete sends me a video of Zaki in a green field strewn with uprooted palm trees and debris. He wears a khaki vest embossed with the logo WE CARE, and he carries a small body wrapped in a sheet. He is back in Banten, Dete says, doing humanitarian aid after a tsunami killed hundreds. The operation was the brainchild of a bunch of former terrorist inmates from prison, who banded together and went out to help.

Back in England, watching the video on my phone, I wonder whether Zaki will stay an aid worker or be drawn back to his old crowd. His loneliness on getting out of prison, and his trouble getting paid work, may make returning to a jihadist network just too tempting. Will his aid efforts morph again into more militant actions? Nobody knows, just as nobody knows whether Amir's or Yudi's admiration for Al Qaeda will harden into something more dangerous. But living with uncertainty, surely, is the price of living in a free and open society. No, it is more than that, I realize. It is the *responsibility* of a free and open society to allow for that uncertainty. Creating monsters whose monstrousness is unexamined, much like locking up people indefinitely in the name of security, allows us the absolution of that responsibility. Indonesia was grappling with what taking responsibility for militants might look like, and while I found it unsettling, it also felt vital.

AFTER INDONESIA, I APPLIED for a visa to Pakistan, which promised to be a perfect place for me to probe both the production and the dismantling of the "Other" and the "terrorist." The specter of Muslim "Otherness" haunted the country's very birth. In 1947 a British colonial administration carved up the subcontinent, creating both India and Pakistan, a homeland for the Muslim minority. More recently, its nuclear capabilities and decades of issues with militancy have led American media and army generals alike to repeatedly label Pakistan "the most dangerous country in the world." Wars in neighboring Afghanistan and Kashmir mean it routinely features among the world's five leading countries for terrorism-related deaths. Less noted is that the country's years of dealing with militants had inspired daring, creative ways of working to rehabilitate them.

GREAT GAMES

MY TAXI JOUNCES DOWN an unpaved road, past cows nosing the green scum of a marsh and boys playing a ragged game of pickup cricket. The air smells of dust, dung, and mandarin peels—a reassuring scent, taking me back to my childhood. In the late 1970s, just before the 1979 Soviet invasion of Afghanistan kicked off a series of wars in the region, my family had lived in Kabul, where my father, a law professor, worked for a year as an adviser to the minister of justice. Our family's stint in Afghanistan was one of a number we spent in Asia during my childhood. These years abroad were driven not just by my father's enthusiasm for Muslim cultures but by his chronic depression. It wasn't quite so crippling when he lived overseas, where life and work felt less stressful to him than it did back in St. Louis.

To a ten-year-old American kid living in Kabul, Pakistan felt downright cosmopolitan in comparison. The State Department orthodontist flew to Islamabad every few months to tighten the braces on American teenage teeth, and the bazaar stalls sold Cadbury chocolate. We'd drive down the Khyber Pass to spend Thanksgiving weekend in Peshawar, where we'd eat at a Chinese restaurant and look at Buddhist stupas. Or farther down, in Lahore, we'd listen to *qawwali* music at the shrines of Sufi mystics. My thrifty father booked us into the cathedral guest house there—not because we were Catholic but because it was cheap. For breakfast, the nuns served oatmeal, every spoonful like swallowing a dry washcloth. Later, we'd walk down the dusty mall to the nearby museum, where Rudyard Kipling's father had been a curator. Its collections prove, in stone, clay, and paint, that Pakistan's history was culturally and religiously plural.

As a journalist in my twenties and thirties, I'd returned many times. In the 1990s, glittering offices of multinational banks appeared in Lahore and Karachi; the old horse-drawn *tongas* were all but replaced by cars—Suzukis for the middle classes, gleaming SUVs for the wealthy. While globalization boosted open markets, it stifled religious and cultural tolerance. President Zia ul-Haq's martial law and Islamization drive drained possibilities in the 1980s, while the Afghan wars brought guns, heroin, and millions of refugees. The Saudis spread a dour, joyless interpretation of Wahhabi Islam that inspired Sunni militia groups to target Shias and attack Sufi shrines. Christians and other minorities felt increasingly threatened by blasphemy laws. For a couple of years, militants actually gained control over swaths of the northeastern corner of the country: from 2007 to 2009, the Taliban managed to take over the Swat Valley, in Khyber Pakhtunkhwa. Today Pakistan remains among the top countries in the world for terrorism-related deaths.

The relationship between the militants and the government has been murky for decades. The conflict with India over Kashmir has empowered some jihadist groups to operate fairly freely, and it's widely assumed that some enjoy support from Pakistan's security services. Particularly since 9/11, under pressure from Western governments, Islamabad has launched periodic crackdowns on jihadist groups. In 2019 the BBC reported that Pakistani officials were again promising to tackle militants, while admitting that there were simply too many to eliminate through force. Among the government proposals for remedies: deradicalization programs, job placement, and "somewhat bizarrely," noted the BBC report, "using them as a kind of 'paramilitary' force."

In spite of—or more likely, because of—the ways militancy has been marbled into their society, Pakistanis have made daring and creative experiments in rehabilitating ex-militants. Among them is the PAIMAN Alumni Trust, a nonprofit whose headquarters sits unpromisingly underneath an Islamabad highway, on a dusty plain pierced by power lines and cellphone masts. The compound is unmarked because many of the young men who come to stay there are targets for retaliation by their former groups.

Such was the case for a young man I'll call Ahmed, who came to meet me at the PAIMAN offices with his younger sister, whom I'll call Salma. (Both siblings asked that I use pseudonyms.) Since my journalist visa restricted my movements, I couldn't travel to their home in Peshawar, so they came to meet me in Islamabad. Ahmed is heavy-browed and bearded, with a quiet intensity. Salma has a round and pink-cheeked face, hair covered with a pink *dupatta,* and an air of still confidence. Together they told me their story.

ONE DAY IN 2014, Ahmed's friend Saleem met him in the street. Some friends from outside the neighborhood were coming for tea, said Saleem. Would he like to come by to meet them? Sure, said Ahmed, who had little else to do. His father's death had made him head of the family, which meant he could come and go as he pleased, without much bother from his mother and siblings. Ahmed was then thirty-three, but without a father and with just a high school diploma, it was hard for him to find a job. He mostly spent his days hanging out in his neighborhood of Gunj Mohalla, in the old city of Peshawar, on the Pakistani side of the Khyber Pass.

The first time he went to Saleem's house, it was just a matter of a cup of chai and a "hello hi," as Pakistanis call the most casual of chats. The two visitors were clearly very pious, what with their long beards and white crocheted skullcaps. Over the next few weeks, "hello hi's" turned into afternoons. The men seemed genuinely interested in Ahmed, asking about his friends and daily routine, commenting on the neighborhood shopkeepers and mosques. Sometimes they brought fruit, which was a treat. Best of all, they had cellphones—and not just the old-fashioned black models sold in the local bazaar but shiny silver ones that could connect to the internet.

One of the men, Imran, showed him something on his Samsung: a cricket game, with little players that you could control pushing the buttons. "Have a try," he urged. And so Ahmed did, picking his team as Pakistan playing against India. He played the next day, too, punching away on the phone as the older men chatted, and the day after that. It became a routine for him to go and drink tea, have a chat, and play a game or three of phone cricket.

After about a month, Imran said that seeing how Ahmed enjoyed the game so much, he might as well take the phone home for a day or two. Not only that, he could receive messages, even videos, right here, with this little green square called WhatsApp. Imran said that whenever he found something that Ahmed might be interested in, he would send it along.

Wait, he'd even show him how to watch a video. He'd send Ahmed one right now. Imran took out another cellphone from his pocket and punched a few buttons. Ahmed's phone pinged. "Go on, press that," said Imran, smiling.

And suddenly there was a video of a bloody scene of Shia Muslims fighting Sunni Muslims in a mosque in Iraq. And then came another one, showing Shiites killing Sunnis in the Baluchistani city of Quetta, just a day's travel down south.

The men watched Ahmed watch the videos. Terrible, they tutted, but these sorts of things were happening wherever there were Shiites. Wasn't this neighborhood full of them?

Ahmed looked up, the phone humming warm in his hand. He'd never given much thought to who was what in Gunj Mohalla. One of Peshawar's oldest quarters, it was home to Hindus, Christians, and Muslims. The people living in its narrow alleyways were just neighbors, attending one another's weddings and funerals, cheering Pakistan's cricketers, sharing tea and the occasional pilau.

"Even if our religions are different, the culture is the same for all of us," Ahmed said. "Maybe the Hindus won't eat meat, but there isn't much difference between us." He'd often come home to find his sisters giggling with their Shia neighbors or just coming from tea in their houses down the alleyway. Sunni or Shiite, both were Muslims.

Muslims? Imran said. No, no, no! Shiites are *kafirs*—unbelievers. In fact, a true Muslim should not have anything to do with them. Better to eat with a Christian, even, than with a Shiite! Eating with them was totally *haram*. ("They never mentioned anything about Hindus or Jewish people," Ahmed noted later, "only Shiites.")

Having never had much religious instruction, Ahmed was vaguely ashamed, in front of these righteous men, that he'd never bothered to learn much about what being a true Muslim meant.

They seemed happy to teach him. Over the next weeks, Ahmed's cellphone pulsed with messages. Imran sent videos of Shia violence against Sunnis, each one a reminder that it was necessary to kill Shiites before they killed true Muslims. He sent Ahmed fatwas from mullahs, explaining that the Shiites were *kafir*. He sent tales of pure Muslim women violated by Shia men, and a quote from the Quran about killing all the unbelievers.

Throughout that hot summer, the chai and chat sessions continued, with the two men talking to Ahmed about what it meant to be a true Muslim. Faith wasn't just about belief but action, they said. It was important to protect pious Muslims from those plotting to destroy them, like the Shiites, they said. ("They made hate in a corner of my heart against the Shia community," Ahmed told me.)

In turn, he began to pass on the men's wisdom to his friends, meeting guys from his neighborhood in the corner of a shop or after dark in a public park and telling them what he'd learned. "We decided we had to do something for our community," he said. "We talked about how they did things to our females, so why shouldn't we do something to their males?"

It's an old calculus, no less toxic for being time-worn: the presumed duty to protect "our" women against the rampages of the invented Other. In my own country, the myth of the predatory Black male violating white females is a cornerstone of racism. In the post–Civil War South, it was used to justify segregation and anti-miscegenation laws, and it was a key engine of terrorist campaigns waged by the Klan through lynchings and pogroms. Claims of the need to protect "our" women from predatory Others echo in today's white supremacist rhetoric. The founder of the Proud Boys claimed that Muslims in Britain were "raping children regularly," while the Christchurch terrorist who murdered mosque-goers in New Zealand fulminated against Muslim migrants as rapists of white women.

AHMED'S MONTHS OF INDOCTRINATION led up to a horrible day. Looking back on this period was like peering into "a dark hole," he told me. "I was perfectly okay before the incident, and I was able to become human again after it. But during it?" All he remembers from those talks with his new friends was an increasing certainty that he had to protect Sunnis by hurting Shiites. "I think the men did their homework," he told me. They'd targeted him as someone without prospects but with the intelligence and charisma to plan an attack. "I have leadership qualities," he said matter-of-factly.

All morning, as Ahmed and Salma told me their story, I found myself thinking of *Kim*, a 1901 Rudyard Kipling novel of British India that I'd read in college. The teenage hero Kim is an orphan of poor Irish parents but rich gifts—charm, smarts, and a mastery of both South Asian and British cultures. Raised on the streets of Lahore during the height of the nineteenth-century Great Game, when Britain and Russia struggled over Afghanistan, Kim is recruited as a spy for the British. The job requires him to travel the Grand Trunk Road, code-switching between his European and Indian selves as he goes.

Much as Ahmed was recruited to extremism through games of cricket on a Samsung, Kim is trained in a different game to serve the British. In "The Play of the Jewels," a British agent scatters precious stones on a tray, then covers them, testing how many of their positions Kim can recall. (Today "Kim's Game" is taught to schoolchildren, scouts, and American snipers as a memory exercise.) After Kim is used in the service of the imperial struggle over Asia, he suffers a breakdown. Playing the Great Game triggers Kim's temporary collapse of the self. "I go from one place to another as I might be a kickball," Kipling's hero says. "This is the great world, and I am only Kim. Who is Kim?"

Listening to Ahmed's talk about his "black hole" reminded me of Kim's collapse. How many people, I wondered, had been groomed in service to the imperial British game, and how many now, in service to transnational games for other, more recent empires? How many have relinquished their sense of self to the collective identity of some group, be it a foreign invader or a local militia? A group of militants, resisting an invasion, or profiting from it?

ONE SUMMER DAY, SOME three months after he first met the men, Ahmed sat in Saleem's house, playing phone cricket. Imran, Saleem, and the other man were huddled in a corner, whispering. Ahmed played distractedly, hurt by his exclusion. Finally, tossing down the phone, he went over to the group. "Hey, I'm your friend, too," he said. "What are you talking about? You can tell me."

Imran and the other men exchanged glances, seeming to hesitate.

"Come on, you can trust me!" Ahmed urged.

A long pause, and then, very slowly, Imran relented. "All right," he said. In fact, there was something that maybe Ahmed could do to help them protect Islam. An opportunity was coming up to avenge Muslims, to behave righteously, to take revenge for all the blood those *kafirs* had spilled. To hurt not just one or two Shia bastards, but many. Remember those fatwas and Quran suras about killing nonbelievers? Well, Muharram was coming up in a couple months, and the usual Shia processions through Gunj Mohalla might provide an opportunity.

Every Muharram, a sacred month in the Islamic calendar, Shia Muslims retell the story of the defeat of Hussain, the Prophet Muhammad's grandson, whom Shiites believe to be the rightful successor to leadership of the Islamic community. Hussain was killed on the tenth of the month by the army of the Sunni caliph. In communities where local or global forces have stoked sectarian divisions, the month's mourning processions can be lightning rods for tensions.

Ahmed seemed to be a resourceful young man, said Imran. Would he happen to have any friends who were God-fearing Muslims and brave?

"I WAS A VERY ordinary girl, with a routine life," Ahmed's sister Salma told me five years after that terrible day. "I never thought of doing anything extraordinary." I suspect that what she managed to do that Muharram had helped endow her with her air of sober authority. She is thirty-two, six years younger than Ahmed, so she was used to deferring to him, like a good Pashtun sister. And yet, after he first brought home that flashy cellphone, she marked the changes in him.

For one thing, she remembered, he was always in a foul mood, his dark brows knit, his eyes narrowed, and the muscles tensed in his cheek. And that scraggly beard didn't suit him. Worse, he began to speak ill of their neighbors. One day when she was having a *gupshup* with a few girlfriends from down the street, Ahmed burst in, took one look, and ordered her into the other room. "Get rid of them," he told her. They were Shiites, not Muslim, he said, and nobody in his household would ever consort with *kafirs*.

"I didn't really take him seriously then," she recalled to me. "These were people we'd shared our sorrows and happiness with." But when he began reeling off the addresses of the neighborhood's Shia families, she became truly alarmed. "He'd memorized them," she said. "He'd point them out, say, 'This house, that house, this colored gate, that colored gate—don't visit with them.' It was as though he were conducting surveillance on them."

Salma knew to watch for warning signs of extremism, because she was a member of Tolana—"Together" in Pashto—a network of local watch groups organized by PAIMAN in which women would gather to share concerns about neighborhood issues, from voting rights to domestic violence. And she had attended a PAIMAN training workshop, where she'd learned to watch for how a person might display early warning signs of extremism, like growing aggressiveness or sullenness, a distracted manner, and intolerant talk. Reserved, even shy, Salma hadn't made any particular impression on her workshop trainer. But when she went out into her community, she really shone: she began training other women, leading groups showing how to challenge their sons and brothers when they saw them behaving badly. "When I saw it in my own house and family, I knew I had to do something," she said.

One day she overheard her brother on the phone, whispering something about the "seventh of Muharram." At this, she decided to take her Shia friends into her confidence. She invited her Tolana group over for an emergency session. Five were Sunni, six were Shia, and all were alarmed when she told them that she didn't know the details, but thought her brother might be planning to do something during the men's Muharram procession. Warn your families to take care, she told the Shia women.

Panicked, the Shia women left quickly to warn their husbands and brothers. Within days, Salma heard that local Shia menfolk were plotting to band together to protect their families from Sunni violence. Suddenly "it felt like it had gone out of control," Salma told me. What had begun as a shared community issue now had the makings of a testosterone-fueled turf war. What's more, the sectarian suspicion seeded by the recruiters was spreading beyond the men, to Salma and her friends. Suddenly, Salma found that she feared her Shia neighbors, feeling "this extremist tendency not just hitting my brother," she said. "Now it was hitting me, too."

She phoned Mossarat Qadeem, PAIMAN's executive director, and the two women came up with a plan. It would be risky for Salma, but worth it if she could stop her neighborhood from turning into a Sunni-Shia battleground. Knowing how high the stakes were "gave me the courage to act," said Salma. The women confided their plan to the imam of the local Sunni mosque, who promised his support.

BEFORE MOVING TO PAIMAN, Qadeem had taught political science and gender studies at the University of Peshawar. She thinks men like Ahmed's recruiters have become key drivers of extremism in Khyber Pakhtunkhwa. There'd always been poverty in Pakistan, and kids who'd been overlooked by distracted parents or who'd not had the chance for education or jobs. What had changed in the last few decades was the presence of recruiters who fanned out across the region, a raft of "very strong and strategic instigators" as she puts it, trained to exploit the poor, bored, or unemployed. "Whoever sent them, sent them to make inroads into our communities," she explains. "And we Pakistanis provided them with the opportunity to do so, because we had these gaps, like weak or poor governance, or lack of opportunities or education."

I'm struck by the responsibility—fault, even—that Qadeem lays not on individuals or even regions but on Pakistani society at large for allowing the recruiters to operate so effectively. One way to thwart terrorism, she believes, is to strengthen community ties. That's why she started PAIMAN's Tolana network, groups in small villages across northern Pakistan formed to tackle neighborhood issues from voter registration to road safety. Tolana women were trained to look for anything in their communities that could signal militant activity. "If you want to know the security situation of a community," she believes, "ask its women, not the police."

Because of this training, Salma had picked up early on her brother's lousy moods and short trousers. Another Tolana volunteer spotted a physical clue in a neighbor's home—a laundry line hanging with clothes for scores of people, in a house where only two families lived. After stopping by the kitchen and finding enough pots to stock a restaurant, the volunteer alerted the police, who raided the house and found a basement stashed with suicide vests and arms. In another village, a local Tolana member knocked on a neighbor's door and found a whole group of women sewing suicide bombers' jackets. They'd been paid 500 rupees apiece by the lead seamstress, who was a militant sympathizer. With a month of work and a little money, PAIMAN was able to teach the women new skills and find them new clients. Increasingly isolated, the recruiter seamstress eventually had to leave the village.

Western critics have suggested that neighborhood interventions like these could run rather too close to the old Stasi kind of system of local state informants. Qadeem, who has lectured on her approach at counterterrorism conferences, the United Nations, and the London School of Economics, says such concerns show why it's vital to start prevention initiatives at the grassroots. Top-down strategies run the risk of alienating targeted groups even further, as happened with the UK's controversial Prevent program and the American CVE programs, both of which aroused suspicion within Muslim communities. "The way their governments have strategized is just adding fuel to the fire," she says. "It's a strategy of surveillance, not prevention. Instead of creating goodwill among these communities, they are putting them on the other side of the fence. They feel suspected, not supported."

Having seen in Khyber Pakhtunkhwa how close links can be between militants and their communities, she's scathing about leaders who deem militants beyond the pale of diplomacy. "It pisses me off, all this theoretical talk," she says. "All this worry about 'Oh, you can't talk to the Taliban.' Well, we have been sitting with them! Interacting with them, dealing with them!" She frowns. "What makes intellect in a person is experience. It's exposure to the unknown. Well, we've had the unknown here in Khyber Pakhtunkhwa. It's living with us. *We've* developed these solutions. *We* are the ones who can teach the world about violent extremism."

THE SEVENTH OF MUHARRAM was an October day, with morning showers damping down the dust in the streets. Rising early, Ahmed skipped breakfast, figuring that he could flee the scene of the attack better on an empty stomach. Even this deprivation was exciting, like he was a leading man in a movie, preparing for the big mission. Heart pumping, he mentally rehearsed the plan he and his recruiters had been through when they met two days before at Saleem's. Ahmed had suggested that they buy pistols in the bazaar, but the men said knives would arouse less suspicion. They'd settled on butchers' knives, just like the ones those *kafirs* had used on Sunnis in Quetta. After Ahmed and his friends did the deed, they were to come back to Saleem's house. The recruiters promised to meet them there and take them to a safe place.

In the morning, Ahmed went around the neighborhood, distributing freshly sharpened knives to eleven friends. He had each man practice sliding a knife up the sleeve of his shirt, the left-handed guys adjusting accordingly. All knew to keep the blades up and the handles down, clenching them in their fists. Ahmed divided the men into groups of three and four, to avoid attracting attention. "It's now or never," he told them. "Let's do this."

In Gunj Mohalla's main street, hundreds of Shia men had begun to gather. Dressed in black, carrying banners and flags, they prepared to merge with mourners from other neighborhoods, who were marching toward them from the upper part of the mohalla. Ahmed's men went to the main thoroughfare and fanned out into the crowd in groups. There'd been no talk of what they would do after they struck, though all the men had agreed to watch Ahmed—if he saw a police sharpshooter on the roof, he'd signal them to call it off.

As Ahmed waited for the procession to start, he scanned the crowd of milling Shiites, picking out the men he planned to knife. "I was thinking about which ones to attack based on which ones I hated the most physically," he said. "I was so highly charged with this anger in me, I couldn't see anything but the enemy."

SALMA AND HER FRIENDS had prepared that morning, too. They put on black *chadars,* a voluminous veil that female mourners wear in Muharram processions. They used the veils to cover the lower half of their faces, just as they did every time they went out in public. Defying tradition, these women would join an all-male march. At least their *chadars* would protect their *ghairat,* honor. Before they set off, Salma told the five Sunni women to stand on one side of the street, and the six Shia women on the other, letting the procession pass between them. "When you see your family members, let your *chadar* fall," Salma said. "Show them your face." Her plan was to shock their male relatives by defying the local code of modesty. By distracting the men, they might prevent the attack.

The women took their places, and a minute or so later Salma saw her brother standing about ten feet away. On letting her *chadar* drop to reveal her face, she stared directly into her brother's eyes. "I had no idea what he would do," said Salma. "I thought he might end up shooting me, or at least hit me. But at least I would be able to save the lives of hundreds of people."

Ahmed was so stunned that he did nothing. "It was like a blackout for me," he said. "My mind and my heart scattered. Everything disappeared, and I only saw her in front of me. It was as though the crowd was gone, and the road was empty." The shock acted as an antidote to the poison that the recruiters had dripped so deliberately into him those past months. He froze. He knew he couldn't hit her here and now, in front of the women she was with—the mother of a friend, the big sister of another. "I grew up with them," he explained. "I couldn't imagine hitting them, or having them seeing me hit Salma."

As he stood rooted in place, the procession started up in earnest. The marchers raised their flags and banners, preparing to walk, when he did "the only good thing I remember doing that day." He shook his head slightly, the signal for the other eleven men to stand down. Assuming there was some sort of danger, they did.

At the time, Ahmed was furious that his mission had been disrupted. Salma dragged him home, where he yelled and hurled books and dishes in their front room. She got him a glass of water and asked him to sit. He ran out of the house and down the alley to Saleem's, where he banged on the door but got no response. He tried again later, but neither the recruiters nor Saleem were there. They'd clearly left the neighborhood. For three days, Ahmed refused to speak to Salma. She endured his fury and hid his Samsung. She tried showing him suras of the Quran forbidding violence and enjoining harmony with people of other faiths. He wouldn't look at them. In the meantime, she asked two members of the local male Tolana group to take him to Islamabad, to PAIMAN, which runs in-house rehabilitation for former militants.

Later, it dawned on Ahmed that the plan had essentially been a suicide mission: had he and his friends gone ahead with the stabbings, they would never have made it out alive, trapped in that narrow street, outnumbered by maybe four hundred Shia men: "I would not have been spared, and I would not be sitting here now."

Salma and her Sunni friends have kept the details of their plan secret to this day, which is probably why Ahmed is still alive. "It remained within those women's families, and they never shared it," she said. She knew that the only way to keep communal peace was to keep silent about the plot. "Even the Shia women on the other side of the street had no idea exactly what the men were planning," she explained. "If they had found out, there would have been real violence."

By removing her veil and showing her face, Salma was using PAIMAN's core rehabilitation philosophy: reminding violent extremists of their own humanity. Recruiters incite people to commit violence for a political goal by stripping away their dignity and identity, says Qadeem. "Your identity is subsumed in the group's identity. The recruiters make you a blank slate, and write what they want to write." Ahmed says he was perfectly normal before meeting Imran, if perhaps a bit aimless. To plunge into the "black hole," as he describes those six months, was to merge with the collective identity the recruiters had prepared for him: a Sunni, yes, but perhaps more important, one of a gang of twelve guys, working together.

I once heard the novelist Mohammed Hanif, a brilliant observer of his native Pakistan, speak at a literary festival. During Partition of the subcontinent in 1947, he said, near the newly drawn border dividing India and Pakistan, there were many rapes. Hindus raped Muslims, and Muslims Hindus. Men told their female relatives to drown themselves in the household well, thus preserving the family honor, if not their lives. But Hanif's ancestors refused. Taking a chance on life above ground instead of guaranteeing shame and silence below it, they chose to face the dangers of resistance rather than the social security of victimhood. "The history of Pakistan," Hanif said, "was made by women who refused to jump into wells."

Salma and the neighbors who joined her at the procession that day remind me of those women who refused the fate of the well. Like the women who resisted Partition-era codes of honor and silence, they braved public life. They refused to let male rage result in their destruction. They scuffed up the lines in the sand that frightened, angry men were working so hard to create.

SHAFQAT MEHMOOD, THE RETIRED brigadier general who started the PAIMAN Alumni Trust in 2004, has the brisk confidence, bristled mustache, and pukka English of the Pakistani army officer class. At his last military post, in Quetta, a city in Baluchistan, he saw firsthand how poverty was a recruiting tool for militant groups. When he retired, the army gave him a large house. He sold it and used the proceeds to start the nonprofit.

Researching how Al Qaeda, Al Shabab, and Boko Haram gain recruits, Mehmood and his staff set out to build their own framework for rehabilitation. It started as a trial and error process, a luxury most programs in the West don't have, since the risks of public scrutiny and fear of terrorism are too great. "In the West, they live on zero error syndrome," says the brigadier general. In Europe and the United States, security concerns can make for cautious programs that can't be tweaked in light of new evidence. But in Pakistan, the threats are so complex and the resources to face them so scarce that there's leeway for experimentation. "We made lots of mistakes," he cheerily admits.

PAIMAN learned from those mistakes and even more from the youths who came for rehabilitation. They taught him not to use the word *peace* because it would immediately rouse militants' suspicions: "They'll assume you're a paid agent of the CIA or MI6." Young men from the Afghan-Pakistan border were weary of hearing Western leaders and the governments they propped up drone on about peace in gilt rooms in Geneva or helicopter tarmacs at Bagram. Decades of war had degraded the word, along with *terrorist, suicide jacket,* and *radicalization*—other words PAIMAN avoids. Instead of *peace,* Mehmood and his staff speak of *social harmony* and even *love.*

It's not what I expected to hear from an army man, much less an officer in a culture dazzled by strongmen and military bluster. Pakistan is besotted with hard-man posturing, electing a playboy-cricketer-turned-politician as its current president, erecting statues of its nuclear missiles at traffic roundabouts. And yet here was Mehmood, extolling the power of emotions and stories. Just upstairs was PAIMAN's purpose-built storytelling room, with a domed ceiling dazzling with mirrored mosaics of flowers. For the brigadier general, getting young men to tell their stories—or even to realize that they have a story to tell—is the engine of rehabilitation. Many of the militants who come to PAIMAN grew up in families or communities where they felt ignored. Many have never been hugged or been wished a happy birthday. "We sit with them," offers Mehmood. "Never have their parents sat with them. Over and over, we are asking these young men, 'Who are you?' We say, 'Look into yourself—tell us who you are.'"

It's easiest to get the young men talking in the evenings. "It's the same anywhere in the world," Mehmood notes. "If you're in a prison, in a barracks, the moment there's a bugle alarm, you're on the hop. When night comes again, that's when you start dreaming." In the dorms at night, Mehmood himself will sit on the floor with the young militants, play a game of cards, and wait for them to relax. Then he will casually ask a young man, "So how is it that you picked up a gun?" And slowly the night seems to soften them, and they'll begin to tell him. By the end of the week, "They call me Baba—father."

He shows me a photo taken after a long talk session: three men in a conference room with him, all with heavy beards and builds. Two of them have their heads down on their desk, as though they are crying. A third one is hugging Mehmood, his head burrowed in the brigadier's shoulder. Pashtun men frequently embrace one another in greeting, but this hug felt more meaningful, says Mehmood. "When you realize that you were away from what your own inner self wants you to be, the grip of an embrace is totally different. You can feel it in the arms."

Seeming on the edge of tears himself, Mehmood coughs and stabs at the keys of his laptop, bringing up more pictures. He shows me a shot of ex-militants out on adventure training in a pine forest in northern Pakistan. Three men in white prayer caps are lifting a fourth man, big-bearded and baggy-trousered in the classic Taliban style, high onto a rope course in the trees. In another photo, ex-militants are in a conga line, laughing.

Still another photo shows a moment in one of the "interactive street theater" performances that PAIMAN organizes. Ex-militants go to a village with a loudspeaker and flags and perform a short play about a social issue. When the subject is domestic violence, some of them take the women's parts. Afterward they engage the crowd in a discussion, coaxing the villagers to talk about subjects often thought to be taboo.

"You would say they would kill you!" Mehmood exclaims. "Highly dangerous men! Highly dangerous! But these activities opened them up; they started enjoying life." Without them, "they'd be sitting in a corner with their weapon, thinking about who they were going to kill! Deciding who is *kafir* and who is not!"

Hypermasculinity is dangerous when intact and messy when it crumbles. But the brigadier general is working to repurpose some of its elements—vigor, determination, paternalism—for good. Aware that the men will need something to keep them busy after militancy, he sends them back to their villages to do community service. He hopes to use the very energy that once pushed them into a terrorist group to rebuild their community's trust in them. "If someone's daughter is getting married, go knock on their door," he urges them. "Ask them, 'I hear your daughter is getting married. What can I do?' Or if someone dies, go to them and ask, 'Can I help you dig the grave? Or light the track to the graveyard for the mourners?'"

Mehmood is wary of academic theories about deradicalization. "Researchers can write down hundreds of reasons for radicalization," he said. "They can write down the method by which you deradicalize. But unless you see the tears running down their faces, the shift in their body language . . ." He pauses and points to his heart.

IT IS THE HEART that Mehmood works on. When Ahmed arrived at PAIMAN, Mehmood took him out to dinner in a restaurant, then to pray in Islamabad's Faisal Mosque. "At the mosque, he lent me his cellphone," Ahmed tells me, "and said, 'Take a selfie. Do you know what a selfie is?' " Over the next ten days, Mehmood would sit for hours at a stretch, asking Ahmed about his home in Peshawar, taking care to avoid mentioning anything about militancy, ideology, or violence. Instead, he asked Ahmed his favorite color. He bought him some jeans at the bazaar.

In the weeks that followed, Ahmed attended workshops on leadership, and learned screen printing in the art studio. An imam taught classes, impressing Ahmed with tales of how the Prophet Muhammad had preached about communal respect even with Christians and Jewish people. "In the Quran, the idea of protecting and respecting your neighbor is very important," Ahmed tells me. "And nowhere does it mention that the neighbor has to be a Muslim."

Since then Ahmed has earned a college degree and now works as a sign printer, designing stationery and signs for bazaar shops. Like Salma, he leads a Tolana group. Among its members are six of the men who joined him with knives that day in Gunj Mohalla. PAIMAN started what has effectively been a rebirth, says Ahmed. At thirty-eight, "I now feel that I am just a boy of five."

If Ahmed sees PAIMAN as creating paths to a new life, so does Mehmood. "As a soldier, let's be frank, I was not a human being," the brigadier general said. "Every soldier speaks in the language of targets. I learned more in the first three years of my life out of uniform than in my thirty-three years in the defense force. The humane part of my life started then."

Everyone I spoke to at PAIMAN seemed motivated not by fear but by a sense of responsibility for their community. Ahmed's notion of responsibility had been twisted into hatred of Shiites by his recruiters. Salma and her neighbors had felt the responsibility to her neighborhood, and she was willing to risk local notions of a woman's propriety to protect it. Frontline proximity to militants means risk, whether you're living with them, like Salma, or fighting them, as Mehmood had in Quetta. As he said, the "zero risk" culture is not something his country can afford.

Read the Pakistani newspapers, and you'll see a robust discourse of blaming the country's militancy problem on some outsider, whether the Afghans, the Saudis, the Indians, the Americans, the poor, or the fanatics. But the people I met at PAIMAN didn't have the luxury of dismissing the threat as coming from some inscrutable "Other." In Khyber Pakhtunkhwa, the people joining these militias were neighbors, relatives, and friends. The seamstress who persuaded her sewing circle to make suicide jackets may have become a social pariah when the rest of the women realized who she worked for, but she wasn't a shadowy foreigner.

As painstaking as embroidery stitches, PAIMAN's counterterrorism strategy pays attention to mundane details: a brother's rancid mood, a laundry line full of unfamiliar clothes, a sewing pattern for vests with a curious number of pockets. If signs of terrorist activity lurked in a house or hamlet, so too, often, did the terrorists. Proximity makes for ambiguity. One continues to love the radicalized brother while loathing his actions, or tolerates the former militant next door.

How very different this strategy is from that more renowned response to Pakistan's terrorist problem, the drone. The Obama administration embraced the new technology enthusiastically, advocating a "kill rather than capture" policy. Where grassroots organizations like PAIMAN deal with the drudgery and uncertainties of rehabilitation, the American security industry, and the military itself, promote drones as a way for soldiers to avoid missions that are "dull, dirty and dangerous." Hunter-killer drones like the Reaper and the Predator have one job: eliminate their targets—or fly home, having failed. The nature of the technology makes missions a matter of "all or nothing," notes the French philosopher Grégoire Chamayou in *A Theory of the Drone*. "Either shoot to kill or take no action at all. Lethal force is the only option available." The ultimate decision of whether to shoot or fly home is marked by a similarly stark calculation about the targets. They are analyzed using data conforming to "patterns of life," note Ann Rogers and John Hill, authors of *Unmanned: Drone Warfare and Global Security:* "In common with other forms of dataveillance, these people and their lives are flattened and reduced to machine-readable binary forms."

Trying to change an extremist in your own living room or street, however, can be dull, dirty, or even dangerous. But Salma had to attempt it, even if it meant risking her life. Her love for her brother meant she had to believe his violent views might be changed. Drones that are launched from the Nevada desert to kill or come home, however, leave terrorists as terrorists until the day they die.

THE WORLD'S BEST
DERADICALIZATION PROGRAM

WHEN I ASKED THE academic John Horgan, who has written extensively on radicalization, to name the world's best rehabilitation program, he immediately replied Sabaoon, a boarding school for former child militants run by the clinical psychologist Feriha Peracha.

Set in the Swat Valley in Khyber Pakhtunkhwa, ringed by the foothills of the Hindu Kush, Sabaoon is a compound of turquoise and white buildings surrounded by playing fields and flower beds. High walls and Pakistani army soldiers guard it, protecting students and staff from militants eager to harm or kidnap defectors or their teachers. Like many women involved on the front lines of peace-building work, Dr. Peracha has received targeted death threats; the army provides her with an escort for the seven-hour drive from Lahore. Despite the dangers, she remains sanguine, crisply observing that she could easily be killed shopping for clothes in Lahore.

Since 2010, Peracha and her staff have worked with hundreds of boys who'd joined the Pakistani Taliban, helping them find paths from militancy back to the mainstream. The Pakistani Taliban emerged in 2007 as an alliance of militia groups bent on overthrowing Pakistan's government. For two years, they established a state in Khyber Pakhtunkhwa that ruled by their interpretation of sharia law. Recruiting poor children in village madrassas, the group compensated for its paltry firepower with a steady stream of young and hungry recruits who would fight as guerrillas or die as suicide bombers.

Sabaoon—"the first light of dawn" in Pashto—has an extraordinary record of success: none of its graduates has ever returned to militancy, says Dr. Peracha. It's provided hundreds of teenage boys with a path not just to peaceful lives but to social mobility. Whatever the boys' aspirations might be, the school continues to help them after they leave, providing them with capital to start a business or fees to attend university. Former child spies and soldiers have found new careers as psychologists, lawyers, and doctors, a nearly unimaginable prospect for poor boys from a region with a rural literacy rate of just 52 percent. Less academically gifted students have become electricians, motorcycle repairmen, tailors, and grocers. When I ask Peracha whether parents of ordinary children angle to get their kids admitted to Sabaoon, she answers emphatically: "All the time."

In other parts of the world, counterterrorism experts debate what kind of support former militants are due. How much and what kind of help is enough? How much is too much? Should programs help formers get jobs and houses? Does counseling simply reward militancy? Critics balk at the ethics of the Saudi state helping former militants by paying for their weddings, dowries, mortgages, and cars. Indonesians grumble about their government giving ex-jihadis seed capital for businesses, while law-abiding citizens struggle to start theirs.

But Peracha argues that the Sabaoon boys' youth makes them victims of terrorism, not perpetrators of it. "Every time I hear of a bomb blast, I'm compassionate about the victims, but also about the young boys who were recruited to do it," she said. "When these boys we work with joined the Taliban, most felt that they were genuinely protecting their culture and their religion. They knew no better, and they were used and abused."

A petite woman with a cut-glass accent and well-coiffed copper hair, she had to convince her family that her work in Swat was worth the danger. "They said, 'You're risking our lives, too,'" she recalled.

"'They'll kill you, and they'll kill us.'" To persuade her brother, she invited him to come up to see the school. When he saw boys in blue and green uniforms playing cricket, he was incredulous: "These can't be militants."

What he witnessed wasn't just a ballgame, but a rehabilitation session in disguise. Sabaoon's late-afternoon sports sessions, where students play cricket, volleyball, and soccer, are part of its strategy to allow former militants to recoup some childhood normalcy. Sometimes the boys play cricket against the army guards, and when that happens, the games take on a larger meaning, as signs of the boys' evolution from outlaws to law-abiding citizens. "Just two months ago these kids were saying, 'We'll cut your head off,'" the guards would gasp. "Now they're saluting us."

The cricket games often unnerved the army guards. The change in their former adversaries so confused and frightened some soldiers that Sabaoon social workers had to spend time talking out their concerns in small groups. Such changes suggest that Sabaoon is deradicalizing not just militants but other Pakistanis as well. "The Pakistani army was fighting its own people," said Peracha. "The soldiers were just as traumatized as the militants and the victims." A Pakistani general who visited Sabaoon wrote in its guest book that it had healed not just former terrorists but the rest of the population, too.

THE DAUGHTER OF A government official, Feriha Peracha was raised in Rawalpindi, where, like many Pakistani girls from prosperous families, she'd attended a Catholic convent school, and she went to university in the West. After earning her doctorate in psychology in London and practicing for twenty-five years in the UK and Canada, she returned to Pakistan with her husband. Setting up a clinical practice in Lahore, she catered to affluent professionals afflicted by the commonplace mental health ills of modern life. "I'd help them with anxiety, depression, psychosis," she said. "But the violent expression of the human mind, I had not confronted until I started to work with these boys." Taking over Sabaoon has aged her, she says, but it is the most rewarding work she's ever done. Before starting there, she thought she wanted to leave Pakistan and return to academia and clinical work in her beloved London. But "I now feel I should stay here," she says. "Not as a Pakistani, but as a humanist. It's a good feeling to know that you can change something that people thought couldn't change."

Her deradicalization work began almost by accident. In 2009 the Pakistani Army secured the Swat Valley after two years of Taliban rule. An army general she knew called to ask her for a favor. His men had rounded up some boys who'd joined the Taliban and were trying to decide what to do with them. Would she come to Swat to give the army her professional assessment? Peracha asked her young colleague, a recently qualified psychologist named Raafia Raees Khan, to accompany her from Lahore to Swat. Though the region remained dangerous, neither woman hesitated.

Having spent summer holidays in Swat as a child, Peracha remembered it as "paradise on earth," with glaciers, lakes, waterfalls, tulips, and fruit orchards. But between 2007 and 2009, the Pakistani Taliban had bombed and banned girls' schools and attacked those who resisted their edicts, most famously Malala Yousafzai. The militants outlawed music and dance and made public lashings and beheadings a common form of discipline.

During their eight-hour drive to Swat, the women passed through countryside pocked with postwar scenes. Families who'd fled their homes thronged the roads. Buildings were sandbagged, and armed soldiers lined the highways. Both women covered their heads, something neither would have done in Lahore. Because they would be meeting young members of the Taliban, they'd packed surgical masks to obscure their faces.

In the end, they forgot to use their masks. That was fortunate, since the boys they met at the army post in Mingora were clearly "more scared of me than I was of them," recalled Peracha. Deeply traumatized, they ranged in age from eight to sixteen, with matted hair, long nails, and ragged clothes, looking "as though they'd come out of another century," said Peracha. (Today, when a new boy arrives at Sabaoon, the staff call in the local barber to trim his hair—and his beard, assuming he's old enough to grow one.)

From nine A.M. till midnight, the two women interviewed the boys, then stayed up till five compiling a psychological assessment of the group. The next morning Peracha spoke to the assembled generals, pronouncing what would become a sort of therapeutic mantra for all future Sabaoon students: "These boys are not dangerous in themselves, but they can be made to behave in very dangerous ways." With the right support, she judged, they could be helped and perhaps even transformed.

She wasn't entirely sure how she'd do it, but when General Ashfaq Parvez Kayani, then chief of army staff, asked her to start Sabaoon, she immediately agreed, and so did her colleague Khan. "It was a split-second decision," recalled Khan, a grave young woman. "But when we've talked about it since, neither of us would ever have done it any differently." The army gave them buildings for the school and pledged to protect both students and staff. They'd drop each boy off along with a sheet of paper describing his militant activities, and they'd retain the final say on whether it was safe to release him or not. But inside the compound itself, Peracha and her staff would work freely.

Initially, both women treated the boys as a group, assuming that since they were all poor Swati boys who had joined the Taliban, they'd share a single road to rehabilitation. But gradually, they realized they'd need to tailor an individual program for each one, shaped by his route into militancy, his relationship with his parents, and his mental state. Peracha credits Sabaoon's success to this labor-intensive approach, along with the long-term monitoring each boy receives after leaving. "The more we worked with them, the more we realized the push and pull factors [into militancy] for each of the boys was so different," she tells me. "There were innumerable variables."

In the West, young people join militant groups of all kinds, from white nationalist groups to violent cults, looking for belonging, identity, or thrills. Many find them online. Not so for Pakistani youth, who live in a country that had only 17 percent internet penetration in 2019. The boys at Sabaoon joined the militants less in search of personal meaning than because of the poverty of possibilities in Swat. While Western prevention programs emphasize motivating factors like boredom, alienation, and racism or Islamophobia, these Pakistani boys are generally drawn to militancy by material need. That makes them, in the words of one Sabaoon psychologist, "dry wood, ready for burning."

After 9/11 many Western counterterrorism experts downplayed the idea that poverty was a radicalization driver, partly because the middle-class World Trade Center bombers and the multimillionaire Osama bin Laden clearly weren't drawn to terrorism for the money. But according to Peracha, boys in Baluchistan's Quetta are hired to plant roadside bombs for twenty dollars apiece. In the Pakistani context, then, "preventing violent extremism starts with that boy who has no clothes and nothing to eat, and who's begging on the street," she observes. "Hopelessness can make for suicide bombers. If life is not good enough here, then heaven can seem much better."

In the early days of Taliban rule, some parents donated their children to the militants as an offering for the cause. When gangs of the men came to villages demanding support, poor mothers, having no money or gold bangles to hand over, would give them a child. Some boys were sold by their parents, or lured by the militants. On village streets—without playgrounds, clubs, or cinemas—bored and broke children are easy prey for militants who dangle the promise of food, a few rupees, or the glamour of a ride in an SUV. Some of the boys were abducted by the Taliban and held hostage for months or years in camps.

Some boys arrive at Sabaoon having been through what Peracha calls a "metaphoric death," in which the militants abduct them, strip them of their old names and identities, and give them new ones. In some camps, they were given new "siblings." Many boys arrived at Sabaoon deeply traumatized, crying in bed at night and fighting one another by day. "At the beginning it was warfare," Peracha said. "I'd never seen such hatred."

One boy, who'd joined the Taliban at seven, was part of a stable of boys kept by a militant commander. When this man went out into the bazaar, he'd order two boys to wear vests packed with explosives and to walk a few paces ahead of him. The commander held the detonators, and if any Pakistani Army soldiers appeared ahead of him, he planned to press the button. If the boys did die, he promised them, they and their families would go to heaven, since the Pakistani Army was allied with the Americans. One boy escaped, turning himself in to the army, which took him to Peracha. "When the commanders hold these children's detonators while they wear the vests, it's murder, not suicide," she tells me.

She refuses to see evil in the militants themselves, however, only in their circumstances. Pushed hard enough, by poverty or fear or brainwashing, anyone can find themselves engaged in horrific acts: "What scares me is that perhaps there is a monster in all of us."

What unnerved me was that these stories of brutality among Pakistani militants fed into a much broader narrative stream. Tales of savageries by brown or black foreigners have been deployed to justify Western invasions and subjugation for centuries. Such stories suggest a population's unchanging essence, implicitly arguing that these savages were incorrigibly violent. But told by Peracha, risking her life to reform other Pakistanis, such stories didn't dehumanize the young militants. Steeped in local dynamics and alive to the basic needs beneath the bad choices the boys made, her account rehumanized them.

DURING THE EARLY DAYS of the school, Peracha and Khan would return after a day's work to Malakand Fort, where Peracha stayed in the room where Winston Churchill slept while in Swat as a war correspondent. For exercise, they'd walk at dusk in the nearby hills, talking over the day's events and wondering which of their charges might possibly try to kill them. Looking back, it was precisely the boys they most feared in those early days who would "protect us the most today," Peracha told me. "I know they would make sure we were safe."

Some Sabaoon graduates would go even further in their devotion to their alma mater. In 2014 Pakistani Taliban bombed a Peshawar school attended by many army families, killing 149 people, 132 of whom were children. A video surfaced of the charismatic leader Mullah Fazlullah asking why there was so much moral outrage over the deaths of the kids of army officers. Militants' children had been taken by force, he claimed, and sent to Sabaoon. Some Sabaoon alumni contacted the school, desperate to go on TV to say they'd been happy there and treated well.

But to do so would have made them targets for retaliation. "We had to prevent them" from going public, said Peracha. "We hadn't done all this to risk their lives again, by having them show their faces on TV."

As dangerous as running Sabaoon could feel, Peracha and Khan knew from the beginning that they couldn't abandon it, not as mental health professionals, not as Pakistanis, and not as Muslims. After 9/11 Peracha had watched the world and her own place in it change. "People used to talk about B.C. and A.D., and now they talk about Before 9/11 and After," she said. "Before, living for twenty-five years in the West, I never thought about my color. Afterward I was made aware that I was of a specific race."

As well as rising intolerance against Muslims abroad, there were spiraling sectarian tensions and violence within Pakistan. The growth "of this Us and Them, black and white thinking, it invoked a sense in me that something had to be done," Peracha said. Khan, who has always lived in Pakistan, also felt the responsibility keenly. "It was not just to these youth, but to the country, and to our religion as well," she explained. "We saw how badly the religion was being misused, misdirecting these boys toward doing something that makes no religious sense at all." In a post-9/11 world, anti-Islamic prejudice had saddled them with an added task: the need to redeem their home and their faith from becoming synonymous with violence and hatred.

Peracha designed Sabaoon's atmosphere of disciplined kindness. There are no punishments: if a boy misbehaves, he merely loses a bit of his afternoon sports session. "I tell my staff never to interrogate—only to interview," she told me. Music and art, banned under the Taliban, are encouraged not merely for therapeutic purposes but because "culture opens you up to everything in this life, while extremists just talk about the next life." At graduation ceremonies, the boys sing and dance. One boy took up playing the *rebab,* a traditional stringed instrument, and began performing concerts. At first some students balked at drawing pictures in the art classes, deeming representation to be un-Islamic. They relented eventually, though some early efforts unnerved the staff. The children drew rain that looked like bullets, and their trees had grenades for leaves and machine guns for branches. The boy who had walked ahead of his commander in a suicide vest kept painting pictures of buckets full of blood. Over time the imagery slowly changed, and today the boy, now grown, works as a tailor.

The boys arrive at Sabaoon with only scant knowledge of Islam—or much else. Right away they are given a standardized test of logical reasoning, and most score in the bottom 5 to 7 percent. Many had dropped out of school, and even those who'd stayed had been limited to rote learning. "They don't ask questions," observed Peracha. "The powerful can ask questions, but the people below them cannot. So much of our work is encouraging these children to ask questions."

Lacking even the most basic critical reasoning skills, the boys are easily exploited by the militants. Some had been told that the Quran commands the people of Swat to kill Pakistani Army soldiers because they were working for the United States. The boys didn't think to question why a seventh-century scripture would name-check countries founded in 1776 and 1947. Taliban commanders pushed the old myth that a verse in the Quran says virgins await jihadis in heaven—and added that you get extra virgins for killing an American. One militant leader found out a boy liked green parrots, so he promised him that he'd turn into a parrot in paradise. Later, when they know better, the boys sometimes tease one another about their former worldviews. "Can you *believe* I used to think that?" they'll ask one another.

Peracha enlisted a renowned Swati religious scholar, Dr. Muhammad Farooq Khan, to teach the boys about Islam. A Vienna-trained psychiatrist and chancellor of the University of Swat, Khan was the author of numerous books on Islam and a bravely vocal critic of Pakistan's violent extremists. Peracha stocked the library with his Pashto-language commentaries on the Quran, so that when talk turned to false claims about virgins and jihad or Jews and Christians, she could direct the boys to sources in a language they could actually read.

She made sure to wrest back the religious concepts the Taliban had hijacked. She would stress that the word *jihad* means not merely "armed warfare" but, more broadly, "struggle." The Prophet Muhammad declared that the "greater jihad," infinitely more important than battle, was the *jihad al nafs*, the struggle against one's own soul. At Sabaoon, a boy's jihad can be his struggle to master fractions, or to find a friend, or to overcome nightmares. "I use the word *jihad* a lot," declared Peracha. While chatting to a boy in the school courtyard, she'll ask him, "And what was your personal jihad this week?"

Posing questions works better, she's found, than directly challenging the beliefs the militants fed the boys. So she will ask a student why the Taliban stockpiled guns in a mosque, a place of peace and prayer. Or why most militants who claim that jihad leads straight to paradise don't send their own children out in suicide vests. "If heaven after death is so beautiful," she'll suggest, "why aren't the militants using their own children for jihad?" (Her larger point stands, but in fact militants occasionally do recruit their own children. The father of one Sabaoon pupil had already sent two of his sons to be suicide bombers. When it was the third brother's turn, he ran away from home and turned himself in to the army, which brought him to Sabaoon.)

At first, Peracha and Khan worried that being female would be a disadvantage in Swat: these boys had been taught the Taliban party line that a woman's place was within the four walls of the house. But their gender turned out to be an asset. Traumatized by the militants' all-male environments, Sabaoon boys welcomed a respite from posturing and machismo. They felt far freer revealing their fears and weaknesses to women. Many adopted Peracha as a mother-figure, while the younger Khan played more of a big-sister role.

Sundays are visiting days for parents. On his parents' first visit, a boy often tells them about his activities with the militants, detailing days he spent spying, extorting, and sometimes, worse. During these confessions, many parents can't bear to look at their son's face, let alone accept his past actions. When this happens, Peracha and Khan will intervene, saying, "Look, he's trying to be open about what he's done. You have to find some part of yourself that is willing to forgive him."

The boys who come from militant families, or who advanced high in Taliban ranks, are often ideologically hardened, and can take years to reform. One handsome and charismatic boy with an IQ of 150 had been groomed to be a Taliban commander, before arriving at Sabaoon. One day he calmly told Peracha, "I could kill you at any time, you know." Using a technique the militants had taught him, he had buried a fish in a nearby field. He knew what to bury next to it so that its body would fill with a poisonous gas. "If I poked it with a stick, the gas would escape, and you'd be dead," he told her. After years of rehabilitation at Sabaoon, he's due to be released soon and is planning on pursuing a career in medicine.

To assess whether a boy is fit to leave, his case worker has him write regular personal statements about his activity with the Taliban. "Whatever true thing you can tell us will help you," he is told. "Because the decision to reintegrate you is ours, but the army has to give the final word." The more closely a boy's statements match up to army intelligence about him, the better. If he neglects to include, say, the fact that he'd been involved in a group that killed people, that's a problem. Peracha had to delay one boy's departure since he had written all about the graves he'd dug to bury bodies but omitted the fact that he'd buried caches of arms, too.

A boy's growing sense of shame over his past actions shows that he is making progress. "Shame is a very significant process which you have to go through," Peracha said. "Guilt gets you nowhere. Shame does." When I ask why she makes the distinction between the two, she says it has to do with the militants' obsession with paradise. "Guilt is an emotion that would allow for penance in the afterlife," she says. "But shame occurs in the context of this life, over something that you did that wasn't acceptable to this society." A lonely, self-absorbed feeling, guilt often remains between a person and God. Shame, on the other hand, is a social emotion, connecting a person to others.

Knitting boys back into their communities remains one of Sabaoon's greatest challenges. Before any boy goes home to his village, Sabaoon social workers work with the family, the local army commander, and the village elders. Each boy is encouraged to find a way to help the community he hurt as a militant, be it by tutoring kids or picking up litter. For the boy, the task provides both penance and therapy; for the community it proves that he has changed. This dynamic often continues for years after graduation: youths trained as motorcycle mechanics or electricians offer free repairs. Those who can drive offer free rides to villagers going to the city for medical appointments.

Though the militants often try to lure the boys back, Peracha says there's not been a single case of recidivism among Sabaoon graduates.

She credits this feat, in large part, to the intensive monitoring of the boys after they leave. Some return to their villages, where a case manager visits to keep track of their progress. For boys who continue their education, or who might be considered high risk because they come from militant families, Sabaoon has a monitoring center in Mingora. The boys board in a dorm while they're adapting to mainstream life, and they're offered tutoring and emotional support from Khan and her team. "These boys need to know that whatever transition they are making to their new life," Khan says, "I'm still there to support them."

I'D PACKED A DOG-EARED paperback biography of Alexander the Great for my trip to Pakistan. The Macedonian conqueror had marched his armies through the regions where, some twenty-five hundred years later, the Taliban would flourish. But the anecdote that haunted me while in Pakistan actually occurred in Persia. After Alexander defeated the Persians in 330 B.C., he was on the road to the vanquished empire's capital, Persepolis, when he happened upon a group of Greeks. They'd been there since the past war between the Greeks and Persians, some years before. Captured by the Persians, these prisoners of war had stayed on as slaves, and their masters had marked them as such by cutting off a nose, ear, or hand. When Alexander's army met them on the road, the young general reportedly cried at the sight of his maimed countrymen, while the former slaves cried at the sight of their liberators.

What, Alexander asked, could he do for them? Would they like to return to Greece? He'd pay for them to do so, if they wanted to go home.

But the men refused. Their wounds made them living embodiments of the Greek defeat, they said. If they went home, they weren't sure if they'd be welcomed or shunned. What they wanted was a village of their own where they could live together, neither as slaves to the Persians nor as symbols of humiliation to the Greeks. Alexander gave them land, and they kept their wives and grew crops, in their own Greco-Persian no-man's-land.

These men knew that the ultimate challenge comes after war, in the homecoming. For an outlaw or warrior, it was far easier to wander than to come to rest. For homecomings don't test the mettle only of the person who returns. They test the character of home, too, exposing the bones of a society that accepts or rejects their returnees—even those who have sided with enemies.

I'M SITTING IN THE hushed and marbled restaurant of a luxury hotel in Islamabad, amid international businessmen finishing expense account lunches and wealthy families taking tea and cake. Across from me sits a young man I'll call Muhammad. Once a Taliban spy, he became a Sabaoon student, and now, armed with a master's degree in psychology, he is working with other ex-militants as a Sabaoon psychologist. He sits ramrod straight and addresses me as "ma'am." Affixed to the lapel of his green corduroy blazer is a pin of the Pakistani flag. "Now I am a peaceful citizen of Pakistan," he says, catching me peering at it. "But as a child, I was a rigid and cruel person. My hobby was killing baby chicks, and my heart was hard, like a stone." He joined the Pakistani Taliban as a boy, and for a time, he was willing to die for its leaders. "My aim was just to harm people. We were worse than animals."

Born in a village in Khyber Pakhtunkhwa, Muhammad felt overlooked at home, which he shared with seven siblings and parents who fought bitterly. When he was around nine, a Swati militant, Maulana Fazlullah, grew prominent by preaching on the evils of female education, Christians and Jews, and the United States. Every night Muhammad would listen to Fazlullah's radio address, often broadcast illegally from mobile transmitters strapped to the backs of donkeys to avoid detection. Every Friday he'd go to Fazlullah's madrassa to listen to his sermon and talk to him.

Muhammad's father was a supporter of the Taliban, so when a group of the militants came to his village and recruited the eleven-year-old, the men raised no objections. The boy's first job was to shake down his fellow villagers for milk and bread for the fighters. Within a few months, he advanced to working as a spy, gathering intelligence on local Pakistani Army outposts. The militants and the boredom of life in his own village convinced him that this life wasn't important. He could achieve paradise in the next life, he figured, and was willing to die for the movement. At thirteen, he was arrested by the army, which kept him in prison for a few weeks, then brought him to Sabaoon. On arrival, he assumed it would be much like jail. But Sabaoon proved to be, he said, "a paradise on earth."

Life with the militants had left him a bit aggressive, a bit fearful, and a bit incredulous, since "he didn't feel that he had done anything to be at Sabaoon," recalled Khan. Though he'd dropped out of school, he was clearly bright. On his first meeting with Peracha, he was defiant. "What do United Nations resolutions say about individual rights?" he demanded. "I'm allowed to speak my mind—to say whatever I want!" Unlike most Sabaoon boys, who spoke only Pashto, he knew Urdu. Short on staff, Peracha and Khan asked him to act as a translator for the tests they gave new arrivals. The gig didn't last long, stopping when he was found to be helping the boys with the answers, but Muhammad liked having responsibility.

After his chaotic, hardscrabble life with the militants, he found the good food, scheduled classes, and the school uniform weird. All his life he'd worn nothing but traditional Pashtun clothes; the Taliban believed that wearing Western-style shirts and pants was *haram*. It took a while for him to agree to wear the uniform's green blazer and button-down shirt.

It took time for him to feel comfortable talking to Peracha and Khan. Back in the village, tradition held that one didn't talk to other families' women. Peracha was the first woman outside his family he had ever spoken to. It was her kindness that struck him most strongly. "Dr. Feriha Peracha started talking to me in a very soft tone," he said. "She called me 'my son.' Those words can't be forgotten by me." As their sessions progressed, it dawned on him that "there was no personal interest there," he says. "She was doing these things for humanity." Over time, "I came to know that women have rights to do jobs like men, to be independent, and to do something for themselves."

Muhammad spent much of his time at the school unlearning what the militants had taught him, particularly about Islam. In Dr. Farooq Khan's classes, he learned that jihad was not one of the pillars of Islam, contrary to the militants' claim. Having once joined a group who bombed girls' schools, Muhammad now learned that Islam actually promoted female education. He read that people of other faiths should be extended kindness and respect, not demonized as infidels. God was not just the god of right-thinking Muslims, he learned, but Rab-ul-Alameen—"God of the Universe, creator of all humans." Where the classes in the village had been a matter of rote learning, Dr. Farooq encouraged students to ask him questions. Even better, he brought candy to class.

Most boys liked Dr. Farooq, but Muhammad, who had just lost his father, formed an exceptionally close bond with him. On October 2, 2010, while the doctor was on a lunch break at his clinic, two members of the Taliban shot and killed him and his assistant. For Muhammad, the loss was devastating.

Working in the school's vegetable garden proved therapeutic, as did teaching the younger kids sports. He discovered he was gifted academically and thought about joining the army or becoming a lawyer. But watching Peracha convinced Muhammad that he wanted to be a psychologist. She moved him so deeply because, as he delicately put it, "she was quite aged." She was only in her early sixties, but it was humbling to see a wealthy city woman, old enough to be his grandmother, working fifteen-hour days on behalf of poor village teenagers. Others might dismiss Sabaoon's students as doomed to lives of militancy or poverty, but not Peracha. "I saw her," Muhammad explained, "and thought, if she can help people, why not me?"

He went off to study psychology at the university in Peshawar, where he told nobody about his past. While studying, he volunteered for the Red Crescent, the Muslim equivalent of the International Red Cross. He donated blood seventeen times and won the award for being the region's outstanding volunteer. When floods hit Khyber Pakhtunkhwa, he headed a team distributing food handouts. After Taliban militants bombed a Christian neighborhood, he held a fundraising drive for the survivors. When someone asked, pointedly, why he chose to raise funds for Christians rather than for Muslim victims of American drone attacks, he replied that the faith of a victim was beside the point. People need help, he said, no matter who they are.

Returning home to a village that had just known him as a Taliban thug was perhaps Muhammad's greatest challenge. His strategy was simply to talk about his change. "I presented my own self," he said. "I told them my own story, of who I was, and who I am." As it turned out, most villagers accepted him. "He was better groomed and better disciplined than they expected," recalled Khan. "Some commented that he didn't seem like he'd gone to prison or a center to be reformed at all. They thought he'd come back from abroad!" Now when a man from the village goes for a job interview, or a boy studies for a school entrance exam, Muhammad helps him prepare. "I am an inspiration for the people," he said. "Parents will say to their children, 'Look at Muhammad—how he was then, and how he is now. See how a person can change!'"

At twenty-six, he seems entirely at ease in the hushed elegance of the hotel. He sips his tea, recites a couplet from the medieval poet Sa'adi, and speaks proudly of his sons and the "beautiful lady" he married. No traces remain of the youth who'd shake down villagers for the Taliban.

"Changing is one thing," I say. "Proving to everyone else that you've changed, that's harder, surely."

They're both tough, he agrees. "But when you accept yourself, you can easily confront the people."

MUHAMMAD'S LIFE STORY HAD a graceful 180-degree arc, a beautiful curve as he moved from militant to mental health professional, from Sabaoon student to Sabaoon staff member. I left the hotel elated, blinking in Islamabad's dusty winter sunlight. I'd hoped to grab a taxi across the road, but the whole thoroughfare was blocked from traffic because the Saudi Arabian prince Mohammed bin Salman was coming to town. A public holiday had been declared; Saudi and Pakistani flags fluttered on streetlights, and signs welcomed the prince "to his second home." The prince would be given a gold-plated submachine gun and the country's highest civilian honor; Pakistan would get a much-needed $20 billion in investments.

Trudging back to the hotel to call a cab, I felt the glow of Muhammad's story fade a bit. The national flags, the signs flattering the prince, all served to remind me just how small Muhammad's story was in the scale of things. Rehabilitation efforts, even those as successful as Sabaoon, can't compete with the geopolitical power plays stoking militancy. For over forty years, partly to counterbalance Iranian influence in the region, Saudi Arabia had been pouring hundreds of millions into Pakistan. It had helped build tens of thousands of madrassas, whose hard-line leaders frequently promoted anti-Shiite and xenophobic mindsets. By some accounts, Saudi sources had provided funding for the region's jihadist groups and supported charities that had siphoned off money to Al Qaeda. Publicly, Western governments lauded it as a major ally in counterterrorism efforts, but it was obvious that the kingdom remained, as Will McCants of the Brookings Institution put it, "both the arsonists and the firefighters." In a 2009 memo later leaked by WikiLeaks, Secretary of State Hillary Clinton called Saudi donors "the most significant source of funding to Sunni terrorist groups worldwide," citing Al Qaeda and the Taliban among them. While the Kingdom of Saudi Arabia was serious about the terrorist threat inside its borders, Clinton noted, it was far less interested in stopping the funding stream to terrorist groups overseas.

To date, I'd been looking at rehabilitation efforts as a matter of individuals, hunting for origin stories by trying to understand one person's problems, reveling in accounts of interventions that made a difference with one troubled boy. It's the nature of the deradicalization arena to focus on individuals, on what led a teen in Minneapolis to leave one's home to fight, or on what combination of imam, psychologist, and social worker might steer a Hamburg youth away from an extremist cell. The successes in Denmark, Pakistan, and Minneapolis convinced me that extremism can and must be healed person by person.

Yet the forces that create extremism are systemic. Just focusing on these bespoke approaches could perpetuate the notion that the problem lay squarely and solely with individuals. Even analyses that took into account local conditions, like a region's economy or the politics of a town often left the bigger picture unexamined. Taking a few steps back, I saw that even the most successful programs were trying to suppress symptoms of the various malaises fueling militancy. How, then, to strategize for a sustainable cure?

ONE SOLUTION MIGHT BE found in the foreign policy of my own country. Back in Jakarta, I'd asked Yudi Zulfahri, the Indonesian Al Qaeda admirer and aspiring politician, how he'd stop recruitment to militant groups. Easy, he said without skipping a beat. The United States and its allies should stop invading other countries. "America acts as if it's the global police," he said. "If it wants to interfere in other people's domestic affairs, then they have to be prepared for a reaction from the country they invaded." I'd heard this line many times before, as has anyone who's read a newspaper since the 1979 Iranian Revolution inspired generations of militants. As a reporter, I'd listened to lots of people—mostly men, mostly young—rail against Western interventions and the inequities of the international order. On street corners, in student lounges, and at rallies, I'd listened to so many speeches about the evils of American imperialism that I was tempted to zone out as Yudi talked. But statistically, his argument was sound, at least according to the work of Robert Pape, a political scientist at the University of Chicago. Having studied patterns among suicide bombers around the world between 1980 and 2003, he found that nearly all shared one characteristic—and it wasn't a Muslim background. Rather, a full 95 percent of them were under some sort of foreign occupation.

I knew Yudi's analysis was simplistic, knew that even if some white witch were to wave her wand so that Washington called all U.S. troops home from the 177 countries where they are stationed, cut off every arms sale to Saudi Arabia, canceled purchases of every last drop of Gulf oil, and stopped every penny of aid to allies who tortured and killed dissidents, there would still be some people ready to fight for a myriad of reasons, ranging from a love of guns to the need for a job or a cause.

And yet Yudi's complaint gave me pause. As we spoke, back home in the United States, the MeToo and Black Lives Matter movements were gaining traction. Both these national protests employed strategies that feminists and Black activists have used for generations: connecting the experiences of individuals, then hunting for patterns that point to institutionalized abuse. Before these movements gained national attention, it was all too easy for some people to dismiss the story of one aspiring actress groped by a studio lech as a bit of isolated bad luck, or the story of one unarmed Black man shot by police in the back as a private drama. Both movements drew attention to power so entrenched and invisible that it could hide in plain sight.

Having begun this project seeking to complicate the popular stereotype of the terrorist as evil and irredeemable, I'd immersed myself in the stories of individuals and in small-bore solutions. As leaders from Jesus to Oprah well know, stories of personal transformation can be powerful tools for shifting people's perceptions. But confining one's gaze exclusively to individual stories can, in fact, disempower. In the long run, keeping the focus on individuals is a diluted version of celebrity culture, distracting us from broader but more insidious structures. My mother's generation of feminists chanted that the personal is political, but my generation, weaned on the post-Reagan cult of individualism, saw power not in coming together as a collective but in the personality cults of Madonna and the Kardashians. Among the many gifts from the MeToo and Black Lives Matter movements was the use of people's stories to illuminate structural problems. The rallying chant of "Say her name," the murders of Breonna Taylor and George Floyd—these stories of individuals galvanized Americans to call for root and branch reform.

Even people who are still grieving can sometimes see that their personal loss is political. One victim I met, mourning the death of a family member in a terrorist attack, was clear-eyed enough to see that her tragedy was far bigger than her. "The victims of terror attacks are actually pawns in a bigger game between the government and the extremist group," she said. "Civilians get caught up in the middle. Every time a government starts to interfere in another country, something happens. It's not like terrorists are attacking governments or parliaments. It's innocent people who are killed. Victims of terrorism are sacrifices to the state."

Though Yudi was an admirer of Al Qaeda, and this woman lost a loved one to a terrorist group, both blamed the violence less on terrorists than on governments. Organizations like Sabaoon worked to rescue individuals who were caught up in societal problems. They crafted solutions for the suffering of individuals, and they hoped that when those individuals returned to their villages, they could help make changes there. But to find a solution to the huge forces that strangled lives like Muhammad's, I'd have to look at institutions designed to address problems at a national and global level. I'd have to see what governments were doing about them.

PART III

A WIDER VIEW

AMERICAN BLOWBACK

IF PAKISTAN HAD SHOWN me the work of miniaturists, trying to make a street, a village, or an individual psyche safe, a conference held by the Organization for Security and Co-operation in Europe (OSCE) provided a glimpse of a massive tableau, large enough to stretch around the world. The OSCE counts countries as disparate as the United States, Sweden, and Azerbaijan among its fifty-seven members, so the meeting was set in the no-man's-land culture of globo-diplomacy. It was held in the spring of 2018 in Rome, under the slightly clinical title "The Reverse Flow of Foreign Terrorist Fighters." The venue was a hotel near the Borghese Gardens. Sunlight glinted off the machine guns of the carabinieri, kissed the security vans parked outside, and bronzed the black rumps of the police horses on patrol.

In the hotel ballroom, the proceedings were as stately as an ocean liner and just as self-enclosed. The photos of militants that flashed on the screen overhead were brown; the faces around the conference table, overwhelmingly white. There were a few exceptions, such as Norwegian parliamentarian Abid Qayyum Raja, who gave a barn-burning address calling for Europe's migrants to integrate. ("Bet you're out of business cards," boomed one American, cutting through the circle of admirers huddled around Raja afterward.) Several delegates used sizable chunks of their speaking time to advertise their own upcoming counterterrorism conferences—in Moscow, or New York, or Vienna. "The circus," said one veteran of such gatherings, referring to the roving bands of experts, intelligence officers, and diplomats who frequent such summits. "Are you going to Madrid?" the Austrian consultant asked the Washingtonian. "I can't unfortunately, since—"

"It conflicts with Paris," they chime as one.

The "circus" had its own patois. When the head of the United Nations Office of Counterterrorism spoke of "the tail end of the former terrorist fighter's life cycle," I had an unbidden image of diagrams of frogs in my seventh-grade biology textbook. But for all that their voices were heard, the FTFs, or foreign terrorist fighters, might as well have been maggots. With few exceptions, the jihadis were framed as spectral threats, showing up on the conference room screen as grainy mug shots, dry statistics, or swooping arrows.

Delegates droned through the prepared texts about their national interventions, like biddable students reading from dull textbooks. We learn that now is not the time for complacency. That we must anticipate the threats of tomorrow. That we are facing a truly global challenge. That we need closer cooperation and immediate information, shared across borders. That the safety of our citizens is at stake. That security must be balanced with a full respect for human rights.

This sheen of gentlemanly consensus was scratched the first morning, when Russia's deputy minister of foreign affairs, Oleg Syromolotov, thundered through a keynote speech, celebrating the "smashing military victory over terrorism" achieved by the Syrian Army "with the support of, first of all, Russian armed forces." A sustained win, he warned, could be assured only by inflicting suitably tough repercussions on returning foreign fighters. In Russia, terrorists face none of the "comfortable" softness that Europe provides them, but "a virtually inevitable, strict, and just criminal prosecution." Respect for human rights just hamstrings Europeans, he said, and plays into the hands of terrorists. The "Western practice of giving absolute priority to the freedom of expression" was "downright dangerous." European attempts at rehabilitation and reintegration of terrorists was "dangerous," turning "'executioners' to victims, by virtue of cunning methods."

Later, a senior prosecutor from Moscow presented a triumphant overview of Russia's antiterrorism laws. "Every individual who participates in terrorism is criminally liable," she announced. A Russian who makes food for someone the government deems a terrorist, or lets him stay on their couch, can get ten years in prison. That's potentially a lot of people looking at jail time, since the Russian government's definition of a terrorist is elastic enough to include Jehovah's Witnesses and anyone who sets off fireworks at a soccer game.

In truth, strongman repression doesn't necessarily deter terrorist activity. Often, it has the opposite effect. Democracies that respect civil liberties, minority rights, and the rule of law are less likely to become targets of terrorism than are nondemocratic societies. A 2016 study found that 93 percent of terrorist attacks between 1989 and 2014 occurred in countries with high rates of state-sponsored terrorism—government forces engaging in extrajudicial killing, torture, and imprisonment without trial. And when the United Nations Development Program asked militants in Africa what push factors led them to join a violent extremist group, 71 percent cited "government action," including the killing or arrest of a family member or friend.

On paper at least, international organizations, including the OSCE, advocate that their member states adopt a multifaceted approach to dealing with the causes and fallouts of terrorist recruitment. The United Nations called for a "global, holistic, multidimensional, and strategic" response to mercenaries, including fighters returning from Syria and Iraq. A 2020 OSCE report would stress "the interconnectedness of human rights and security, and the critical need to address violations, injustice, inequality," and other incubators of terrorist groups. It applauded "prevention, prosecution, rehabilitation and reintegration."

And yet, the report continued, "in practice, far greater emphasis still appears to be placed on repressive and punitive approaches than on preventive or rehabilitative ones."

———

I'M NOT NAÏVE. EXPECTING an international conference on security to spend much time on the sociopolitical roots of terrorism would be about as misplaced as asking a Marvel superhero to talk about his mommy issues. And to be fair, the Rome conference was focused on the return of foreign fighters, not on what drove them to go. But I remained skeptical. Bloviations from the Russians aside, the conference was scrubbed clean of any hint that global geopolitics might play a role in fomenting violent extremism. There was no mention of OSCE members' involvement in, say, the invasions of Iraq and Afghanistan, or their support of dictatorships in Saudi Arabia and Egypt, or the rise of the far right's popularity among electorates from Hungary to the United States.

What was missing, I realized, was any acknowledgment of responsibility, any admission of a link between what these governments did abroad and the threats they faced at home. There was no official version of the two A.M. self-interrogations that Nicola, the British mother of an ISIS fighter, and the other mothers I'd interviewed, had described. Indeed, Nicola had warned me about these international conferences. A veteran of many counterterrorism meetings, she recalls attending a conference where delegates were discussing what drove people to become militants. Noting that nobody mentioned Western foreign policy, she stuck up her hand and offered her analysis. "Of course it's got to do with foreign policy!" she explained. "If you're a Somali or an Arab, your life has been shaped by Western foreign policy. Even if you've been raised in Europe, you've been brought up on your parents' stories of how it affected your family's life and culture. How can you say it's not important?"

Silence. Suggesting that terrorism might be not just an outgrowth of the discontents of powerless young brown men but partly a product of policies set by powerful, mostly white ones didn't get an answer, not in that auditorium.

On the afternoon the Rome conference ended, I wandered outside the hotel into the nearby cool and green of the Borghese Gardens, a park beloved of Romans eager to escape the city's heat and diesel fumes. In the Villa Borghese, the park museum, there is a painting depicting the story of the ancient Greek strongman Polydamas of Skotoussa, whose strength was so spectacular that he killed a lion with his bare hands, stopped a four-horse chariot, and vanquished three Persian fighters. But his faith in his own strength proved his downfall. One hot summer afternoon, he and some friends sought refuge from the noonday sun in the cool of a cave. The roof began collapsing, and while his friends fled, Polydamas stayed, certain he could hold up the ceiling with his great arms. Instead, he was crushed to death. An aging strongman, muscle-bound, vanquished by a blind belief in his own omnipotence.

NOT LONG AFTER RETURNING from Rome, I spoke with Larry Attree, a longtime analyst studying counterterrorism efforts and head of global policy and advocacy at the peace-building organization Saferworld. When it comes to working on the root causes of violent extremism, "most governments aren't willing to look at their own behavior," he told me. "They're so busy asking, 'Why do these individuals sign up and use violence?' that they're not thinking about solving the bigger problem, which is, Why do these movements exist? Who else is responsible for violence and abuse in this context? What role do foreign governments play?"

Too often, he noted, both media and government pay far too much attention to violent extremism and too little to the conditions feeding its appeal, such as government corruption and human rights abuses. Take Yemen, he suggested, which Western governments saw primarily as a haven for Al Qaeda rather than a country governed by a corrupt elite. The West gave the Yemeni government money to take on Al Qaeda, which led it to quash legitimate internal dissent. This led to a violent civil war, which in turn gave ISIS and Al Qaeda opportunities to exploit the chaos. Training a lens on "violent extremism" rather than on broader issues, like corruption or repression, can be risky in the long run.

"Read Sarah Chayes," Attree counseled me at the phone call's end.

An American journalist and consultant with more than ten years of experience in Afghanistan, Chayes managed to get top U.S. officials to see that corruption is intrinsically linked to security. In her 2015 book,

Thieves of State: Why Corruption Threatens Global Security, Chayes argues that most insurgencies take place where government corruption is deep and broad. For citizens facing the daily humiliation of system-atized corruption, the language of moral purity that extremist groups offer can sound pretty good. If you've watched your sister be groomed by a bureaucrat, or your grocer father pay protection money to the local police, why wouldn't you join a group fighting to impose an in-terpretation of sharia law that would severely punish both sexual ha-rassment and usury? As Chayes testified to the Senate Foreign Relations Committee in 2016:

> [Corruption] gives credence to the arguments of militant religious extremists such as the self-proclaimed Islamic State, and has helped them gain recruits or submissiveness from Afghanistan and Iraq to Pakistan, Central Asia, the Sahel, and West Africa. The pitch is a simple one, rooted in the manifest moral deviance of the corrupt: "They were saying the truth about the violations committed by government agencies," residents of Maiduguri, Nigeria, told me during an outdoor conversation on November 21, 2015, explaining the early preaching of the extremist group Boko Haram. "They said, if our constitution were based on the Islamic system, all these things wouldn't be happening; it would be a just and fair society."

The illusion of moral purity was a powerful pull for these groups. Christianne's son Damian had sent texts from Syria decrying what he saw as the decadent mores of his family back in Canada. Afifa, the In-donesian teenager who'd joined ISIS, had identified corruption in her home country as one reason for migrating to the Islamic State. But Chayes charts how entrenched systemic corruption allows militants to cast themselves as righteous fighters for morality.

Reading her book, I remembered back to 1996, when the Taliban swept into Afghanistan, claiming they'd come to restore justice, dig-nity, and order. Many Afghans, weary of the corruption and violence of the warlords ruling much of the country, believed them. Of course, the professed puritanism became a reign of terror, at least in Kabul. Despite their harshness, the group continued to attract followers—and corruption continued to be a useful recruiting tool. After the 2003 U.S. invasion and installation of the Karzai government, disgust at government corruption helped recruitment: "Out of a hundred Taliban, elders would tell me, fewer than a quarter were 'real,'" Chayes writes. "The rest had taken up arms in disgust with the Government."

Revulsion at another form of systemic injustice—patriarchal culture—can boost militancy's appeal too. In Nigeria, the limited life choices for many rural women make joining Boko Haram seem a liberation of sorts, notes Dr. Fatima Akilu, a psychologist and founder of the Nigerian government's deradicalization program. For women in villages where they'd be married off at nine or ten, a pitch from a combatant to join up or to marry him could sound very attractive: "They'd say, 'If you join our group, you can actually choose what you want to do,'" Dr. Akilu explained. "'You can have slaves, run the show as my wife.'" Women could work as cooks or assemble bombs. Breaking with the customs in many villages, Boko Haram promised women that they would have the right to divorce in the case of an unhappy marriage. "For the first time in their lives, they were offered so many choices, and actually achieved great power within Boko Haram," she observed. When the Nigerian government tried to rehabilitate former Boko Haram recruits, "it was harder to deradicalize the women than the men." The men simply had less to lose.

I'M OLD ENOUGH TO remember when *blowback* was a favored buzzword among American foreign policy pundits. Coined by an American CIA analyst in 1954, the year after Washington ousted Iran's democratically elected prime minister, Mohammad Mossadegh, in order to protect British oil interests, it refers to the unintended fallout from covert government actions overseas. Blowback's exhibit A is the Afghan mujahideen, whom the United States armed to fight the Soviets during the 1980s, and who then morphed into global jihadis in the following decade.

Human rights organizations and military analysts have long argued that America's targeted drone strikes in Yemen, Somalia, Iraq, Pakistan, and Afghanistan are producing contemporary versions of blowback. In 2002 the Bush administration pioneered the use of Predator drones to target overseas terrorists. Their use grew exponentially under the Obama administration, and Trump expanded the acceptable area for their use beyond the battlefield to any "area of active hostilities."

But human rights organizations, security analysts, and military figures—those who've watched drone fallout from up close—argue that drone warfare is counterproductive. Strikes that accidentally kill civilians, coupled with the anxiety and fear that drones produce, serve only to alienate populations and stoke militancy. Two fellows at the conservative Cato Institute, security expert A. Trevor Thrall and retired U.S. air force colonel Erik Goepner, found that countries the United States invaded had 143 more terror attacks annually than other countries; those where the United States used drone strikes averaged 395 more terror attacks a year than those with no drone strikes. A former U.S. diplomat in Yemen estimated that for every drone strike there that kills an Al Qaeda operative, Americans create between forty and sixty new enemies. Drone strikes "cause enemies for the United States that will last for generations," warned George W. Bush's counterterrorism czar Richard Clarke. "All of these innocent people that you kill have brothers and sisters and tribal relations. Many of them were not opposed to the United States prior to some one of their friends or relatives being killed. And then, sometimes, they cross over, not only to being opposed to the United States, but by being willing to pick up arms and become a terrorist against the United States. So you may actually be creating terrorists, rather than eliminating them." In 2015 four veteran U.S. Air Force drone pilots wrote to President Obama about drone campaigns, declaring that "this administration and its predecessors have built a drone program that is one of the most devastating driving forces for terrorism and destabilization around the world."

I'd seen how local conditions can also be powerful engines for militancy, as when a poor boy in Peshawar meets a canny recruiter or falls in with a neighborhood gang working for jihadis. Just as too much focus on individual stories blinds us to the geopolitical forces at work, the converse is true, too: the blowback theory, when used by Americans, perpetuates our myopia. It too hinges on Us, the prime mover of events, and Them, the reactive population. It's a self-absorbed method of analysis: what matters is less Their local realities than how They react to American power.

THERE WAS NO US and Them in the case of Bryant Neal Viñas, the first American after 9/11 to join Al Qaeda. His story was a one-man example of blowback. For as he told it, it was an American drone strike that led him, in 2008, to plot to blow up the Long Island Rail Road.

I took that same rail line from Manhattan to Bayside, Queens, to meet him at his lawyer's office. Walking the avenue lined with pizza joints and cheap nail salons, my LIRR ticket still in my pocket, I wondered how somebody decides to destroy a train line they'd traveled in their youth, with the aim of wounding the city where they were born. We were meeting at the office of Bryant's lawyer because he doesn't have much of a home; he rents a room in a woman's house in Flushing. He's not speaking to his family or to any of his childhood friends. "He's not my son no more," his mother told the New York *Daily News* after his arrest. "I don't know him if he's able to do this. He has no family anymore."

Bryant arrived at our meeting late, full of apologies: he'd been kept overtime at his job scrubbing pots at an Italian restaurant. His baby face, his gray T-shirt, and the baseball cap perched over the do-rag on his head made him look more like a teenager than a thirty-five-year-old man. He has slightly hooded eyes and a subdued, studiously polite air, hinting at decades of disappointment. Nothing in Bryant's upbringing predisposed him to join Al Qaeda, let alone explained the fact that in just seven months with the group, he managed to get access to top commanders. American counterterrorism officials called him "the Forrest Gump of jihad" for his uncanny ability to show up at key Al Qaeda meetings. Here was a guy with a high school education, who'd headed out from Long Island with few contacts and no Arabic, Pashto, or Dari, yet was determined to die as a martyr.

Born in 1982, Bryant had been raised Catholic in Medford, Long Island, by his father, an engineer from Peru, and his mother, from Argentina. When he was fourteen, his father left his mother, who a few years later renounced custody of him. Moving in with his father and his stepmother only created more tensions, and for a time, he lived in his car and bunked with a neighborhood family. He started taking some courses at a technical college but didn't finish them. Six months after 9/11, gripped by fervent patriotism, he enlisted in the U.S. Army as a petroleum supply specialist, but left after three weeks. He received a chapter 11 discharge, which meant he'd failed to adapt to life in the military.

Bouncing between jobs as a truck driver, a forklift operator, and a car wash attendant, Bryant filled his free time with boxing. He first encountered Islam at a Long Island mall, after flirting with a girl working at a T-shirt kiosk. When he asked her out, she said she couldn't, because her family said that Muslims shouldn't date. Bryant started asking around about Islam; a Pakistani friend gave him a child's primer about it. Attracted by the discipline of regular prayers, the avoidance of pork and alcohol, and the emphasis on keeping your body strong, he toyed with the idea of converting. He even fasted during Ramadan in solidarity with Muslims. One day he stopped by a mosque to make a Ramadan donation. Standing at the entrance with his checkbook, he was invited in by a group of guys, and before he knew it, they had him saying the *shahada,* the phrase whose recitation makes one a Muslim. "Now, you're Muslim," said the man. Bryant wanted to convert but was not ready yet. "I still had a lot of sinful stuff I wanted to do," he told me. For the first time in the half hour we'd been talking, he flashed the most fleeting of smiles.

In the years following his conversion, his outrage at American actions in Muslim countries grew. He watched the influential YouTube talks by the New Mexico–born extremist Anwar al-Awlaki, who denounced the evils of nonbelievers and American oppression in idiomatic English from his base in Yemen. (In 2011 Al-Awlaki was killed, along with his sixteen-year-old son, by an American drone strike.)

The ultimate impetus for Bryant's departure for Pakistan, however, was an email exchange with a friend about the Western interventions in Iraq and Afghanistan. "You're one of those people who just talks," the friend accused him, "and never really does anything about the stuff they see as wrong." The accusation cut deep, and Bryant became con-

vinced it was his duty to defend his fellow Muslims from foreign occupation. He asked a Pakistani American friend for contacts in
Pakistan, telling him he wanted to study Islam at a madrassa. In fact,
he was secretly planning to join a militant group. His hope was to end
up dead on an Afghan field, a martyr in a fight against a Western army.

On September 10, 2007, he flew to Lahore, and made his way up to
Peshawar. Soon he had a nom de guerre, Bashir al-Amriki—Bashir the
American—and an introduction to join the Shah-Shab, a group affili-
ated with both the Taliban and the ISI, Pakistan's intelligence service.

When Bryant joined, Shah-Shab had been tasked with waging attacks in Afghanistan's Kunar province to prevent the Afghan government from building a dam stopping the flow of water to Pakistan.
Suddenly the purity of purpose he'd hoped to find among the militants
didn't seem so pure. Moreover, he found that the group was using him
"like a mascot," touting its young American recruit as a talking point
to raise funds. "Once I found out they were ISI, I was like, 'I gotta get
out of here,'" he told me. "I didn't want to do their dirty work. That
wasn't for me." He left, hoping to find a group to take him to fight on
the flatlands of Helmand, in Afghanistan.

"Why Helmand?" I asked.

"I was a disaster in the mountains," he said, his vowels New York–
long. "The altitude was terrible; I got so sick. I'm from Long Island.
I'm used to sea level!" He felt so wretched that he offered to undertake
a suicide mission, figuring that martyrdom would be an honorable
way to end his misery.

He was turned down. In March 2008, he made his way to North
Waziristan, where he was able to join another group. He didn't know
its name until he asked a fellow recruit, a Kuwaiti, who told him. He
was shocked. "I was like, 'This is Al Qaeda? Really? It's not like the stuff
I saw in the videos.'" When he was back on Long Island, he'd thrilled
to the Al Qaeda propaganda videos he'd seen on YouTube, with their
scenes of men in black crawling under barbed wire and firing AK-47s.
But life in the mud-brick house in Waziristan was boring. He spent his
days waiting, usually in vain, for deployment on a mission, choking
down a diet of okra, potatoes, and rice and killing time talking to fellow volunteers. "Most of them were nerds and bookworms, not the

vampire killers who drink blood you read about in the media," he said. Nights, he slept in a flea-infested sleeping bag.

When the house radio could get a signal, the men caught bits of news on the BBC. Bryant heard about Usain Bolt's victory at the Beijing Olympics, and John McCain's and Barack Obama's bids for the U.S. presidency. The wealthier volunteers, usually from the Gulf States, had money to spend on goats, chickens, and specialized combat training. Bryant didn't, so he had to settle for the three courses required for Al Qaeda volunteers: basic training, projectile weapons theory, and explosives theory. To avoid the U.S. drones overhead, classes were conducted inside the house. Bryant learned how to take apart an AK-47 and how to prepare shrapnel for a bomb, sticking glue and ball bearings together "like a sandwich." By July, his training was complete, and not long afterward he was assigned to a group tasked with launching a mortar attack on a U.S. army base in Afghanistan. But the first time they tried, the radio spotter wasn't at his post. The second day, the rockets didn't reach the base, and the mission was aborted.

TALKING TO BRYANT WAS an exercise in cognitive dissonance. I could discern no trace of an aspiring suicide bomber in this guy from Queens. Nor could I see in him any anger, let alone enough to want to bomb the LIRR. "What made you propose it?" I asked. "Was it to impress your commanders? Was it that you hated Americans? New Yorkers?"

Bryant paused, and then spoke in his low, even voice. "When you're in a war zone," he said, "you hear about violence all the time." Its constant hum helped to normalize it, he said.

I pressed on, trying to tease out what made him change from someone who would attack Western targets in Pakistan to someone who would attack New York commuters.

Finally he told me: it was the U.S. drones. At first, the Predators and Reapers flying overhead were simply annoying and anxiety-producing. "Sometimes you could hear them," he said. "On a clear day, you could see them. There's always that awareness that any day could be your last day."

Once while traveling through Waziristan, he and a few other militants stopped at an orphanage to drink tea. Not long afterward a drone bombed the orphanage. On hearing the news, and imagining the dead children, something hardened in him. His notion of jihad shifted from fighting local battles to targeting American civilians. He wanted to get back at the people who had done it, he explained, his voice steady. "It's not something I'm proud of, but in that environment, it becomes normal."

A beat later he added softly, "War is very ugly."

So it was that, in an Al Qaeda safe house in Waziristan, Bryant found himself explaining to a senior commander that a bomb on the Long Island Rail Road could cripple New York City. He had floated other plans—bombing a Walmart, setting up training camps in Peru—but the LIRR plot was the only one to pique his commanders' interest. Late one night, over dinner with senior commander Younis al-Mauritani, Bryant sketched a map of his native Long Island, explaining the key stations, the most crowded times, and crucially, the way all the trains bound for Manhattan merged into a single tunnel. The best plan of attack for a suicide bomber, he explained, was to blow up the tunnel from a train inside it. Al-Mauritani was intrigued. The importance of a bombing like that lay not in the number of casualties, he told Bryant, but in how it could wreck the economy.

The plot never came to fruition, though in the run-up to Thanksgiving 2008, I remember hearing on the radio that New York City travelers were warned of "plausible but uncorroborated information" that an Al Qaeda plot was planned for the holidays. That information was from Bryant.

If the first part of Bryant's story was a lesson about blowback, the second was about the complexities of his homecoming. He turned out to be what even the U.S. government acknowledged was probably the greatest source of Western intelligence on Al Qaeda during his time there. "To say that the defendant provided substantial assistance to the government is an understatement," wrote the U.S. government prosecutor.

HIS ARREST CAME IN the fall, in Peshawar, where he was waiting until the militants' fighting season started again in spring. One day while he was haggling with a shopkeeper over a rifle scope in a bazaar, Pakistani police picked him up. They handed him over to the Americans, who took him to Bagram Air Base in Afghanistan and, from there, to the United States. Don Borelli, the FBI supervisor of his case, recalled watching the FBI plane land in Newburgh, New York, and "a skinny, frail-looking kid" disembark.

Nearly immediately after his arrest, Bryant began telling the authorities what he knew. When I pressed him on why he cooperated so quickly, he struggled a bit, hedging that he gave "some info when I first started, but wasn't willing to give them everything."

When you talk to people working to rehabilitate militants, they will stress that it is a slow, multipronged, and highly personalized process. Rehabilitation usually takes years, with the individual zigzagging between minor successes and setbacks. The best programs draw on teams of people who are carefully selected for the person's needs. For the guy hung up on radical theology, they will enlist an imam, a social worker, and a psychologist. For the neo-Nazi addicted to pills, they will use a drug counselor, as well as a mentor familiar with the local white supremacist scenes.

In his rehabilitation, Bryant had none of these. Indeed, it's difficult to see his transition as real disengagement. It seems more like opportunism, that he flipped sides simply to survive. When I asked him to pinpoint the moment when he started to seriously think about cooperating with U.S. intelligence, he described sitting in a solitary lockdown cell of a Brooklyn prison, freezing, listening to the screams of other inmates, and thinking back through past disappointments, "all the people that ratted on me, the promises that were made."

One day two detectives signed him out of the prison, put him in a car, and drove him to Nathan's Famous, where he got a hot dog and some fries. Knowing he was a lifelong Mets fan, they then took him to the stadium where the team's minor league affiliate, the Brooklyn Cyclones, played. One of the detectives knew the general manager and asked if they could walk around the diamond, explaining the inmate's situation in the broadest of terms: "Hey! Bryant here just got back from Afghanistan! He was in the mountains up there." Bryant chuckled as he recalled the scene. "The look on the general manager's face was like—what?"

With his handcuffs attached to a chain around his waist, Bryant walked around the diamond. The moment gave him a sense of contentment, even joy, "like a kid seeing something that he loves."

Later, as he was waiting in the parking lot for one detective to get the car to drive him back to prison, the other turned to him. "Do you want to go back to maximum security for the rest of your life?" he asked. "Or"—he spread out his arms, looking around the parking lot— "do you want to have a life again? Not many people get a second chance at life."

It was at that moment that "they got me," said Bryant.

As soon as he began to talk to the FBI, the U.S. Army swung into action. Based on his information, CIA-operated drones bombed the places he'd trained and lived, including the mud-brick safe house in Waziristan. It's highly likely that the information he shared resulted in the deaths of his former comrades.

Was it painful to think about? I asked him.

"A little bit, but the way I look at it, if I'm going to leave my old life behind, they can't be my friends anymore." He shrugged. "It was a little tough, but I figured that this is the way it's going to be now."

Bryant wore his allegiances lightly even in retelling his story. Repetition had buffed the account to a sheen; he answered my questions courteously, but without much emotion. The ease with which he had moved from one militant group to another, serving as an informant first for Al Qaeda, then for the Americans, reminded me that not every jihadi harbors an ideology, let alone unshakable political beliefs.

Bryant's lawyer, Steve Zissou, insisted his client was not quite as glib as he sounded. "I don't think he ever felt good about it," he said. "Knowing that you caused some of the deaths [of former comrades] is a difficult thing to live with." There's no way of knowing how many people were killed because of what Bryant told the FBI, but given how important the U.S. government deemed his information to be, Zissou inferred that "a lot of people died."

When I asked Bryant exactly when he truly gave up his former goals as a militant, he shrugged and said: "When you plead guilty, that's when you renounce your old life."

"But did your worldview change?" I persisted. "I mean, you're helping the same army you went out to fight to bomb your former buddies. Did you change how you viewed the injustices that you wanted to fight in the first place?"

He said he still believed it wrong for Western powers to meddle in Muslim countries, but "now I've seen the other side, and it gives me a better understanding that both sides are wrong."

I remained mystified by how Bryant managed to shift so seamlessly from a would-be suicide bomber to a U.S. intelligence asset. The judge in his case, Nicholas G. Garaufis, implied a similar bewilderment, noting that the man's spectacular volte-face complicated his sentencing: "The juxtaposition of Mr. Vinas's atrocious crimes and his remarkable post-arrest cooperation is what makes the task of sentencing Mr. Vinas so difficult."

Later, when I asked Zissou why he thought his client changed allegiances so quickly and completely, the lawyer exhaled slowly. "Well . . . yeah. I'm not sure. It may be as simple as not wanting to spend the rest of his life in prison."

It's not uncommon, the FBI's Borelli told me later, for captured militants to start talking within days, even hours. Many are simply eager to tell their stories. There's often a void within them, the one that was previously filled by joining a group. "When that's taken away, when they're caught, sometimes telling their story may keep it alive for them," he said. "Or it may fill some other void, give them some kind of purpose."

As with Willy Loman, in *Death of a Salesman*, whose dreams are dashed, attention should be paid. And attention was paid to Bryant: over the nine years he spent in prison, he participated in one hundred interviews, reviewed one thousand photographs, and helped in more than thirty law enforcement investigations, both in the United States and overseas. "The number of faceless, nameless victims he has saved," Zissou said, hitting the desk for emphasis. "Soldiers! Muslims! Non-Muslims! Men, women, children, people who never knew they'd be victims!"

Bryant and Zissou had both expected that his cooperation with the government would earn him a place in a witness protection program. When Zissou learned, a day before Bryant's prison release, that he'd been denied entry into the program, he was incandescent. "Now what the fuck do we do?" he wondered. Without a family, friends, or money, Bryant had nowhere to go. Zissou got the authorities to agree to pay for him to spend a month in an extended-stay hotel. Farbod Azad, the FBI agent assigned to his case, visited, bringing him a box of Fruity Pebbles and some milk—then told him the bureau was finished paying for his room. Another government agency paid for a month, and after that he was sent to a three-quarters house for former offenders. He was on his own, needing to look for work. "It was like, 'Goodbye, thanks. Good luck in the homeless shelter,'" Zissou said, still a little bitter one year on. "It's almost like they were trying to get him to go back to extremism."

Avuncular and silver-haired, a veteran of numerous terrorism cases, Zissou believes mentoring ex-militants to be "a moral and professional responsibility." If they're denied the tools to create new futures after leaving prison, former jihadis "aren't just at risk of committing another crime," he says, "but of committing a crime of insane violence."

The lawyer's relationship with Bryant goes well beyond the duly diligent. Zissou gave him an anthology of famous essays, and over takeout lunches at his office, the two men discussed philosophy and history. One lesson Zissou wanted to drive home informally was that Muslim populations hadn't always viewed American foreign policy with suspicion. For a young man who'd come of age in a post-9/11 world, it was a shock to hear that Middle Eastern crowds used to cheer visiting American dignitaries, and that there's a Rue John Kennedy in Beirut.

They also tried to puzzle out the future for a guy who had barely graduated from high school, who had no support from family or friends but did have a major felony charge. Bryant calls Zissou his consigliere; Zissou calls Bryant "son." "When I haven't heard or seen him in two or three days, I send him a text message: 'What the fuck is wrong with you? Where the fuck are you?'" Zissou grins fondly. "He'll say, 'Whaddaya mean?' And I'll tell him, 'You don't go this long without checking in!'"

The terms of his probation ban Bryant from owning a computer, so he checks his email at Steve's law office. He's a familiar figure there, running out for coffee for the office, photocopying, or helping install wireless routers. "Everybody loves him here," said Zissou. "There's nothing he wouldn't do." Midway through my conversation with Bryant, he put his head around the door to josh the former terrorist: "Don't talk about the stuff you want to blow up, okay?"

I laughed nervously, but the warmth between them was palpable. Even more, it was clearly crucial to the rickety strategy devised to keep Bryant from sliding back toward extremism.

Zissou hopes that Bryant will eventually transition into counterterrorism work. Initially, he resisted. "All he wanted to do is get into the witsec"—witness protection—"and kind of disappear," he told me. It took the consigliere weeks to coax his client to accept the potential benefits of living in the open. "I said to him, 'Listen, you're thirty-five years old. Do you really want to live a life of fear? Or do you want to live a life that has some meaning? Do you really want to hide out with a different name? Here's an opportunity for you to make a difference in your life.'"

Despite his social stigma, and the potential danger of retaliation from Al Qaeda, living out in the open gave Bryant the possibility of doing meaningful work. Mitchell Silber, the NYPD's former director of intelligence analysis, hired him as a part-time consultant at the counterextremist project Parallel Networks, and the two of them have co-authored an article and given talks at D.C. think tanks. There's also hope that Bryant might eventually make some money from Hollywood: Zissou's been talking to some people in L.A. about dramatizing his life story.

Until then, the former militant supports himself by working as a lead and asbestos remover for New York City. Asbestos removal is a bizarrely appropriate job, jokes Zissou—just an extension of his work exposing Al Qaeda's toxicity for U.S. intelligence services.

WALKING BACK TO THE LIRR station, I reflect that Bryant's path, powered not by ideology but by survival and opportunism, was profoundly American. That this country essentially abandoned him at the prison gates, after he spent eight and a half years inside, speaks to the lack of a U.S. rehabilitation strategy. More broadly, being cut loose so abruptly is standard operating procedure in a nation where individuals are left very much on their own. He can't expect help from a welfare state or a government-funded safety net, as he could in Northern Europe. He can't get support from his tribe or extended family, as he could in many Muslim countries. If you're from suburban Long Island, you have no village to go home to, no elders to steer you. Except perhaps your lawyer, if you're lucky.

Ours is a culture in which the rootless thrive, and which prizes dynamism and individualism over tradition or kinship. More than any other militant I interviewed, Bryant was self-made, propelling himself into Al Qaeda on luck and his wits, then using those wits in prison to become a high-level FBI asset. His story's third act was quintessentially American, too: he was dropped from the witness protection program, then left to exit prison without family, money, or formal rehabilitation.

We're a country where the son of South American immigrants can become a jihadi in the Hindu Kush. And he, in turn, doesn't need much time to turn, flipping and talking to the FBI quickly to survive. But he learned that agility in a land that can afford to take things lightly when it comes to other countries, one that can move fast and break things, to borrow Facebook's early motto. A country whose own power is such that it doesn't seem to learn much about blowback, to connect the dots between the fear it produces overseas and the fear many of its citizens feel at home. When we fly our drones out from the base in the Nevada desert to Waziristan, we know they'll fly home again. With our eyes trained on our domestic political dramas at home, what happens in Waziristan stays in Waziristan.

FOR A COUNTRY THAT prides itself on imagining the future, we Americans are lousy at understanding the past. Until very recently, white people were able to overlook the cornerstone crimes of our history: the theft of Native Americans' lands and slavery. For generations, Black people have demanded a reckoning with our country's racism and a rethink of the systems that perpetuate it; most recently, movements like Black Lives Matter have forced a national conversation and, in some areas, change. Taking responsibility for this past is a fraught and clumsy process, requiring Americans to unpack our national mythologies, forcing families and institutions to scrutinize the origins of their wealth and power. It's slow work.

If an honest account of atrocities that Americans committed at home is proving difficult, facing up to our complicity in faraway conflicts is infinitely harder. For many of us, it takes a feat of the imagination to see how the long tail of slavery lashes our society today. It's even more challenging to see how centuries of Western imperial power have stoked violence abroad. It's fearsomely hard to comprehend the global fallout from our foreign wars. Or to see that the wars we fight may make us less safe, rather than more so. Or to see that the strongmen we subcontract to fight terrorism may ultimately stoke the conditions for it. Or to grasp the ways that corruption or state-sponsored violence nurture it.

Terrorist origin stories aren't found only in homes or neighborhoods, but in national institutions, too. I knew I had to look at a larger landscape, to a country once ruled by violent extremists. A country whose hatred of Others hobbled it, and for a few years, threatened the world order. A country that has since done some serious self-reflection on how violent extremism once rotted its democracy.

The obvious place to go next was Germany.

QUANTUM ENTANGLEMENT

IF ANY WESTERN COUNTRY has been forced to reckon with a history of violent extremism, it is Germany. Modern Berlin is a monument to the condemnation of the country's Nazi past. The streets are studded with *Stolpersteine*—"Stumbling Stones"—squares of brass set in sidewalks, etched with the names and dates of every Jewish Berliner taken away to the Nazi concentration camps. Near where Hitler's center of operations once stood is the Memorial to the Murdered Jews of Europe. At the Topography of Terror, a museum built on the site of the Nazi SS headquarters, visitors shuffle aghast, trying to absorb the history of the rise and reign of the Third Reich. To walk around Berlin is to see a nation's therapy playing out on streets and stones—a city taking responsibility for its past by deliberately exposing it.

I go to a temple of this state-sanctioned push for tolerance—a bookstore on a side street near Checkpoint Charlie, the famous guardpost that stood at the Berlin Wall. It's the Medienzentrum of Germany's Federal Agency for Civic Education, where floor-to-ceiling shelves hold books to educate Germans on pressing topics of the present (fake news, hunger, environmentalism, Salafi Islam in Europe) and the past

(Auschwitz, East Germany, and World War I). For millennials, there's *Fluter,* a sleek magazine addressing issues from plastics to migration. Office managers can pick up free posters displaying the warning signs of homophobia or anti-Semitism. Children can play card games that teach Germany's political vocabulary. A video screen plays episodes of the cartoon *Hanisauland,* featuring a community of animals building a democratic state, thwarting the dastardly "Hatey Hares," nasty rabbits in red suspenders, led by wannabe dictator Hahaboss.

High-minded and heavily subsidized by the German state, the offerings at the Medienzentrum have a hint of determined desperation about them, like Gatsby tossing out his shirts in the hopes of winning Daisy Buchanan's heart. When I asked the store clerks about their customers, they said they were usually older people, raised in the shadow of the war, and a few curious young people. Sometimes far-right extremists came in, not to browse but to harass. The publications on the shelves are fake! they scream. The truth lies not in democratic values, but elsewhere. Bring back the old days, they say, when Germany was for Germans.

Stacked high beside the cashier are pocket-size copies of the German Basic Law, or constitution, free for the taking. Inscribed in it is Germany's postwar commitment to *streitbare Demokratie,* or "militant democracy," the idea that the country must defend its liberal democratic system—even if it means curtailing some freedoms to do so. Mindful that Hitler came to power by parliamentary democracy, the constitution's framers included the "Eternity Clause," which states that certain principles endure forever. Not even a majority vote in the Bundestag can snuff out human rights or the separation of powers. The country's supreme court can ban associations or political parties if they are deemed to undermine democracy or threaten the republic. Among the curbs on expression in the interests of preserving democratic norms: a ban on the public display of Nazi symbols or salutes, unless they are used for educational or artistic purposes. As concerns about hate speech on the internet have grown, Germany has been at the forefront of countries monitoring content. A 2018 law known as NetzDG requires social network platforms to swiftly remove "manifestly unlawful" content or to face stiff fines.

———

GERMANY KNOWS THE DIFFICULTIES of trying to deradicalize a whole nation. How did it seek to build a tolerant society out of one in which nearly half the doctors had been Nazi party members, and where the university science departments had taught racist theories? Nazi ideology had been so pervasive that after the war, "a veil of forgetfulness was allowed to settle over all but the very worst offenders," wrote historian James Hawes. Each of the Allies attempted its own postwar Nazi reeducation program, bearing the stamp of its respective political culture. The Russians started "antifascist schools," in which German POWs were made to publicly renounce the Nazi creed, then to study a Marxist-Leninist curriculum. American "idea factories" schooled former soldiers of the Third Reich on the vices of fascism and the virtues of democracy and capitalism. British rehabilitation efforts drew on the Oxbridge education system and the history of parliamentary debate. Later, after its founding in 1949, East Germany would prove far better than West Germany at denazification, notes Susan Neiman in *Learning from the Germans: Race and the Memory of Evil.* "East Germany put far more old Nazis on trial, and out of office, than the West," she writes. "The occupying forces in the American and British zones initially planned a large denazification program that would divide Germans into five categories according to their degree of guilt, and would absolve, punish or reeducate accordingly, but the task was overwhelming." There were too few Allied soldiers whose German was fluent enough to read the questionnaires that powerful Nazis were required to fill out. The Cold War soon distracted Americans and Britons, who turned their attention to cultivating allies against new enemies rather than pursuing old ones. West Germany's denazification program sputtered out, the government opting to focus on recompensing victims instead of rehabilitating Nazis.

Even as it failed at comprehensive denazification, however, West Germany worked to prevent renazification. Beginning in the 1950s, the government energetically erected a scaffolding for democracy and pluralism. The best defense against the rise of another Hitler was to be a muscular civil society. Well-educated citizens, sturdy nongovernmental organizations, and a free press could check the power of government if totalitarianism ever threatened Germans again. The West German philosopher Jürgen Habermas articulated the official postwar ideal for German citizenry: to be attached primarily to the liberal democratic order rather than to any ethnic or nationalistic concept of Germany. "No other country in the world," wrote Julia Berczyk and Floris Vermeulen in a survey of German deradicalization programs, "has articulated the defense of democracy against extremism so explicitly."

Other Western countries have framed violent extremism as something foreign or freakish, walled off from wider cultural currents. Given its history, Germany can't afford such illusions. Tellingly, it has more programs devoted to countering extremism than any other country on earth: some 720, with roughly half run by the government, and the other half by civil society. Modern Germany started its earliest formal violent extremist exit programs in the 1990s, a response to the spike in right-wing violence after the reunification of East and West Germany.

As concerns over Islamist militancy have grown, practitioners have used what they learned from rehabilitating right-wing extremists to work with former and aspiring jihadis. The range of German programs to help extremists leave their groups dazzles, as does the variety of schemes designed to stop them from joining in the first place. Deradicalization practitioners use tactics ranging from counseling to youth cultures to counter the lure of extremism. One-on-one mentoring can last for years. Some groups echo the national project of facing and condemning the Nazi legacy by *Vergangenheitsbewältigung*—"working through the past." Some programs require individual extremists to take responsibility for their past crimes. The Berlin deradicalization group the Violence Prevention Network has trademarked a process called Verantwortungspädagogik, or "Responsibility Education," which encourages violent extremists to account for their actions in front of a group of fellow offenders.

In contrast to the British practitioners I talked to, the Germans working in the prevention and exit sphere were well funded enough to tailor-make programs for each of their clients and to continue their work for as long as it took. They were steeped in the local scenes, down to knowing which Nazi heavy metal band had a neighborhood following, but they were also able to call on regional and national resources for support. Here in Germany, I'd found a country that acknowledged a national, systemic issue but was tackling it person by person.

I SEE THE PATIENCE it takes to wean young people away from the right-wing scene when I travel to Bremen, a gritty industrial city in northeastern Germany. In a spare, street-level office I meet Ole, a counselor with the government-funded antiextremist program VAJA. (Because of the nature of his work, he asked that I not use his last name.) Bespectacled and blond, with the air of an earnest graduate student, Ole tells me that it can take years to pry right-wing extremists away from their old networks: "We are talking, talking, talking."

Every Friday, teams of VAJA street workers go to where marginalized youth hang out, haunting parking lots, playgrounds, and bus shelters. To be transparent, so they won't be mistaken for the police, they wear VAJA hoodies. They'll bum a cigarette and try to strike up a conversation. In the first month or so, the youth often test the street workers, seeing how they'll react to an anti-Semitic joke, say, or a story about beating up an immigrant. The VAJA counselors listen and reassure. "You're right-wing extremists," they'll say to the youth. "We want to talk to you, no matter what your crimes."

VAJA practices Acceptance-Based Youth Work, which means "we make a distinction between what a person does and what they think—and the person herself," explains Ole. "So she's a Nazi, but she's also a human being. We accept the human being, but we don't accept the attitudes." Most clients work with VAJA for over a year. "Our work is to look at a person as someone with a lot of different layers," he said. "You don't focus on the fact that he's just a fascist or Nazi, but look at the person as a whole."

Ole works one-on-one with right-wing "followers and sympathizers," youth who are involved in the right-wing scene but aren't hardliners—yet. When he encounters a right-wing leader, someone whose exit will mean he needs a new identity and perhaps a move to a new city or country, he calls in the specialists from ARUG, a group in Wolfsburg, two hours south of Bremen, that is trained to help formers start new lives.

For younger "followers," it's often more a case of nudging them in a new direction. VAJA's rules for its clients are nonnegotiable. They have to break off from their old contacts in the neo-Nazi scene and erase all their numbers from their phones. They can't attend right-wing rallies or concerts, and they can't wear clothes with white supremacist symbols or slogans. "If they claim they have no clothes, well, we help get them some new ones," says Ole. "Half of the work is taking away, and half of the work is finding something new. If you don't find something new, and the person is not a stable situation and doesn't have hobbies, or anything to do all day long, they will go right back in."

When I meet him, Ole has been working with fifteen-year-old Sascha for two and a half years, with no end in sight. One of his main goals has been to help the neo-Nazi find new hobbies, something to replace his passion for listening to the five hundred banned white power songs on his cellphone.

Every week for months, Sascha begged Ole to take him swimming, so his mentor, slightly mystified but looking for new activities for the boy, finally obliged and took him to a pool. In the changing room, he saw a huge bandage on Sascha's thigh. "What happened there?" he asked, though half-certain he already knew.

Sascha peeled back the bandage, revealing a homemade swastika tattoo. By exposing it in a public place, the boy broke Law 86a of Germany's Criminal Code, which bans the display of Nazi signs and symbols.

"He couldn't say it, but he'd wanted to show me," Ole explains. "That's why he wanted to go swimming." Flaunting the tattoo was just one way he tested Ole. "It was always an experiment to see what he could get away with. A little bit of provocation, then at the same time 'Help me!'"

Finally, Sascha's mother paid to have his swastika covered over. The new tattoo blotting out the swastika was a Viking—a less overt white power symbol.

Disengagement is a process, and in Sascha's case, it looks as though it will be a long one.

————

OLE'S IS NOT A popular job. "It's donkey work," he says. German de-radicalization counselors much prefer working with Islamist extremists to working with neo-Nazis, several people in the field tell me. "Everyone wants to work in the field of Islamists," says André Taubert, head of Legato, a Hamburg program that works with the families of youth at risk for Islamist extremism. The reason, he believes, is fairly simple: while the far-right extremists frequently threaten prevention workers, Islamist extremists don't, not in Germany. "None of these religious extremists was ever interested in me. But if you work in right-wing extremism, you're targeted. If you work in a youth club and you have a special program against the far right, then your club may be burned the next night. You can be beaten up in the street, or have your house covered with graffiti. People are afraid."

Between 2014 and 2017, membership in right-wing extremist groups increased from 21,000 to 24,000, with roughly half of the members linked to violence. The year after Chancellor Angela Merkel's 2015 decision to open the doors to a million Syrian refugees brought 3,533 attacks on migrants and asylum hostels. Perhaps most unnerving: many of the arsonists were not known right-wing agitators, but Germans without criminal records. In 2020, the German interior minister Horst Seehofer warned that right-wing extremism was the "biggest threat" facing the country. Compared to actions by Islamist extremists, Taubert tells me, "right-wing extremism is a thousand times more violent in Germany."

Still, for many years and for many Germans, extremism was overwhelmingly linked to Muslims. In 2017 Demokratie leben!, a government organization designed to strengthen civic values against extremism, funded twenty-eight showcase projects on Islamic extremism—and a mere twelve on far-right extremism. But in a country where polls show 20 percent of citizens harbor racist views, and where the right-wing Alternative for Germany (AfD) is the opposition party, a focus on Islamist rather than right-wing extremists simply plays to the majority. White Germans see themselves as potentially endangered by jihadist bombers but not by right-wing extremists, explains Taubert. "A normal

German person is not afraid of a right-wing extremist," he says. "We are mostly blond and blue-eyed. We aren't their target."

NICO DI MARCO IS a natural blond, but a target for the far right nonetheless. He's had his tires slashed and was once barricaded inside an antifascist meeting while scores of Nazis hammered on the windows outside. Wire thin, alert as a lizard, the forty-year-old wears a sleeveless black T-shirt emblazoned with a pissed-off-looking cat—the logo of an anticapitalist trade union. His hair is a nest of snarls and short braids. Over the years, he's worn it sunset red, even bubblegum pink. "Some people don't talk with me, they talk with my hair," he says, smiling.

The hairstyle signals Nico's love of punk music, but it's also a tool for his job. In the style code of German youth, it telegraphs that he's a leftist, implicitly against the far right. For the neo-Nazi youth he meets at work, his leather jacket with its red anarchist symbol marks him as both a challenge and a target. His look is an "irritation"—a visual bit of grit, designed to scratch an extremist's too-smooth vision of the world. "When I'm doing a workshop on Nazism or racism, they know I am the enemy," he said. "Often in school classes, youngsters say I have to go into the gas chambers."

Nico works for Cultures Interactive, an antiextremist organization that harnesses the power of subcultures to show people possibilities beyond rigid extremist thinking. Its workshops on punk, graffiti, skateboarding, and DJing are aimed at young people who are either involved in or attracted to violent extremist groups. These activities, born of Germany's rich and complex youth subculture scene, help expand horizons, says Nico, by sparking dialogues on racism, violence, gender, and identity.

He once worked with a group of "very violent" girls of fourteen and fifteen who were in a neo-Nazi group. They had beaten up a guy with a baseball bat, falsely claiming he was a pedophile. It later emerged that they'd all been forced to have sex with the older neo-Nazi guys in the group, and had taken out their rage on the stranger. In the year that Nico worked with the girls, he noticed that they reserved their anger for other people. With one another, they were tender, even loving. He called up a rap artist, Sookie, who'd achieved a certain amount of fame in the queer rap scene, and arranged for her to give a concert specially for the girls: "The girls saw it, left the Nazi group, and are now all gay!"

Much of Nico's work involves helping young fantasists to nail down their opinions with facts. When neo-Nazi youth spout tirades about how Jews or the Illuminati run Germany, he shows them a list of the five hundred richest Germans, to teach them that the powerful aren't members of some shadowy cabal but have names and public faces.

He recalls one teenager who was adamant that he wanted to build a Nazi society. After a year of getting nowhere with him, Nico resorted to a strategy of pointed questioning called the subversive irritation method (*subversive Verunsicherungspaedagogik*). The next time the boy began spouting off about sending Muslims and migrants to camps, Nico seized the opportunity. "So okay," he parried. "Are you going to use violence to round up all these people and take them to the camps to die?"

The boy wasn't sure.

"Maybe they won't want to go," Nico persisted. "After all, they're living here, like you. When they answer the door, they might not go willingly. So you'll probably have to use violence."

Maybe not violence, the boy said slowly.

"Okay, then what will you do instead?"

Maybe, the boy ventured, he could drive the train, taking them to the camps.

Nico nodded. "Of course, then you'd be taking them to be killed."

On reflection, the boy didn't want to drive the train. Maybe, he guessed, he could clean up at the camp.

"So you'll let the others do the bad stuff, and you'll support them?" Nico asked.

A long pause. "Perhaps," said the boy, "I don't want to kill people."

Not long afterward the boy left the far-right movement—only to join a violent group of rockers. "I reached the goal, but it wasn't a happy ending," says Nico. The experience revealed an all-too-common problem in counterextremism work: neo-Nazi affiliations are often just the topsoil of deeper problems. The boy abused drugs and alcohol and had an absent father. "You can work on the right-wing thinking but, in doing that, cover up his real situation," muses Nico. "It shows what we can do—and what we cannot."

NICO UNDERSTANDS THE COMPLEXITIES of young far-right extremists so well, in part, because he was briefly one himself. The son of an Italian father and German mother, he lived in Italy until he turned six. When he moved to Rudow, a working-class neighborhood of Berlin, nativists called him a foreigner for his Italian-accented German; some parents forbade their children to play with him, claiming Italians had lice. The local ice cream shop, run by Italian immigrants, found itself targeted by nasty competition from a shop that set up directly across from it, with a sign featuring the pointed slogan "Our Land, Our Ice Cream." Nico learned early to be scared of the neighborhood neo-Nazi gangs and the regular beatings they meted out to anyone they deemed an immigrant.

If Nico's accent marked him as an outsider to some Rudow Germans, his blond hair made him a target for the children of migrants. When he was fourteen, some boys of Arab and Turkish descent beat him up. His mother called the police, who sent an officer over, a man whose beer belly and mullet made Nico think he was a trucker, not a policeman. When the boy described his assailants as having darker skin and hair than he, the man told him that the description didn't help at all. "That's what they all look like," he said grimly.

Sitting on Nico's mother's couch, tut-tutting about how violent the neighborhood was getting these days, he advised Nico to band together with some other Germans for safety's sake. At the time, the advice felt sweet, offering both a practical solution to Nico's fear—and an affirmation that he belonged: "For the first time, someone was calling me German."

One night, in a basement meeting of the youth wing of the neo-Nazi National Democratic Party, he was listening to speeches about the need to protect "real Germans" from "foreigners." A man raised his hand and said that what Germans needed was patrol groups, to keep order on the streets.

The meeting jolted Nico. It gave him his first glimpse of the workings of the vicious circle: how right-wing racism stokes jihadist racism, and how fear works as an engine for division, pitting one frightened, angry group against another. Fear—whether of bomb plots by global networks or thuggery by Berlin schoolboys—swells the ranks of extremist groups. Getting beaten up by the gang of the children of migrants had planted fear in him, had sent him scuttling for protection from neo-Nazis. But the talk of "patrol groups" and "real Germans" woke him up, scaring him more than the scuffle with the gang.

At seventeen, he drifted into Rudow's punk scene, which managed to evade the tensions between the children of native Germans and the children of migrants. While there were "many violent moments with punks," Nico recalls, he felt free to opt out of them. "I was able to say 'I don't want to be part of this violence.' Weakness and fear were accepted."

MARIE JAGER, NICO, AND I are sitting in a café in the Neukölln neighborhood of Berlin, on a gritty street of kebab shops and nightclubs. Marie is channeling a Weimar-era cabaret star who arrived in the twenty-first century by way of a punk gig. Her black hair is spiky, her eyes are kohl-lined, and she's draped strings of fake pearls over her tank top. In the 1990s, while she was coming of age in a small town in East Germany, hip-hop, punk, and graffiti were her escapes from the local far-right sympathizers. On a school trip to the Buchenwald concentration camp, she watched some classmates use pebbles to make swastikas. In her teens, she fled to Berlin, gravitating toward its queer and feminist scenes, and studying Islamic studies, philosophy, and politics at university.

Today, where Nico focuses on the far-right scene, Marie works with Muslim youth at risk of joining extremist groups. She gives workshops on DJing and graffiti, both stealth routes to open discussions about racism, gender issues, and extremism. Like Nico, she spends lots of time trying to get the youth to question their own beliefs and dreams. Where Nico tries to puncture fantasies of building a pure Aryan Germany, Marie does the same with Muslims' beliefs about building a pure caliphate, or about fleeing back to some romanticized Old Country.

Often she finds herself trying to inject nuance into young Muslims' discussions of history. "One of the most popular videos on YouTube is this horrible movie connecting what happened to the Jews in the 1930s to what is happening now," she tells me. "It suggests we're really close to putting Muslims into concentration camps. After they watch it, the kids are saying 'Oh, the Jews are so safe now,' while they feel more fear and rage than ever." Some question the country's focus on the Nazi past, when they feel so marginalized in its present. "We hear about anti-Semitism all the time," young Muslims will tell her. "Can we talk about racism against Muslims for a while?"

"I see your point," Marie responds. "Maybe we can see a connection between them?"

IN RECENT YEARS, GERMANY'S right wing has grown increasingly strident—and more mainstream. Signs of the country's lurch to the right surfaced in 2010, when Thilo Sarrazin, a board member of Germany's central bank, published a book called *Germany Does Away with Itself,* claiming that Muslim migrants were "dumbing down" the country. It became a bestseller. Another spasm of far-right activity came in 2015, when Chancellor Angela Merkel allowed a million migrants from the Middle East and Africa into the country. The next year brought 113 arson attacks, 10 bombings, and 1,313 physical assaults, all from right-wing extremists. In 2017, the far-right Alternative for Germany became the country's third-largest party, and the nation suffered the highest number of violent right-wing attacks since the downfall of the Third Reich. "The really right-wing, hard-core movements are the same as they were a decade ago, but the middle of our society has stepped to the right," Ole tells me. "What people can say about refugees, they wouldn't have dared to ten years ago." In 2016 the respected *Frankfurter Allgemeine Zeitung* noted, with concern, that some forms of racism and intolerance had become *salonfähig,* or socially acceptable.

Antifascist activists have long asserted that far-right groups enjoy protection by police across Germany. The suspicion of official complicity in the far-right scene gained traction during the trial of the National Socialist Underground, a far-right group which committed ten murders—nine immigrants and one police officer—between 2000 and

2007. The conviction came in 2018, after years of police insisting the killings were not a right-wing plot, but the result of gang warfare among Germany's Turkish community.

The national mood was such that even some of its heroes felt marginalized. The month I first met Nico, Mesut Özil, a German soccer player and star of the 2014 World Cup, resigned from the national team. Born in Germany of Turkish ancestry, he'd once been given a prestigious award for symbolizing successful integration into German society. But after he posed for a picture with Turkey's president Recep Tayyip Erdoğan, critics questioned his loyalty to Germany. In his resignation letter, Özil said he'd left the team because of racially charged criticism in the wake of Germany's poor showing in the 2018 World Cup. "I am German when we win," he wrote, "but I am an immigrant when we lose." The words were a chilling echo of Albert Einstein's, nearly a century before: "If my theory of relativity is proven successful, Germany will claim me as a German, and France will declare that I am a citizen of the world. Should my theory prove untrue, France will say that I am a German, and Germany will declare that I am a Jew."

Einstein once described the idea of "quantum entanglement," in which the properties of particles far away from one another are entwined, and action on one affects the other, as "spooky action at a distance." While in Germany, I kept hearing of a sort of quantum entanglement between far-right and jihadist extremists, noticing how similar their appeals were, albeit to different audiences. Recruiters for both types of extremism play on people's yearnings for belonging, meaning, and transcendence. Both paint a glorious, imagined past, be it a strong nation of Aryans or a Muslim caliphate purportedly modeled on the Prophet Muhammad's Medina. They share parallel visions of how to solve societies' problems, writes Julia Ebner, who has chronicled both movements and their mutual reinforcement in *The Rage: The Vicious Circle of Islamist and Far-Right Extremism*. "They are built on zero-sum games and call for 'absolute' solutions," she wrote. "It is the nature of their stories that unites jihadist and neo-Nazi groups."

In Germany as elsewhere, right-wing and Islamist extremists have no formal links. Still, their discourses echo each other. "When Salafists say, 'We as Muslims need to retreat into the Muslim community, and to find strength in the umma, it's a mirror image of the narrative promoted by right-wing extremists," notes Götz Nordbruch of Ufuq, a civic education and extremism-prevention organization in Berlin. "You have two homogenous collectives, built on identities—white German and Muslim. Both are similar in the sense they claim an authentic character, either based in nature or in the will of God, and both are very exclusive."

Nico saw this vicious mirroring at his old high school, which he visited to try to deescalate friction between two groups of fifteen-year-old boys, one far right, the other styling itself Islamist. The neo-Nazi gang was a powerful force in Rudow, burning down houses of Arab and Turkish immigrant families. A group of Salafi Muslim boys tried to assert their own show of power at school. They petitioned the principal for a prayer room, which they pretty much ran as their own domain, and they began harassing Muslim girls to dress modestly and cover their heads.

One day Nico found some stickers with Islamophobic messages on a wall near the school and stopped to remove them. Scratching away at the sticker with his keys—using bare hands is dangerous, since neo-Nazis sometimes stick razor blades beneath their stickers, slicing the fingers of anyone trying to remove them—he heard one of the neo-Nazi gang members yelling at him to stop. While they were talking, some guys from a Turkish Muslim gang came by and backed up the neo-Nazi: Nico should leave the sticker up, they agreed.

The two groups had formed a twisted alliance due to a shared goal of separatism. Each bolstered the other's testosterone-fueled quest for cultural apartheid; both had an interest in Muslims sticking with other Muslims. The kids of immigrants had internalized the logic of segregation. Tellingly, the stickers had begun dotting the neighborhood right after rumors spread that a Rudow Muslim family had slaughtered a sheep in their backyard. The right-wingers had jumped on this as a sign of barbaric immigrant ways. The Muslim gang, for its part, had no problem with the slaughter—only that it had occurred in full view of their white neighbors. "Both of these groups were saying, 'We have a white culture,' and 'We have a Muslim culture,' and they shouldn't mix," said Nico. There have been similar parallels between neo-Nazi and Salafi Muslim gangs in their treatment of women. "The whites say, 'No sex with Arab guys,'" says Marie, "and from the Arab and Turkish side, it's 'Don't date a German.'"

Particularly since Germany's reunification in 1990, its reckoning with Nazi history has been vigorous but far from unanimous. Despite state-sanctioned efforts to face the memory of the Holocaust and the horrors of the Third Reich, the country has endured a resurgence of far-right hatred in recent years, with some groups building on historical anti-Semitism, and many reviving with a new target: Islam. As Nico well knew, the alliances formed by extremist groups are so complex as to seem contradictory. Some neo-Nazis have partnered with Islamist extremists, sharing anti-Semitic ideas, joining forces at pro-Palestine marches, and planning attacks on Israelis.

The rise of ISIS and a new wave of immigrants gave the far-right scene a new focus and fire, with Muslims now fashioned as public enemies. Though anti-Semitism remained an animating hatred for many far-right groups, Islamophobia emerged as the unifying factor among them. National polls show that a quarter of Germans hold anti-Semitic views—but half hold Islamophobic ones.

The violence gave ISIS recruiters grist for their sales pitches. "They can use the evidence of the rise of right-wing populism and Islamophobia," said Julia Reinelt of the Berlin-based Violence Prevention Network. "They can say, 'See? You're not wanted here in Germany. You can't live like a practicing Muslim here. You'll never be accepted, so come to the caliphate.'"

Jihadist terrorist attacks, in turn, provided compelling fodder for right-wing recruiters. The far-right populist party AfD grew in popularity after December 2016, when a Tunisian-born man killed twelve by driving a truck into a crowd. There was mutual inspiration on a tactical level, too: ISIS's slick propaganda videos reminded the right-wing extremists of the power of online spectacle. A sense of victimhood irrigates both streams of extremism. "When we raise the issue of the Holocaust at schools," says Marie, "the right-wing students are like, 'Do we still have to feel guilty about this? Can't we stop? I want to be proud of being German again.' But memories of the Nazi past work very differently for the country's Muslims. More and more they say what the Salafis are telling them: 'We are the new Jews.'"

I LEFT GERMANY WITH cautious admiration for its attempts to confront historical hatreds and to counter contemporary ones. Its past teaches a painful lesson in the work it takes to keep a country from sliding into hatred. Guilt, along with affluence, powered German programs, making them much better developed than other European approaches. The country's diffuse and diverse approach to deradicalization seemed less punitive than the French strategy, which tends to be centralized, security-oriented, and until recently almost entirely focused on incarceration. Local German programs seemed to receive more support than British ventures, many of which were starved for cash. The bans on Nazi expression unnerved me slightly, as an American raised on the gospel of free speech. But Germans viewed them as protections for "militant democracy" and as part of a national effort to take responsibility for past horror.

The question remains, however, as to what extent *Vergangenheitsbewältigung*—"working through the past"—is actually working. The rise of hate crimes committed by the far right, as well as its infiltration into elite army units, suggest the limits of lavish government programs. Indeed, the national vow to "never forget" may have created a paradox at the heart of the contemporary German identity. Esra Özyürek, an anthropologist at the University of Cambridge, argues that enshrining the Holocaust as a primal historical moment, whose weight must be borne by all Germans, has created a new narrative of exclusion for its country's Muslims. "Despite its opposition to hyper-nationalism, Germany's Holocaust memory culture fails to include those members of its society who are not ethnically German," she wrote in the Israeli newspaper *Haaretz*. "Today, Germans of Muslim origin are commonly accused of being unable to relate to Holocaust history, incapable of establishing empathy with its Jewish victims, and of importing new forms of antisemitism to a country that is assumed to have dealt successfully with its own anti-Jewish racism."

When history weighs so heavily, it can be wielded as a tool not only to promote unity but also to stoke divisions. Memory can help a nation work through its shame on the world stage, but crafted just so, it can also be weaponized to divide. Getting the balance right, in a country of 85 million people, is proving exceedingly difficult.

On a smaller scale, it might be possible to reconcile the memory of the past with the realities of the present. In fact, in one small city in Belgium, the mayor was able to convince residents that combating extremism and polarization was the work not of one migrant group, or of mothers, or of the security services. As he saw it, it was the work of every citizen.

HOW TO DERADICALIZE YOUR TOWN

THE SUMMER OF 2018, when I first went to Mechelen, was hot and angry. Leaders everywhere seemed to be building ever-higher walls and declaring restrictive new definitions of "Us" and "Them." In the United States, the Supreme Court upheld Trump's Muslim ban. In Israel, the Knesset passed a law formally enshrining Palestinians as second-class citizens, rendering the right to self-determination a privilege "unique to the Jewish people." In Hungary, Viktor Orbán's far-right government criminalized anyone who assisted asylum-seeking migrants.

In such a season, Mechelen felt like a refuge. The Belgian city's pretty river, gabled houses, and cathedral tower evoke a chocolate-box version of Old Europe, that mythical place that the far-right claims it must defend from Others. Yet the word I kept thinking of as I walked its cobbled streets was "cosmopolitan." It's an unfashionable concept these days, much maligned by populists and nationalists as the purview of globe-trotting elites, untethered to anything but their passports. But done right, cosmopolitanism allows for people to be rooted in a place or culture, even while they look beyond them and out onto the world. "Cosmopolitanism is an expansive act of the moral imagination," the

British Ghanaian philosopher Kwame Anthony Appiah once wrote. "It sees human beings as shaping their lives within nesting memberships: a family, a neighborhood, a plurality of overlapping identity groups, spiraling out to encompass all humanity. It asks us to be many things, because we are many things." In Mechelen, I would find a city government working to build a similar vision.

In earlier eras, Mechelen savagely rejected pluralism. During World War II, the Nazis used the city's barracks to transport Belgian Jews and Roma to Auschwitz. At the turn of the twenty-first century, nearly a third of Mechelaars, as the city's residents are called, supported Belgium's extreme-right party. That started to change when a new mayor was elected in 2001, someone determined to lead the town away from extremist intolerance. His drive to change the place came, in large part, from a reckoning with his own family's complicity in violent extremism.

LIKE SEVENTEEN GENERATIONS OF his ancestors, Bart Somers was raised in Mechelen. The Somers family has lived there since 1520, the year it built the tower on its cathedral, hoping that it would be the highest in Europe. Born in 1964, Somers studied law in Leuven before going into politics, becoming a leading light in the Open Flemish Liberals and Democrats party, then mayor of Mechelen. When I met him, he had enjoyed such success during his five mayoral terms that he was rumored to be slated for a big job in the European Union. Tall, with a salt-and-pepper crop and pink cheeks, he had a manner that mixed the erudition of a German philosopher with the enthusiasm of an Italian soccer coach.

When he first heard that hundreds of young Muslims were leaving Belgium to join ISIS, he saw something of himself. At sixteen, he'd been dazzled by the commitment of the IRA hunger strikers, protesting British rule in Northern Ireland from their prison cells. A generation before that, his own family had embraced a poisonous political ideology, with tragic results for his uncle Jan. "Every time I hear about children recruited by the Islamic State, I cannot see only a terrorist," he told me. "I also see the uncle I never knew."

The Somers family's slide toward violent extremism had started in idealism. His grandfather Ludwig, civic-minded and sophisticated, had been a schoolmaster, head of the local drama society and author of a guidebook to Brussels. He'd also been a Flemish nationalist since his boyhood in the 1920s, feeling that the Belgian state hadn't truly appreciated the sacrifice of the Flemish soldiers during World War I. In 1933 Ludwig joined the nationalist Vlaams Nationaal Verbond. His frustration grew at what he saw as Belgian discrimination against its Dutch-speaking citizens, so when the party lurched rightward, aligning itself to the Nazi new order, Ludwig went with it. Late in World War II, his two sons joined the Volkssturm, Hitler's last-gasp militia, formed in 1944. Fifteen-year-old Jan was killed fighting the Russians in a Nazi battalion on the Eastern Front.

Somers recalled a childhood visit to his uncle Jan's grave with his father and grandfather. The older man dissolved in tears. "My grandfather was asking himself, 'How is it possible that a cultured person like me, fighting for a cause that could be called democratic, could fall into extremism out of frustration, anger, and negativity? How did it happen that I could embrace violent extremism and join a regime that is indefensible?'" The moment taught Somers "how dangerous politics can be," he observes. "How at certain moments, for certain reasons, you get gripped by radical ideas. These movements can go further and further and further, till at the end of the day, you are like my grandfather, standing at the grave of your son, killed in a Nazi uniform."

When white Belgians ask him why young Muslims would leave Europe to join militant groups in Syria, he invokes his uncle Jan. "Just go back a few decades in European history, and you'll find that millions of Europeans embraced the idea that Jews were the cause of all misery, and that democracy was something bad," he said. "A crazy ideology, but it killed fifty million people. It destroyed Europe." The "crazy ideology" was buried not just in Somers's family's history, of course, but in Mechelen's. During World War II, the city's Dossin barracks was a transit camp for Belgian Jews and Roma. Between 1942 and 1944, over twenty-five thousand people were deported on trains from Mechelen to Auschwitz-Birkenau.

A few generations later the Mechelen train tracks would sit squarely on the richest seam for Islamic State recruits in the Western world. For a few years, the twenty-six miles of track between Brussels and Antwerp were the epicenter of departures for Syria. Belgium had Europe's highest per capita number of foreign fighters in Syria, thanks in part to groups like Sharia4Belgium, whose firebrand volunteers would travel along the Brussels-Antwerp train line to find fresh recruits. Brussels, just to Mechelen's south, had some two hundred residents leave for Syria. Antwerp, to the north, lost one hundred young people. And in Vilvoorde, a commuter town a thirteen-minute ride from Mechelen, recruiters found the most receptive audience in Belgium—and thus in the West. The town of forty-two thousand would see twenty-nine departures for Syria. Nearly every Vilvoorde high school lost students to Syria; a few of them even achieved high positions in ISIS's foreign ministry.

Vilvoorde's dire foreign fighter statistics meant it had to move swiftly. Choosing a strategy of support and reintegration, it set up a seven-person team headed by a young doctoral student in Islamic studies, Jessika Soors, in charge. When it came to figuring out who was at risk for radicalization, Soors focused not on religion but on social exclusion: "It wasn't a case of looking for long beards, but bad social conditions." Much of her job as policy coordinator for radicalization and polarization involves trying to help youth suffering from isolation, long-term unemployment, or parental neglect. As Vilvoorde's foreign fighters started coming back from Syria, they were sent to prisons throughout Belgium. The mayor, Hans Bonte, traveled to visit every returnee, in six different prisons. "He's adamant about doing it," says Soors. "He tells them, 'You're a citizen of Vilvoorde and have the same rights as other citizens. But because of your profile, we'll be there to monitor you.'"

IF VILVOORDE SERVES, IN Mayor Bonte's words, as "a laboratory for Belgium, and beyond that, for Europe and the world," on how to deal with homegrown violent extremists, Mechelen is a lab for preventing extremism in the first place. While the surrounding towns lost many young people to the Islamic State, not a single person left from Mechelen. Like Vilvoorde, the city has a hyperdiverse population. Like Vil-

voorde, it's undergone rapid demographic and economic changes over
the past generation. When Bart Somers was a boy, Mechelen was overwhelmingly white and Belgian: now its eighty-five thousand residents
are drawn from 138 nations. Both Vilvoorde and Mechelen watched their
economic fortunes plummet in the 1980s and '90s: Vilvoorde's Renault
plant closed down, and Mechelen's name became a byword in Belgium
for crime and shuttered shops. But in 2011, when the Sharia4Belgium
recruiters got off the train in Mechelen, the leaders at the mosque and
the youth club told them to get back on it.

That nobody from Mechelen left for Syria was partly luck, Somers
concedes. He knows well from his own family history that every population has people who are vulnerable to radicalization. But a key reason ISIS failed to recruit any Mechelaars remains Somers's drive to
make everyone in the city feel they belonged. The strategy wasn't simply about creating a warm and rosy glow but about ensuring safety. If
you build a web of strong civic institutions and promote a sense of
belonging, Somers reasons, the few people attracted to extremist ideology will be connected enough to the community that someone in
their circle will notice and alert the police or social services. Beyond
that, cultivating a sense of belonging robs the extremists of a major
grievance: social exclusion. "To say it a little bit provocatively"—
Somers grins—"we try to recruit them for our society, before people
of a radical ideology can recruit them."

Relying on traditional identity politics doesn't work, he believes, because "labeling people is actually organized segregation." Instead, viewing radicalization as stemming from isolation, he set out to strengthen
Mechelen's social connective tissue. In a hyperdiverse city, citizens
needed to be allowed to thrive as multifaceted beings rather than simply be defined as "Muslim" or by their countries of origin. To think of
people in terms of a single identity "makes a caricature of each of us,"
he says. "If I reduce you to an American and I am only a European,
then you become Donald Trump in my eyes." Worse, this kind of re-
ductionism "allows people to get control over who you are." Political
opportunists prey on single-faceted identities, and all too soon "you've
got leaders who are defining what we have to do to be a good American, a good Muslim, a good Belgian. Then, you lose your freedom."

To deny the multitudes in each person makes for a brittle civic life. Politicians and groups promoting single-faceted identities would miss, for example, that Mayor Somers is simultaneously "a citizen of Mechelen, Flemish, Belgian, European, a father, a liberal, someone who likes to read books, and someone who doesn't like to watch soccer," he says. Each of these identities serves as a way for him to connect with his fellow citizens. "All these identities allow me to have something to bridge to other people, to have something in common with them. And if you have three or four things in common, then the two or three things that are different are not a threat—they get interesting! And we can talk about them, because we have enough in common." His exuberant concept of a self of many parts, and his faith that it can be put to use for a vigorous, healthy democracy, remind me of those famous lines from an earlier, equally passionate champion of pluralism. "Do I contradict myself?" wrote Walt Whitman. "Very well then then I contradict myself. / (I am large, I contain multitudes.)"

DURING EUROPE'S 2015 MIGRANT crisis, Mechelen bucked regional trends by actively asking migrants to settle there. But the following year its commitment to inclusion was tested when a coordinated terrorist attack on Brussels claimed thirty-five lives and wounded three hundred more people; just twenty minutes from Mechelen, at the Brussels Airport, two of the terrorists' bombs exploded. Somers publicly condemned the killings and the killers. But his message, with its pointed inclusion of Belgium's Muslims, had a different timbre from those of most politicians. The country's Muslims were victims of such an attack twice over, he said: once as Belgium citizens, and once as people whose religion was used to justify the attacks. "The attacks were done by people born in Belgium," he made sure to tell Mechelen. "They are terrorists, but they are *our* terrorists. They were born here, grew up here, go to our schools. They're our problem, and we have to work on it."

In short, Somers refused to cast the attackers as Other. Their crimes were not the box-ticking banalities of Hannah Arendt's Nazi bureaucrats, but by reframing the perpetrators as "our terrorists," he not only sent a signal of inclusivity to Mechelen's Muslims, but called for his fellow Belgians to reflect on their own complicity in the creation of terrorism.

The night of the attacks, the crowd at one of the Mechelen youth clubs were glued to the TV, watching the mayor's statement. When they heard it, a few of the guys started crying. "You're the first politician who said something like that," a young man later told Somers, "the first one who told us that we're still a part of this society."

In the days that followed, the Belgian government deployed eighteen hundred soldiers to patrol cities, and carried out stop and searches in heavily Muslim neighborhoods. But not in Mechelen. Somers asked police officers to work longer hours for a couple of months but didn't feel the need for a conspicuous show of militarization. He wanted a police presence in Mechelen, but not a threatening one. Officers rarely brought guns on patrol and never wore bulletproof vests. Instead of building barriers or walls in public areas to prevent attacks, the police learned to park their vehicles at inventive angles in particular spaces to protect the public. Since he was first elected, Somers wanted to "make Mechelen look safe, but not securitized," the city's police commissioner, Yves Boegarts, told me. The city embarked on the appearance of what theorists have called "desecuritization," or moving from emergency mode to the ordinary rhythms of civic life. As the international relations scholar Patricia Owens once wrote, desecuritization makes for a "genuine public sphere, where humans can, in an Arendtian fashion, 'debate and act to build a common world.'"

IN THE 1990S, MECHELAARS had little sense of a common world. Tales of Moroccan immigrants dealing hash, a high rate of petty thefts, and streets of shuttered shops earned it the nickname "Chicago on the river Dijle." "Migration, in many people's minds, was something negative," Somers said. By 2001, a third of Mechelen's shops were vacant, it had the highest crime rate in Belgium, and a consumer magazine rated it the dirtiest city in Flanders. Fear among its white residents helped boost the fortunes of the far-right Flemish party Vlaams Belang: in 2004, 32 percent of Mechelaars voted for it. "Right-wing politicians try to make a connection between diversity and decline," observed Somers. "We tore it apart."

He did so by trying to make the city green, clean, and safe. Landmark projects, like transforming an old brewery into a heritage center, wooed first private investment and, later, middle-class residents. Young professionals moved into heavily migrant areas in the nineteenth-century houses on the edges of town. In England or the United States, this might have been the start of gentrification, in which rising rents hit migrants and poor people hard and force them to move out to make way for fancy condos. But in Mechelen, this didn't happen nearly as much. Most Mechelaars from foreign backgrounds own their homes. Often racism meant they couldn't rent, and most people in Belgium are homeowners, as the government promotes buying. When Somers started putting money into the parks and streets in poorer neighborhoods, housing values went up. But when middle-class professionals started buying in areas with lots of migrants, the original residents didn't move. Instead, notes Somers, they said, "My house doubled in value—thank you, city! And I'm going to stay here."

Neighborhood culture morphed as more middle-class people moved in. Residents became more actively involved in their common life, complaining to city hall when the playground swings or streetlights broke, and holding street parties and barbecues. Minor stuff, one might imagine, but Somers sees these microevents as muscular challenges to polarization, which can serve as an incubator for extremism.

Deft politician that he is, he explains it by telling a story. "Say you're a guy named Pieter, and you're eighty-two years old, and for a while now, you've been feeling strange in your own city because there are so many new people of Moroccan ancestry. For the first time in years, someone knocks on your door, from a Flemish background, and says, 'Come.'"

You go to the street party and wash down a plate of your neighbor Rashid's tagine with your favorite ale. A few days later, when Rashid's son is playing too loudly in the street, "you're not going to call the police, because you spoke with his father at the barbecue," says Somers. "You ring his doorbell and say, 'Rashid, your son is really annoying me.' And Rashid will not be defensive. He won't think 'This is a white, middle-class person being racist, coming here to give me a lesson.' Because he, too, has been at the barbecue, and he knows Pieter is a normal person."

If Mayor Somers's vision sounds simplistic, it's worth noting that these neighborhood changes are supported by broader integration policies. In Belgium, parents can choose which school their children attend. For a long time, this created the usual divide: some Mechelen schools drew students from the white middle class, and others from recent arrivals. Somers's team persuaded 250 middle-class parents to send their children to schools with heavily migrant populations, guaranteeing the quality of the education and working with school heads to make sure they delivered it. Then the city hall started in on migrant families, persuading parents to send their kids to the middle-class school. "The migrants would say exactly the same thing the middle class had said at first: 'We don't feel at home there, and it's not really our school.' And we'd say, 'Yes, it's your school, because your kid is smart enough to go there.'"

By one metric, the drive seems to have created a greater sense of belonging among second-generation Muslims. A recent study asked Flemish children about their identity, says Alexander Van Leuven, an anthropologist and Mechelen's deradicalization officer. Throughout the region, many children of immigrants said they felt Muslim or Turkish or Moroccan. But in Mechelen, the children overwhelmingly responded they were "Mechelaars."

Tolerance, believes Somers, grows from social mixing, carefully tended. When a group of Muslim citizens petitioned him to start an Islamic school, he turned them down, explaining that Mechelen didn't do segregation. A Moroccan community soccer team was persuaded to throw open its doors to include youth of all backgrounds. Joining the Scouts is a traditional rite of passage for Belgian kids, but city workers, noting that Scout troops were uncannily white, went out to persuade migrant parents to let their children join.

Somers sponsored what he jokes is Mechelen's "speed dating" program, in which every foreign newcomer is matched with a Mechelen native, choosing a potential friend from a panel of five volunteers. The matched pairs sign a contract to meet weekly for six months, so that the newcomer can practice their Dutch and learn the basics of Belgian life. "I thought it would be the multiculti types who would volunteer for the scheme," Somers muses. "But there are also people who say, '*They* have to adapt, and *I* will teach him.'" In the program, Mechelen old-timers tutor newcomers in skills like opening a bank account and shopping. But often, on a stroll or over a coffee, the migrant will confide to his teacher about the mother he misses, or his loneliness, "and it's a human moment," he says. "And people come together, and there's change." It's not just migrants being trained to be good Belgians, but Belgians being taught to embrace Europe's twenty-first-century reality. After six months, at the "graduation" ceremony, both newcomers and old-timers are awarded certificates.

TO REFORM MECHELEN, SOMERS drew on ideas from both the left and the right of the political spectrum. When conservatives accuse him of being "a lefty," the mayor points to Mechelen's streets, clean as dinner plates, and the security cameras watching above them—the most such surveillance in Belgium. He hired more police and embraced the "broken windows" theory made famous by former New York mayor Rudolph Giuliani, which holds that petty crimes lead to more serious ones. In the United States, this approach has been widely discredited, as it led to excessive targeting of minorities by police. Mechelen largely avoided such an outcome by making conscious attempts to desecuritize the police force. "We frame it so that the police are only one small piece of the chain of institutions working together," says Commissioner Boegarts. "We try to have a global view when problems arise."

Somers pushed for a more visible police presence, in large part, to tackle xenophobia. If people don't feel safe in the streets, he reasons, "they'll blame two groups: democratic politicians and migrants." They'll vote for populists at the polls, and they'll scapegoat newcomers in the streets. But if everyone, from frail retirees to high school dropouts, feels safe in the city, "you strengthen trust in democracy, you create more openness for diversity, and you disconnect diversity from decline. We've showed that diversity and progress can go hand in hand."

While many European politicians have cast integration as a job for recent migrants, like scrubbing toilets or sweeping streets, Somers believes it's the responsibility of every European, from bankers with bloodlines dating back to Charlemagne to Aleppo-born refugees. "Everyone has to adapt to the new normal," he says. "My family may have lived in Mechelen for seventeen generations, but I'm the first generation to live in the reality of diversity." One in five Mechelaars are Muslim, a statistic that led Somers to extend an impish public invitation to Hungary's president Viktor Orbán, a far-right populist who has called refugees "Muslim invaders," to visit the city. "We have more Muslims than Hungary and Slovakia put together," the mayor says. "Yet we're safer, more prosperous, and more vibrant."

Mechelen's success makes it "a weapon against populism," Somers says, "and not with multiculti naïveté, but with facts and figures." Muggings fell by 91 percent, and other forms of crime plummeted. The consumer magazine that had previously ranked Mechelen the dirtiest city in Flanders recently gave it top marks for cleanliness. Where once Mechelaars scraped the bottom of polls in civic pride and trust in fellow citizens, now they rank in the top three cities in Flanders in both categories. Mechelen's turnaround boosted Somers's career. He won a prize for being the world's best mayor in 2016, lectures internationally on combating extremism, and became a minister in the Flemish government.

Not all Mechelaars are convinced by their mayor's vision. In the Great Market square, I ask Karina—blond, zaftig, and stern—how she feels about the city's hyperdiversity. She observes that her forty years of work as a waitress and cleaner have yielded her only 720 euros a month in pension, "while these migrants come and automatically get 1,110 euros. They come and they get. For us, they take away." Nor does she feel safe. "At night, all the Blacks come out, and as a woman, you're not safe." She does have one friend from a migrant background, she finally concedes. Her husband drives a cab for a Moroccan, who is a fair boss. The two couples sometimes go for dinner at one another's houses. It was easily done, she says, because the other couple is essentially Belgian: "They aren't wearing coverings on their heads, and they have very good morals."

Not fifty feet from where we are talking, in a prime position on the

Great Market square, stands the local branch of Vlaams Belang (VB), the far-right Flemish nationalist party. Before Mayor Somers took office, VB won about a third of the city's vote in the regional parliamentary elections. By 2014, as the mayor proudly told me, local support for the party had plummeted to 6 percent.

But in the 2019 elections, VB more than doubled its support, garnering 15 percent of the Mechelen vote. To be sure, VB support was weaker in Mechelen than in the region at large, where the party held 23 percent of seats in parliament. But I find the numbers troubling, and am shocked by the nativist hatred I see when I surf to VB Mechelen's online social media sites: "The massive influx of foreigners is causing the Mechelaars to become a minority in their own city," reads one typical post. "Nothing will remain of our Flemish identity. Action must be taken now to combat this. STOP mass immigration! Protect our identity." A second constant target: "Big left guru #Somers." Posts sneer at his "woke madness" and his "pamper policy for anyone who doesn't have or want our nationality." In 2021 Somers endorsed the young politician Sihame El Kaouakibi. A post on the VB Facebook page calls her his "pet," and alleges she harbors "sympathies" with her brother, who is "considered dangerous by belgian [sic] state security" for his association with Islamist groups.

Trumpian in its crude racism, the message clearly targets white voters, stoking fears that the presence of migrants will cost them their security and their identity. As with so much populist rhetoric, these posts hinged on zero sum logic: that newcomers—or even third- and fourth-generation Belgians with non-European ancestry—inevitably take something from Belgium. "For populists, if we change anything in how we are organized as a society, it's like submission," Somers told me. "It's like they think there's only one kilo of freedom, and if They get any concessions, then We are giving up some of Our freedom or are somehow losing Our rights."

An outsider would have a hard time grasping how radically Belgium's sense of self has changed in the space of a lifetime. I get a glimpse of the rate of flux when I meet Erwin Wauters, a garrulous, ruddy-faced retired man of sixty-nine and a graduate of Mechelen's "speed dating" program. Over a beer at a Mechelen tapas bar, he pulls a photo album out of his blue backpack and flips it open to a page with two pictures on it. The first shows Erwin as a boy in a bow tie and double-breasted suit, on an outing to the 1958 World's Fair in Brussels. He is standing between two men from the Congo, which was then a Belgian possession. The fair featured a "Congorama," a human zoo, in which hundreds of Congolese were imported for the viewing pleasure of the Belgian public. Below the childhood snapshot is another picture, in which Erwin appears in exactly the same pose, next to his newcomer "buddy," a Senegalese musician, Lamine Sambou. The two men met through the "speed dating" program three years ago and now consider each other family. Erwin and his ninety-four-year-old mother have just returned from his annual trip to Lamine's village in northern Senegal. We pored over Erwin's pictures: Lamine, a virtuoso musician who used to play with the Senegalese star Youssou N'Dour, with his kora, or harp, Erwin and Lamine smiling broadly, arms wrapped around one another. Not every "buddy" pair is so successful, Erwin admits, but "slowly, person by person, we educate people, and bring them together."

But there is a noticeable lag between changing a society "person by person," and changing its power structures. Though over a third of Mechelen's residents come from a migrant background, only 23 percent of the city's administration in 2019 came from a non-Belgian background.

If there's a gap between the administration's aspirations and its structural realities, there is also one, it turned out, between Erwin's emotional life and his voting record. On my second trip to Mechelen, I learned that Erwin—a man who advocates paying reparations to Belgium's former African colonies and who leads Mechelaars on culture tours of Senegal—supports Vlaams Belang. He revealed his political affiliation quite calmly—indeed, he seemed taken aback to be pressed on the subject. He didn't hold with the party's nativist message, he insisted, but was drawn to it as a supporter of Flemish rights. It was the same reason that, some eighty years earlier, Bart Somers's grandfather had joined a party that eventually supported the Nazis. Erwin had been a supporter of the Flemish nationalist cause for most of his life, he said, ever since grade school, when his teachers forced him to speak French rather than his native Dutch.

But what if VB's deputies in the Flemish parliament, I asked, crafted policies that denied his friend Lamine work, support, or even Belgian residency?

Erwin looked incredulous. "That," he insisted, "would never happen."

Do I contradict myself? / Very well then then I contradict myself. / (I am large, I contain multitudes.)

Erwin may be naïve, but I don't believe he's a racist. A sense of victimhood, some sixty years old, led him to cast a vote for right-wing xenophobes. His vote was a reminder that successful extremist groups braid a broad range of grievances into their hatred. The deftest of them leverage unresolved needs or injustices, whether perceived or real, that governments hadn't addressed. I thought of the Pakistani boys whose parents couldn't afford to feed or educate them, so sent them to so-called "jihadi factory" madrassas in the 1990s. I thought of Afifa's aunt in Indonesia, who'd joined ISIS because she needed medical care for her disabled son. Of the Nigerian women who didn't want to leave Boko Haram because the group had given them status and jobs, neither of which they'd have had back in their village. The recruitment successes of militant groups serve as maps of a society's mistakes.

ON BOTH TRIPS TO Mechelen, I visited the Kazerne Dossin, a Holocaust and Human Rights Museum, built beside the barracks where 25,685 Jews and Roma were held before being deported to Auschwitz. On the wall opposite sepia-tinted portraits of people deported from the region is a wall-length photo. It's contemporary—probably taken at some outdoor music festival, the kind my teenagers petition to attend every summer. The image is massive. You can feel the crowd's electricity, its heave and crush. The flailing of forearms, the scent of hot sweat, the ecstasy of togetherness. A euphoric young woman, arms aloft, stands on the shoulders of some Ray-Banned man. Far from sinister, the photo is immersive, sweeping you into the collective rapture.

It's a daring choice for the entrance of a Holocaust museum, this photo of innocent fun. It's the cornerstone image on the first floor, whose theme is "Mass"—a force, the museum catalog informs me, that can "build up a destructive and deadly power that spares nothing and no one, as the Leader looks on, encouraging and inciting." The floor above, themed "Fear," tells the story of the persecution of Jews in Belgium, and the top floor, "Death," details their extermination in concentration camps. On another floor, the scope widens beyond the Holocaust to human rights. One section chronicles contemporary immigrants in Belgium. Another examines global atrocities born of racism. I force myself to look at a 1904 photograph of slaves on a rubber plantation in the Congo. Flanked by two mustachioed Europeans in pith helmets, the men hold up the severed hands of laborers killed by guards. The museum catalogue showed an image I recognized from history books of my own country, shot in Indiana in 1930: the corpses of two Black men, Thomas Shipp and Abram Smith, hanging from a tree as "a cheerful group of men and women looks on," reads the caption.

Still, I remained most haunted by a photograph of ordinary life. To me, the photo of a music festival suggested the possibilities for extremism that lurk within us all, ready to surface given the right conditions. Those who successfully connected with militants and extremists, who worked to rehabilitate them, knew well their own potential for being drawn in. I'd seen that knowledge in Figen Murray, who used her own memories of falling prey to a controlling Christian sect to find empathy for the suicide bomber who killed her son Martyn. I'd seen it in Nico Di Marco, the Berliner working to reform followers of the far right, who'd flirted with the neo-Nazi scene himself; and in Noor Huda Ismail in Jakarta, who insisted that the jihadis he helped were "fucking normal."

In Mechelen, I saw it in Bart Somers, whose grandfather's feelings of cultural marginalization had driven his family to support a genocidal regime. But the mayor's fight for community cohesion was about something more fundamental than just trying to thwart extremism. At its heart, it was a fight to preserve democratic norms. Segregation of different ethnicities or social groups into parallel societies, or even just the dearth of a feeling of a shared civic space, can pit citizens against one another. "We speak a lot [in Europe] about the benefits of diversity," he once said. "But in reality, in cities, we live in separate worlds."

When a society's connective social tissues shrivel up, "we get jealous. We ask, 'Why do *They* get a park and not me?'" It's only a short road from these grievances to social and political polarization, which, as Americans can attest, can imperil the workings of democracy itself.

Fear also can corrode democratic norms. As I write, over 64,000 people from fifty-seven countries, mostly women and children formerly living in the Islamic State, sit in the Al Hol and Roj camps in northeast Syria. Urging their countries to take them back, the UN Human Rights Council said "the continued detention, on unclear grounds, of women and children in the camps is a matter of grave concern and undermines the progression of accountability, truth and justice."

I think of the controversial British case of Shamima Begum, who'd joined ISIS as a fifteen-year-old London schoolgirl. In 2019, the British home secretary stripped her of her British citizenship on grounds of national security. From a camp in northern Syria, she petitioned to return to fight her citizenship case, but in 2021, the Supreme Court concurred with the Home Office. Though it accepted that she couldn't get a fair trial while detained in Syria, the court refused her return on grounds of national security. Human Rights Watch strongly disagreed with the decision—not least on grounds of public safety. "To turn its back on [Britons in Syrian camps] is not only a legal and moral aberration, but a long-term security risk," wrote the organization's UK director Yasmine Ahmed. "Leaving them in detention camps leaves them vulnerable to radicalization and the dire conditions can serve as a recruitment tool. If we have learnt anything from the last 20 years, it's that our security is never served by undermining human rights."

BOTH THE COUNTRY OF my birth and the country where I live have felt an impulse to erase those they deem terrorists from public life. We hide them in prison, strip them of their nationality, or refuse them the right to return home. The logic of our throwaway culture now stretches beyond cheap consumer goods to people: if they're broken, it's simpler to remove them from circulation than it is to repair them. This punitive, resigned approach makes a marked departure from the virtues that power American life at its best: a sense of optimism, and a vision of the common good large enough to harbor the fragile and the marginalized.

When I think about it, that's one reason I began this exploration by listening to mothers. Nicola, Christianne, and Figen all feel a fierce sense of responsibility to their children, yes, but in addition they all use their individual loss to broaden their engagement with society. They started listening to other parents' children who had been radicalized and found unlikely allies in former extremists. Their responses to personal tragedy are primers in building connection, in reinvigorating a sense of a common good. Perhaps because they knew their sons so well, they could see beyond the religious, political, and socioeconomic reasons given for their sons' radicalization. They could identify a larger void these children wanted to fill, could see a search for meaning and purpose, connection, and dignity. The wiliest extremist recruiters know this as well, and so do those doing the slow and complex work of rehabilitation.

Everyone I met during this exploration reckoned with isolation or loneliness. All humans do, but those working in grassroots mechanisms for radicalization and deradicalization find isolation at the core of the problem. It's a feeling that recruiters exploit, and one for their mentors to remedy. "Loneliness is the common ground of terror," cutting off dialogue, connection, and debate, wrote Hannah Arendt in *The Origins of Totalitarianism.*

I type this during a pandemic, when an epidemic of loneliness has spread along with COVID. In locked-down Britain, we generally hold conversations with anyone outside our household on our computers, other people appearing in grainy, dancing squares of light. We have lost what the American legal theorist Cass Sunstein has called the "architecture of serendipity"—the spaces where we can unexpectedly encounter new ideas or worldviews. With shops closed, streets empty, and pubs and theaters dark, the chance of talking to anyone who might challenge us—save for squabbles about what Netflix show to watch, or whether the chicken in the fridge is too old to eat—is slim. Particularly at the start of the pandemic, fear had me reaching for purity, not just by spraying surfaces and wiping hands with antibacterial agents but by retreating from the mess of the world in the interests of certainty and security. I shrank from strangers in the streets, flattening myself against walls to avoid them and the germs they might carry.

My oldest friend called from Washington, D.C., to say that abandoned Italian hamlets were selling for a euro apiece; we whiled away an hour, talking about setting up our families on some hillside in Puglia, away from the crush and mix of city life. We'd grow our own vegetables, read and write, start a tiny community. The plan was pretty ludicrous—spending more than a week in the countryside bores me, and I unfailingly kill even the potted basil plants I buy in supermarkets. But the fantasy was also spookily familiar, a potent mix of fear, nostalgia, and longing: a willful self-isolation in the pursuit of purity and simplicity.

Not long ago, I read that a Federal Reserve Bank of New York study had found a correlation between Germany's deaths from the 1918 flu pandemic and support for the Nazis during the 1932 and 1933 elections. Controlling for other possible influences like unemployment and city budgets, the researchers found that high death rates boosted a locality's support for Adolf Hitler's party. Preliminary evidence suggests extremist groups are taking advantage of the isolation and grief of the COVID era. Hate crimes and violence against Asian Americans spiraled. Online, far-right groups encouraged followers to deliberately infect Jews and Muslims with the virus; Islamist extremists claimed that COVID was God's punishment for Western "degeneracy."

In the United States, COVID brought boredom, isolation, and rocketing screen time—a "perfect storm for recruitment and radicalization," Cynthia Miller-Idriss, who runs PERIL, an extremism research project lab, told National Public Radio. "For extremists, this is an ideal time to exploit youth grievances about their lack of agency, their families' economic distress, and their intense sense of disorientation, confusion, fear, and anxiety," the American University professor said. Physically out of school, denied real-life connections to adults like teachers and coaches, "youth become easy targets for the far right," she said.

And yet the same pandemic year that had brought isolation, fear, and suspicion to Americans had also seen streets fill with peaceful protests for months, as young and old, black and white, urban and rural protested police violence after George Floyd's murder. The season before the pandemic stopped the world, some 4 million people, mostly young, marched for action on climate breakdown. OUR STREETS FLOOD, SO WE FLOOD THE STREETS, read a sign in Houston. In San Francisco, a marcher waved a placard: THE SEA IS RISING, SO MUST WE.

Nights, I worry about my native country becoming the loneliest one in human history. A place where people are sealed off from each other in their cars and cul-de-sacs, where we now see only the Amazon delivery person. I comfort myself with recent images of people taking to the streets to connect and to express a shared sense of rage and responsibility for a dying planet. If extremists prey on people's yearnings for an existential threat, surely climate change is the ultimate one? If they leverage people's needs for common cause, then what better cause for the common good could there be?

ON A SATURDAY MORNING before the world had ever heard of COVID, I watched weddings at the Mechelen city hall. Beneath a Gothic facade so towered and turreted that one expects to see Sleeping Beauty skipping out, a Muslim couple emerged. The bride was wearing a white bouffant dress, while the groom was suited up and grinning sheepishly. The wedding's female guests, many in hijabs, surrounded the newlyweds, beating small drums and ululating loudly. I listened to the Arab women's traditional cry of collective joy, rising right across from the cathedral tower that medieval Mechelen hoped would be the tallest in Europe.

When I met with Mayor Somers, I asked him whether he thought his carefully curated civic policies might actually backfire. I mentioned George Orwell's observation, in his prescient 1940 review of *Mein Kampf,* that people don't necessarily long for peace and harmony but rather for something to believe in fervently and to act on. "Human beings," Orwell wrote, "don't only want comfort, safety, short working-hours, hygiene, birth-control and, in general, common sense. They also, at least intermittently, want struggle and self-sacrifice, not to mention drums, flags and loyalty-parades."

Citing this Orwell quote, the anthropologist Scott Atran argues that just providing people with good jobs and access to a ballot box won't stop young people in the West from being drawn to extremism. According to the World Values Survey, most Europeans don't believe that living in a democratic country is "absolutely important" for them, he points out. Over one-third of young high-earning Americans actually favor army rule. Compared to the willingness of militants to fight and die for jihad, Atran sees scant appetite for making such sacrifices for democratic values.

So where, I ask Somers, does that leave the clean streets of prosperous Mechelen? If humans do need to struggle for a cause, how does Mechelen's cozy strategy satisfy it?

"People want to be bigger than life," Somers agrees. But he sees Mechelen's integration drive as a cause in itself. For him, Mechelen is a story of collective heroism, a challenge offering much the same pride and camaraderie that people desire and populists exploit. The struggle to create a town that reflects Europe's twenty-first-century hyperdiversity is a glorious one, particularly in an era of discord and division. "We are a beacon of hope," he says. "That's the biggest thing that this small city can do: prove that the populists are wrong!"

That's a cause that can produce zeal without violence. It's a cause, he says, "bigger than Mechelen's church tower."

ACKNOWLEDGMENTS

THE STORIES IN THIS book appear thanks to the generosity and courage of a great many people, a number of whom were willing to share the details of the worst times of their lives. The optimism and dedication of the people working to rehabilitate violent extremists remains an inspiration.

I'm grateful to Tom Dodd for sharing his expertise and encouragement when I first embarked on this project. An early draft benefited enormously from a writers' workshop at Stanford University's McCoy Family Center for Ethics in Society, which offers nonfiction writers the luxury of spending a day with a roomful of Stanford professors critiquing the manuscript. My thanks to Joan Berry and Anne Newman, who not only participated but assembled experts from around the Stanford campus: Eamonn Callan, Collin Anthony Chen, Martha Crenshaw, John Evans, David Laitin, Alison McQueen, Salma Mousa, Rob Reich, Shirin Sinnar, Sharika Thiranagama, and Jeremy Weinstein. Jane Coyne was my wingwoman for the day—thank you.

In addition to the people quoted in the book, many academics, researchers, and rehabilitation practitioners shared their expertise with me in interviews, providing invaluable background. My thanks to Nasir Abas, Rashad Ali, Zahed Amanullah, Chaula Rininta Anindya, Rania Awaad, Moustafa Ayad, Byron Bland, Jean Decety, Julia Ebner, Leanne Edberg, James S. Gordon, Todd Green, Rüdiger José Hamm, Georgia Holmer, Melinda Holmes, the staff of Legato in Hamburg, Shashi Jayakumar, Muhammad Asfandiyar Khan, Khalid Koser, Shiraz Maher, Emmanuel Mauleón, Wissem Missoussi, Charlotte Moeyens, Alaina M. Morgan, Jeffrey Murer, René Hedegaard Nielsen, Nina Noorali, Jamuna Oehlmann, Philipp Oswalt, Faiza Patel, Lt. Col. Edward W. Powers, Béatrice Pouligny, Jeremy Richman, Sara Savage, Edit Schlaffer, Aneela Shah, Mitchell Silber, Amrit Singh, Anne Speckhard, Henry Tuck, Robert Örell, Bernd Wagner, Harald Weilnböeck, Fabian Wichmann, the staff of VAJA/Kitab in Bremen, Melissa Yeomans, and Michael Zekulin.

It was a privilege to work with the brilliant Chris Jackson, whose edits manage to be light but profound, subtle but transformative. Emi Ikkanda was the book's early champion; I'm grateful for her editorial vision of what the book could be, and for Julie Grau and Cindy Spiegel's enthusiasm for the project. Huge thanks to Sun Robinson-Smith for being a delightful ally in the final stages. Carla Bruce-Eddings, Lulú Martínez, and Mika Kasuga, and the rest of the team at One World were wonderful advocates for the book. Thanks, too, to Janet Biehl for careful copyediting. Alan Zarembo was a brilliant editor for some of the Indonesia section, which appeared as an article in the *Los Angeles Times*. Mayolisia Ekayanti, Pascale Müller, and Petra Tank provided translations from Bahasa Indonesian and German. Shan Vahidy offered accomplished editorial advice on tone and structure. Jaclyn Jacobs lent her photographic expertise; Kai Eston helped puzzle over a suitable title. Erin Harris has been my agent for nearly a decade now, but I still can't believe my luck in landing on her list.

Thanks to Sarita Choudhury, for the daily dose of your FaceTimed grin and brilliance. And to Liz Unna, Caro Douglas-Pennant, Frances Stonor Saunders, and Camilla Bustani for dinners, spare rooms, and general hilarity on research trips to London. Elke Van Campenhout was the best of hostesses at her urban monastery in Brussels. Nina Berman, always a peerless collaborator, made reporting trips to Belgium and Germany adventures. Rebecca Goldsmith, Neena Jain, and Anne Treeger offered transatlantic wisdom. Anita Dawood shared her thoughts on Pakistan's art scene. Moni Mohsin read early drafts of chapters and provided valuable contacts in Britain and in Pakistan. Selina Mills always gave wise counsel at our sessions at the British Library and Le Pain Quotidien. Beth Gardiner, Natasha Randall, and the other members of Women Who Write cheered, commiserated, and advised via Zoom. And every Sunday at four P.M., Hanna Clements, Amy Dulin, and Jill Herzig would buoy me up for another week of writing.

Finally, my love and gratitude to Antony Seely, who makes me laugh harder and think more deeply than anyone else on the planet. And to Julia and Nic Seely-Power: you were there all the way, reminding me what a better world looks like.

NOTES

EPIGRAPH

vii **"At any moment a bomb":** Virginia Woolf, "Thoughts on Peace in an Air Raid," *The Death of the Moth and Other Essays* (London: Hogarth Press, 1942), p. 211.

INTRODUCTION

4 **asking deradicalization experts:** J. Patrick Coolican, "How Do We De-Radicalize? Three Experts in Political Extremism and Violence Share Ideas," *Ohio Capital Journal,* February 8, 2021, ohiocapitaljournal .com/2021/02/08/how-do-we-de-radicalize-three-experts-in-political -extremism-and-violence-share-ideas/.

4 **"spiritual leadership":** Simon Shuster, " 'Everyone Thinks I'm a Terrorist': Capitol Riot Fuels Calls for Domestic War on Terror," *Time,* January 18, 2021.

4 **"Our most serious threats":** Chuck Hagel, "Advice for the Next Secretary of Defense," *Defense One,* January 19, 2021, www.defenseone.com/ideas/ 2021/01/advice-next-secretary-defense/171466/.

5 **"To be truly radical":** Jane Ronson, "Raymond Williams Papers at the Richard Burton Archives, Swansea University," *Archives Hub,* October 2,

2017, blog.archiveshub.jisc.ac.uk/2017/10/02/raymond-williams-papers-at -the-richard-burton-archives-swansea-university/.

7 **"But if they repent":** Verse 9:5, *The Quran,* trans. Thomas Cleary (Chicago: Starlatch, 2004).

8 **most important form of jihad:** John L. Esposito, *Unholy War: Terror in the Name of Islam* (New York: Oxford University Press, 2002), p. 28.

8 **one in thirty million:** Alex Nowrasteh, "More Americans Die in Animal Attacks than in Terrorist Attacks," Cato Institute, March 8, 2018, www.cato .org/blog/more-americans-die-animal-attacks-terrorist-attacks.

8 **one in ninety-two:** "Odds of Dying," *Injury Facts,* National Safety Council, 2019, injuryfacts.nsc.org/all-injuries/preventable-death-overview/odds-of -dying/.

8 **Political violence has dropped:** Florence Gaub, "Trends in Terrorism," European Union Institute for Security Studies, March 2017, www.iss .europa.eu/sites/default/files/EUISSFiles/Alert_4_Terrorism_in_Europe _0.pdf.

8 **357 percent more press:** Mona Chalabi, "Terror Attacks by Muslims Receive 357% More Press Attention, Study Finds," *Guardian,* July 20, 2018.

8 **seven and a half times:** "Equal Treatment? Measuring the Legal and Media Responses to Ideologically Motivated Violence in the United States," Institute for Social Policy and Understanding, April 2018, www.ispu.org/ public-policy/equal-treatment.

8 **Far-right terrorists killed:** "Right-Wing Extremism Linked to Every 2018 Extremist Murder in the U.S., ADL Finds," Anti-Defamation League, January 23, 2019, www.adl.org/news/press-releases/right-wing-extremism -linked-to-every-2018-extremist-murder-in-the-us-adl-finds.

9 **"There was a failure":** Eddy quoted in Mark Mazzetti et al., "Inside a Deadly Siege: How a String of Failures Led to a Dark Day at the Capitol," *New York Times,* January 10, 2021.

9 **"inappropriate concentration":** Praveen Menon, "NZ's Ardern Apologises as Report into Mosque Attack Faults Focus on Islamist Terror Risks," Reuters, December 8, 2020.

10 **"blessed ban":** Joby Warrick, "Jihadist Groups Hail Trump's Travel Ban as a Victory," *Washington Post,* January 29, 2017.

10 **"Islam hates us":** "'I Think Islam Hates Us'" (editorial), *New York Times,* January 26, 2017, www.nytimes.com/2017/01/26/opinion/i-think-islam -hates-us.html.

11 **"command and control center":** "Trump Opens Global Center for Combating Extremist Ideology," *Washington Post,* May 21, 2017, www .washingtonpost.com/video/politics/trump-opens-global-center-for -combating-extremist-ideology-with-egypts-al-sissi-saudi-arabias-salman/ 2017/05/21/2875d228-3e4f-11e7-b29f-f40ffced2ddb_video.html.

12 **"Drive them out":** "Transcript of Trump's Speech in Saudi Arabia," CNN, May 21, 2017.

12 **"the work of the devil":** Adam Gartrell and Mark Kenny, "Paris Attacks: Malcolm Turnbull Calls the Paris Assault the 'Work of the Devil'" *Sydney Morning Herald,* November 14, 2015.

12 **"the evil ideology of Islamist":** J. Weston Phippen, "Theresa May's Terrorism Strategy," *Atlantic,* June 4, 2017.

13 PURE**, began the headline:** Kevin Rawlinson, "How the British Press Reacted to the Manchester Bombing," *Guardian,* May 23, 2017.

14 NOW THEY KILL: Ibid.

15 **16 percent:** Colin Clark, "Counterterror Costs Since 911: $2.8 TRILLION and Climbing," *Breaking Defense,* September 11, 2018, breakingdefense .com/2018/09/counterterror-costs-since-911-2-8-trillion-and-climbing/.

15 **jihadist militants tripled:** Erik W. Goepner, "Measuring the Effectiveness of America's War on Terror," *Parameters* 46, no. 1 (2016): 113, publications .armywarcollege.edu/pubs/3323.pdf.

15 **1,900 percent:** A. Trevor Thrall and Erik Goepner, "Step Back: Lessons for U.S. Foreign Policy from the Failed War on Terror," Cato Institute, June 26, 2017, www.cato.org/policy-analysis/step-back-lessons-us-foreign-policy -failed-war-terror.

15 **rose by 41 percent:** "Race and Religious Hate Crimes Rose 41% after EU Vote," BBC News, October 13, 2016.

16 **"bring destruction":** "Terrorists Have Nowhere to Hide, Says Defence Secretary," BBC News, December 7, 2017.

16 **"Unfortunately the only way":** Stewart quoted in "British IS Fighters 'Must Be Killed,' Minister Says," BBC News, October 23, 2017.

17 **one hundred definitions:** D. Elaine Pressman, "Risk Assessment Decisions for Violent Political Extremism," Public Safety Canada, 2009, www .publicsafety.gc.ca/cnt/rsrcs/pblctns/2009-02-rdv/2009-02-rdv-eng.pdf.

17 **"something used by":** Jonathan Powell, *Talking to Terrorists: How to End Armed Conflicts* (London: Vintage, 2015), p. 10.

17 **Loujain al-Hathloul:** "Saudi Activist 'Loses Appeal Against Sentence,'" BBC News, March 10, 2021.

17 **finally had to give up:** "Government Abandons Attempts to Define 'Extremism' in Law," *Irish Legal News,* April 8, 2019, www.irishlegal.com/ article/government-abandons-attempts-to-define-extremism-in-law.

17 **Birmingham jail:** Martin Luther King, Jr., "Letter from Birmingham Jail," letterfromjail.com/.

18 **"All terrorists, at the invitation":** Gaitskell quoted in Jonathan Powell, "How to Talk to Terrorists," *Guardian,* October 7, 2014.

18 **"If you imagine Osama":** Michael Burleigh, *Blood and Rage: A Cultural History of Terrorism* (London: HarperPerennial, 2010), p. ix.

18 **Martin McGuinness:** Luke Byrne, "McGuinness' Widow to Receive Letter of Condolence from Queen," *Irish Independent News,* March 22, 2017.

19 **"We don't negotiate with evil":** Cheney quoted in Jonathan Powell, "Negotiate with ISIS," *Atlantic,* December 7, 2015.

19 **"torment":** Rothko quoted in Gabriella Angeleti, "In Pictures: Rothko Chapel's 50th Anniversary Celebrated in New Publication," *Art Newspaper,* March 5, 2021, www.theartnewspaper.com/feature/in-pictures-or-rothko -chapel-s-50th-anniversary-celebrated-in-new-publication.

20 **"tell the story":** Allyn West, "Houston's Rothko Chapel Vandalized with Paint, Handbills: 'It's Okay to Be White,'" *Houston Chronicle,* May 22, 2018, www.chron.com/houston/article/Houston-s-Rothko-Chapel-vandalized -with-paint-12931429.php.

THE LOST BOY

23 **"an ethics that properly":** Ian Ward, *Law, Text, Terror* (Cambridge: Cambridge University Press, 2009), p. 147.

25 **"Policy makers in Washington":** Sanam Naraghi-Anderlini, "Debunking Stereotypes: Which Women Matter in the Fight Against Extremism?" International Civil Society Action Network, April 7, 2016, icanpeacework .org/2016/04/07/debunking-stereotypes-which-women-matter-in-the -fight-against-extremism-by-sanam-anderlini/.

31 **"are the times when":** Robert M. Sapolsky, *Behave: The Biology of Humans at Our Best and Worst* (London: Vintage, 2018), p. 155.

36 **"poisonous ideology":** Cameron quoted in Nadia Khomami, "David Cameron Urges Swift Action Against ISIS," *Guardian,* August 16, 2014.

36 **"the single evil ideology":** May quoted in Gordon Rayner and Jack Maidment, "Theresa May Says 'Enough Is Enough' in Wake of London Bridge Terror Attack as She Confirms General Election Will Go Ahead," *Telegraph,* June 4, 2017.

36 **Religious belief clearly didn't:** Zaman al-Wasl, "Leaked ISIS Documents Reveal Most Recruits Know Little on Islam," *Haaretz,* January 10, 2018, www.haaretz.com/middle-east-news/leaked-isis-documents-reveal-recruits -ignorant-on-islam-1.5424990.

41 **Green Lane Mosque:** Jamie Doward, "Revealed: Preachers' Messages of Hate," *Guardian,* January 7, 2007.

42 **"perpetrators take teenagers":** Nazir Afzal, "Young People Are Easily Led. Our Anti-Radicalisation Schemes Need to Be Cleverer," *Guardian,* April 8, 2015.

42 **After newspapers stoked:** John Holmwood, "The Birmingham Trojan Horse Affair: A Very British Injustice," www.opendemocracy.net, Decem-

ber 13, 2017, www.opendemocracy.net/en/birmingham-trojan-horse-affair
-very-british-injustice/.

43 **"better in the past":** Mark Easton, "The English Question: What Is the Nation's Identity?" BBC News, June 3, 2018.

43 **64 percent of people:** Steven Levy, "Facebook Can't Fix What It Won't Admit To," *Wired,* January 15, 2021.

47 **no conveyor belt:** On the conveyor belt theory, see, for example, Clark McCauley and Sophia Moskalenko, "Understanding Political Radicalization: The Two-Pyramids Model," *American Psychologist* 72, no. 3 (2017): 205–16, www.apa.org/pubs/journals/releases/amp-amp0000062.pdf, and Arun Kundnani, "A Decade Lost: Rethinking Radicalisation and Extremism," Muslim Association of Britain, January 2015, mabonline.net/wp -content/uploads/2015/01/Claystone-rethinking-radicalisation.pdf.

47 **People who hold:** Tore Bjørgo and John G. Horgan, eds., *Leaving Terrorism Behind: Individual and Collective Disengagement* (London: Routledge, 2009), p. 1.

47 **"Despite decades of research":** *Ayman Latif v. Loretta E. Lynch,* U.S. District Court, District of Oregon, Civil case no. CV 10-00750-BR, "Declaration of Marc Sageman in Opposition to Defendants' Cross-Motion for Summary Judgment," p. 6, www.aclu.org/sites/default/files/field _document/268._declaration_of_marc_sageman_8.7.15.pdf.

48 **"push factors":** United Nations, *Plan of Action to Prevent Violent Extremism,* 2016, p. 14, www.un.org/counterterrorism/plan-of-action-to-prevent -violent-extremism.

49 **"some parts of the country":** *"Prevent* Strategy," HM Government, June 2011, p. 3, assets.publishing.service.gov.uk/government/uploads/system/ uploads/attachment_data/file/97976/prevent-strategy-review.pdf.

49 **in Staffordshire:** Randeep Ramesh and Josh Halliday, "In Staffordshire Student Accused of Being a Terrorist for Reading Book on Terrorism," *Guardian,* September 24, 2015.

49 **Nursery school staff:** "Radicalisation Fear over Cucumber Drawing by Boy, 4," BBC News, March 11, 2016.

49 **University conferences on:** "Liberty's Written Evidence to the JCHR's Inquiry on Freedom of Expression in Universities," *Liberty,* March 3, 2020, p. 6, www.libertyhumanrights.org.uk/wp-content/uploads/2020/02/ Libertys-Evidence-to-the-JCHRs-Inquiry-into-Freedom-of-Expression-in -Universities-Dec-2017.pdf.

50 **Future Attribute Screening Technology:** "Privacy Impact Assessment for the Future Attribute Screening Technology (FAST) Project," U.S. Department of Homeland Security, December 15, 2008, www.dhs.gov/xlibrary/ assets/privacy/privacy_pia_st_fast.pdf.

50 **Many analysts have:** Mark C. Niles, "Preempting Justice: "Precrime" in Fiction and in Fact," *Seattle Journal for Justice* 9, no.1 (2010), law.seattleu .edu/Documents/sjsj/2010fall/Niles.pdf.

50 **"frustration at U.S. policy":** "Terrorism Indicators Chart," in Faiza Patel, Andrew Lindsay, and Sophia DenUyl, "Countering Violent Extremism in the Trump Era," Brennan Center for Justice, 2018, www.brennancenter .org/our-work/research-reports/countering-violent-extremism-trump-era.

51 **Global Terrorism Index:** "Global Terrorism Index 2019," *ReliefWeb,* November 20, 2019, reliefweb.int/report/world/global-terrorism-index-2019.

"YOU'RE THE MOTHER OF A TERRORIST"

53 **"No one can tell":** Rita Dove, " 'Persephone Abducted,' " *Mother Love* (New York: W.W. Norton, 1995), p. 13.

55 **"the gray zone":** "Dabiq VII Feature Article: The World Includes Only Two Camps—That of ISIS and That of Its Enemies," Middle East Media Research Institute, February 18, 2015, www.memri.org/jttm/dabiq-vii -feature-article-world-includes-only-two-camps-%E2%80%93-isis-and-its -enemies.

63 **"crack babies":** Enid Logan, "The Wrong Race, Committing Crime, Doing Drugs, and Maladjusted for Motherhood: The Nation's Fury over 'Crack Babies,' " *Social Justice* 26, no. 1 (1999): 115–38, www.jstor.org/ stable/29767115?seq=1.

63 **"de-pluralization of political":** Sara Brzuszkiewicz, "An Interview with Daniel Koehler, German Institute on Radicalization and De-Radicalization Studies," *European Eye on Radicalization,* January 2, 2019, eeradicalization .com/an-interview-with-daniel-koehler-german-institute-on-radicalization -and-de-radicalization-studies/.

63 **"global struggle against Islam":** United States v. Abdullahi Mohamud Yusuf, U.S. District Court, District of Minnesota, File no. 15-CR-46, vol. 1, Daniel Koehler testimony, pp. 3–34.

63 **A deft recruiter can:** Daniel Koehler, *Understanding Deradicalization: Methods, Tools and Programs for Countering Violent Extremism* (New York: Garland, 2018), p. 75.

63 **"then all of these problems":** United States v. Abdullahi Mohamud Yusuf, U.S. District Court, District of Minnesota, File no. 15-CR-46, vol. 1, Daniel Koehler testimony, p. 34.

65 **"We are all sisters":** Mothers for Life, "Open Letter to Our Sons and Daughters in Syria and Iraq," German Institute on Radicalization and De-Radicalization Studies, June 3, 2015, girds.org/mothersforlife/open-letter -to-our-sons-and-daughters.

66   **"tricked by those":** Mothers for Life, "A Second Letter to Abu Bakr al-Baghdadi from the Mothers for Life," German Institute on Radicalization and De-Radicalization Studies, n.d., girds.org/mothersforlife.

70   **"We lost our sons":** Murray in dialogue from *Victoria Derbyshire*, BBC News, May 21, 2018, archive.org/details/BBCNEWS_20180521_080000 _Victoria_Derbyshire.

70   **When the British tabloid:** Alex Green, " 'We Lost Our Sons to the SAME Monster': Mothers of Man Killed in Manchester Attack and Man Who Died Fighting for ISIS Forge Unlikely Bond," *Daily Mail*, May 21, 2018, www.dailymail.co.uk/news/article-5754557/Mothers-man-killed -Manchester-terror-attack-man-died-fighting-ISIS-forge-bond.html.

70   **"Except one was an innocent":** Comments from Readers, ibid.

71   **"The terrorist scrum [*sic*]":** Viewers' comments on *Victoria Derbyshire*, Facebook, www.facebook.com/VictoriaDerbyshire.

THE GODMOTHER AND HER GODDAUGHTERS

75   **"Care Bears":** Quoted in Gillian Slovo, *Another World: Losing Our Children to Islamic State,* performed at National Theatre, London, 2016.

76   **The money Charlotte sent:** Abdullah Mustafa, "Belgium: Mother of Extremist Killed in Syria Charged with Financing Terrorism," *Asharq Al-Awsat*, May 20, 2016, eng-archive.aawsat.com/a-mustafa/world-news/belgium -mother-extremist-killed-syria-charged-financing-terrorism.

84   **Yassine Lachouri, an Islamic State:** Julien Balboni, "Julie a enlevé sa fille pour rejoindre Daesh, elle a 'plongé sa fille dans un enfer,' " *DH Les Sports*, January 12, 2017, www.dhnet.be/actu/faits/julie-a-enleve-sa-fille-pour -rejoindre-daesh-elle-a-plonge-sa-fille-dans-un-enfer-5876834ccd70717 f88f148de.

84   **"plunged her daughter":** Jacques Laruelle, "Pas de double peine pour Julie B, partie en Syrie avec son enfant," *La Libre*, February 9, 2017, www.lalibre .be/actu/belgique/pas-de-double-peine-pour-julie-b-partie-en-syrie-avec -son-enfant-589b5e10cd702bc31911e17e.

85   **"a little Zionist-nationalist":** Amos Oz, *Dear Zealots: Letters from a Divided Land,* trans. Jessica Cohen (Boston: Mariner Books, 2019), pp. 8–9.

TRUST EXERCISES

92   **"seething at his death":** Dave Merritt, "Jack Would Be Livid His Death Has Been Used to Further an Agenda of Hate," *Guardian*, December 2, 2018.

92   **"near-perfect" conditions:** Peter R. Neumann, "Prisons and Terrorism:

Radicalisation and De-Radicalisation in 15 Countries," International Centre for the Study of Radicalisation and Political Violence (ICSR), 2010, www.clingendael.org/sites/default/files/pdfs/Prisons-and-terrorism-15-countries.pdf; and Gabriel Hoeft, "'Soft' Approaches to Counter-Terrorism: An Exploration of the Benefits of Deradicalization Programs," International Institute for Counter-Terrorism, 2015, www.ict.org.il/UserFiles/ICT-Soft-Approaches-to-CT-Hoeft.pdf.

94 **But remedies do proliferate:** Sources on the range of deradicalization approaches include "Preventing Radicalization to Terrorism and Violent Extremism," from the European Commission-sponsored Radicalization Awareness Network (RAN), and Koehler's *Understanding Deradicalization*.

95 **box and play soccer:** Nic Robertson and Paul Cruickshank, "Cagefighter 'Cures' Terrorists," CNN, July 23, 2012.

95 **put on plays and dance:** Jess Gormley and Alex Healey, "How a German Prison Is Using Theatre to De-Radicalise Young Isis Volunteers—Video," *Guardian,* March 6, 2017.

95 **auto maintenance and welding:** James Khalil et al., "Deradicalisation and Disengagement in Somalia: Evidence from a Rehabilitation Programme for Former Members of Al-Shabaab," Royal United Services Institute, January 2018, rusi.org/sites/default/files/20190104_whr_4-18_deradicalisation_and_disengagement_in_somalia_web.pdf.

95 **painting lessons:** Marisa L. Porges, "The Saudi Deradicalization Experiment," Council on Foreign Relations, January 22, 2010, www.cfr.org/expert-brief/saudi-deradicalization-experiment.

95 **"Proust's Madeleine":** Elisabeth Zerofsky, "France: How to Stop a Martyr," Pulitzer Center, September 2, 2016, pulitzercenter.org/reporting/france-how-stop-martyr.

95 **traditional shadow puppets:** Setyo Widagdo and Milda Istiqomah, "Development of Counseling Model of Deradicalization Program in Indonesia," *International Journal of Advanced Research,* March 2019, doi.org/10.21474/IJAR01/8710.

95 **The U.S. approach to:** United States v. Abdullahi Mohamud Yusuf, U.S. District Court, District of Minnesota, File no. 15-CR-46, vol. 1, Daniel Koehler testimony, September 26, 2016, p. 63.

95 **toll-free lines for help:** Koehler, *Understanding Deradicalization*, p. 146.

95 **freelance mentors for at-risk:** Helen Warrell, "Inside Prevent, the UK's Controversial Anti-Terrorism Programme," *Financial Times,* January 24, 2018, www.ft.com/content/a82e18b4-1ea3-11e9-b126-46fc3ad87c65.

96 **Adam Shafi, a Bay Area:** Matt Apuzzo, "Only Hard Choices for Parents Whose Children Flirt with Terror," *New York Times,* April 9, 2016.

97 **Adam ended up:** Nate Gartrell, "In Rebuke of Feds, Judge Frees East Bay

Man Once Accused of Terrorism," *Mercury News*, March 30, 2019, www
.mercurynews.com/2019/03/30/in-rebuke-of-feds-judge-frees-east-bay
-man-once-accused-of-terrorism/.

97 **"We know how to find":** Townsend at "Deradicalization: Oasis or Mirage?" panel at Global Security Forum, 2011, Center for Strategic and International Studies, www.csis.org/events/global-security-forum-2011
-'deradicalization'-oasis-or-mirage.

98 **world's busiest jailer:** "Mass Incarceration," American Civil Liberties Union, n.d., www.aclu.org/issues/smart-justice/mass-incarceration.

98 **"distinctly more punitive":** Joseph Margulies, "Deviance, Risk, and Law: Reflections on the Demand for the Preventive Detention of Suspected Terrorists," *Journal of Criminal Law and Criminology* 101, no. 3 (2011), scholarlycommons.law.northwestern.edu/cgi/viewcontent.cgi?referer
=&httpsredir=1&article=7402&context=jclc. See also James Forman, Jr., "Exporting Harshness: How the War on Crime Helped Make the War on Terror Possible," *NYU Review of Law and Social Change* 33, no. 3 (2009): 333, digitalcommons.law.yale.edu/cgi/viewcontent.cgi?article=4018&context
=fss_papers.

BY THE BOOK

100 **nicknamed "Bones":** Dina Temple-Raston, "He Wanted Jihad. He Got Foucault," *New York* magazine, November 27, 2017, nymag.com/
intelligencer/2017/11/abdullahi-yusuf-isis-syria.html. For details of Abdullahi's early life, I've relied heavily on Temple-Raston's excellent reporting on Abdullahi Yusuf, as well as United States v. Abdullahi Mohamud Yusuf, U.S. District Court, District of Minnesota, Defendant's Position with Regard to Sentencing and Motion for a Downward Variance.

102 **those who were stopped before:** Alexander Meleagrou-Hitchens, Seamus Hughes, and Bennett Clifford, "The Travelers: American Jihadists in Syria and Iraq," George Washington University Program on Extremism, February 2018, p. 2, extremism.gwu.edu/sites/g/files/zaxdzs2191/f/Travelers
AmericanJihadistsinSyriaandIraq.pdf.

109 **"I'm in the reservation":** Harriet Staff, "'I'm in the Reservation of My Mind': Sherman Alexie's Early Inspiration," Poetry Foundation, October 2013, www.poetryfoundation.org/harriet/2013/10/im-in-the-reservation
-of-my-mind-sherman-alexies-early-inspiration.

110 **"This Is Water":** David Foster Wallace, "This Is Water (Full Transcript and Audio)," *Farnam Street*, January 14, 2021, fs.blog/2012/04/david-foster
-wallace-this-is-water/.

112 **"The fanatic," wrote Amos Oz:** Oz, *Dear Zealot*, p. 20.

113 **Germany's deradicalization programs:** Michael Herzog zu Mecklenburg and Ian Anthony, "Preventing Violent Extremism in Germany: Coherence and cooperation in a Decentralized System" (working paper), Stockholm International Peace Research Institute, August 2020, www.sipri.org/sites/default/files/2020-08/wp_2005_violent_extremism.pdf.

113 **France's short-lived program:** Maddy Crowell, "What Went Wrong with France's Deradicalization Program?" *Atlantic,* September 28, 2017.

113 **"the legitimacy and religious":** Angel Rabasa et al., "Deradicalization Process Is Essential Part of Fighting Terrorism," RAND Corporation, November 29, 2010, www.rand.org/news/press/2010/11/29.html.

114 **Minneapolis police officers:** Arun Kundnani, *The Muslims Are Coming!: Islamophobia, Extremism, and the Domestic War on Terror* (London: Verso, 2015), pp. 212–16.

115 **The morning Warsame:** Laura Yuen, Mukhtar M. Ibrahim, and Doualy Xaykaothao, "Latest: ISIS Trial in Minnesota," MPR News, June 3, 2016, www.mprnews.org/story/2016/05/09/isis-trial-minnesota-updates.

116 **many CVE programs:** Faiza Patel, and Amrit Singh, "The Human Rights Risks of Countering Violent Extremism Programs," *Just Security,* April 7, 2016, www.justsecurity.org/30459/human-rights-risks-countering-violent-extremism-programs/.

116 **"broad swaths of political speech":** Emmanuel Mauleón, "It's Time to Put CVE to Bed," Brennan Center for Justice, November 2, 2018, www.brennancenter.org/our-work/analysis-opinion/its-time-put-cve-bed.

116 **With the Muslim travel ban:** Peter Beinart, "Trump Shut Programs to Counter Violent Extremism," *Atlantic,* October 29, 2018.

116 **"suggestive of a national security":** Faiza Patel, Andrew Lindsay, and Sophia DenUyl, "Countering Violent Extremism in the Trump Era," Brennan Center for Justice, June 15, 2018, www.brennancenter.org/our-work/research-reports/countering-violent-extremism-trump-era.

116 **"CVE discriminatorily targets":** Email to Mary McKinley, November 7, 2017.

117 **"flawed models":** Kundnani, *Muslims Are Coming!,* p. 289.

117 **"a terrorist organization":** Davis quoted in Laura Yuen, "3 of 9 Twin Cities Men Sentenced in ISIS Conspiracy Trial," MPR News, November 14, 2016, www.mprnews.org/story/2016/11/14/first-day-of-sentencing-isis-trial.

119 **"Hug a Terrorist":** " 'Hug a Terrorist' Program in Denmark," *Federalist,* August 12, 2017, thefederalist-gary.blogspot.com/2017/08/hug-terrorist-program-in-denmark.html.

THE "TERRORIST DROP-OFF CENTER"

121 **Denmark would make it a crime:** "Denmark: Extremism and Counter-Extremism," Counter Extremism Project, February 18, 2021, www .counterextremism.com/countries/denmark.

122 **"I'd say it's for the best":** Anthony Dworkin, "The Problem with Western Suggestions of a 'Shoot-to-Kill' Policy Against Foreign Fighters," *Just Security*, December 13, 2017, www.justsecurity.org/49290/problematic -suggestions-western-shoot-to-kill-policy-citizens-fighting-isis/.

122 **"Aarhus does want these young people":** Gilles de Kerchove et al., "Rehabilitation and Reintegration of Returning Foreign Terrorist Fighters," Washington Institute for Near East Policy, February 23, 2015, www .washingtoninstitute.org/policy-analysis/rehabilitation-and-reintegration -returning-foreign-terrorist-fighters.

122 **right-wing populists made a strong:** Richard Orange, "Denmark Swings Right on Immigration—and Muslims Feel Besieged," *Guardian,* June 10, 2018, www.theguardian.com/world/2018/jun/10/denmark-swings-right -immigration-muslims-besieged-holbaek.

122 **Life Psychology:** Preben Bertelsen, "Danish Prevention Measures and De-Radicalization Strategies: The Aarhus Model," *Panorama: Insights into Asian and European Affairs,* January 2015, psy.au.dk/fileadmin/Psykologi/ Forskning/Preben_Bertelsen/Avisartikler_radikalisering/Panorama.pdf.

126 **the Saudi program:** Andreas Casptack, "Deradicalization Programs in Saudi Arabia: A Case Study," Middle East Institute, June 10, 2015, www .mei.edu/publications/deradicalization-programs-saudi-arabia-case-study.

126 **sang "La Marseilleise":** Crowell, "France's Deradicalization Program," *op cit.*

127 **"In spite of its egalitarian":** Jeppe Trolle Linnet, "Money Can't Buy Me Hygge: Danish Middle-Class Consumption, Egalitarianism, and the Sanctity of Inner Space," *Social Analysis* 55, no. 2 (2011): 21–44, doi.org/10 .3167/sa.2011.550202.

136 **"ghetto plan":** Billy Perrigo, "What to Know About Denmark's Controversial Plan to Eradicate Immigrant 'Ghettos,'" *Time,* July 2, 2018, time .com/5328347/denmark-ghettos-policies/.

ON MEETING THE BEHEADER

144 **prestige among their fellow:** I Gede Widhiana Suarda, "A Literature Review on Indonesia's Deradicalization Program for Terrorist Prisoners," *Mimbar Hukum* 28, no. 3 (2016): 526–43, journal.ugm.ac.id/jmh/article/ view/16682.

144 **By early 2018:** Emma Broches, "Southeast Asia's Overlooked Foreign Fighter Problem," *Lawfare* (blog), June 5, 2020, www.lawfareblog.com/southeast-asias-overlooked-foreign-fighter-problem.

145 **National Counter Terrorism Agency (BNPT):** Agustinus Beo Da Costa, "Indonesia Brings Together Former Militants and Attack Survivors," Reuters, February 28, 2018, www.reuters.com/article/uk-indonesia-militants-conciliaton-idUKKCN1GC1T6.

145 **"mutual respect and understanding":** "Mitigating Terrorism by Soft Skills," *AsiaViews,* March 9, 2018, asiaviews.net/mitigating-terrorism-soft-skills/.

146 **Western jihadis tend to be:** Diego Gambetta and Steffen Hertog, *Engineers of Jihad: The Curious Connection Between Violent Extremism and Education* (Princeton: Princeton University Press, 2018), pp. 7–8.

146 **people with shameful:** Nafees Hamid, "What Makes a Terrorist?," *New York Review of Books,* July 10, 2020. www.nybooks.com/daily/2017/08/23/what-makes-a-terrorist/.

146 **"Terrorism would be a trivial problem":** Clark R. McCauley, "The Psychology of Terrorism," Social Science Research Council, n.d., essays.ssrc.org/sept11/essays/mccauley.htm.

147 **"Where did this man learn":** Anthea Butler, "Shooters of Color Are Called 'Terrorists' and 'Thugs.' Why Are White Shooters Called 'Mentally Ill'?" *Washington Post,* June 18, 2015.

147 **"Wanted: 100 more Christian heads":** "Militant on Trial for Allegedly Beheading 3 Girls in Indonesia," CBC News, November 8, 2006, www.cbc.ca/news/world/militant-on-trial-for-allegedly-beheading-3-girls-in-indonesia-1.600621.

149 **"Maybe," Huda remarked:** Huda quoted in Carla Power, "'We Have Four Generations of Former Terrorists Here Today': Rehabilitating Extremists in Indonesia," *Los Angeles Times,* April 20, 2018.

150 **Hamas offers clinics:** "Council on Foreign Relations Backgrounder: What Is Hamas?" PBS NewsHour, November 20, 2012, www.pbs.org/newshour/world/hamas-backgrounder.

150 **Hezbollah has been providing:** Shawn Flanigan and Mounah Abdel-Samad, "Hezbollah's Social Jihad: Nonprofits as Resistance Organizations," *Middle East Policy,* June 2009, onlinelibrary.wiley.com/doi/10.1111/j.1475-4967.2009.00396.x/pdf.

150 **Lashkar-e-Taiba has helped:** Saeed Shah, "Pakistan Floods: Islamic Fundamentalists Fill State Aid Void," *Guardian,* August 3, 2010.

150 **relief to the poor in lockdown:** Jessica Watkins and Mustafa Hasan, "The Popular Mobilization and COVID-19 Pandemic in Iraq: A New Raison d'être?" *LSE* (blog), April 28, 2020, blogs.lse.ac.uk/crp/2020/04/28/the

-popular-mobilisation-and-covid-19-pandemic-in-iraq-a-new-raison-detre/, and Nisha Bellinger and Kyle Kattelman, "How the Coronavirus Increases Terrorism Threats in the Developing World," *Conversation,* May 26, 2020, theconversation.com/how-the-coronavirus-increases-terrorism-threats-in -the-developing-world-137466.

151 **Al Qaeda was looking to Hamas's:** Dina Temple-Raston, "Al-Qaida: Now Vying For Hearts, Minds and Land," NPR, July 13, 2012.

151 **Ku Klux Klan sponsored:** Linton Weeks, "When the KKK Was Mainstream," NPR, March 19, 2015, www.npr.org/sections/npr-history-dept/ 2015/03/19/390711598/when-the-ku-klux-klan-was-mainstream.

151 **Black Panthers ran free breakfast:** Erin Blakemore, "How the Black Panthers' Breakfast Program Both Inspired and Threatened the Government," History.com, February 6, 2018, www.history.com/news/free-school -breakfast-black-panther-party.

151 **mother of three in Gaza:** Richard Jackson, "Constructing Enemies: 'Islamic Terrorism' in Political and Academic Discourse," *Government and Opposition* 42, no. 3 (2007): 394–426, doi.org/10.1111/j.1477-7053.2007.00229 .x. Jackson provides a detailed critique of how "terrorism" is foregrounded in Western discourse about jihadi militants.

151 **Holy Land Foundation:** Robert Chesney, "Fifth Circuit Affirms Convictions in Holy Land Foundation," *Lawfare* (blog), December 8, 2011, www .lawfareblog.com/fifth-circuit-affirms-convictions-holy-land-foundation.

151 **"People were very happy":** Sarah Chayes, "Corruption and Terrorism: The Causal Link," Carnegie Endowment for International Peace, May 12, 2016, carnegieendowment.org/2016/05/12/corruption-and-terrorism -causal-link-pub-63568.

152 **"rampant extreme capitalism":** Sanam Naraghi-Anderlini, in "COVID-19 and Violent Extremism" (online webinar), Monash Gender, Peace and Security Center, June 3, 2020, www.monash.edu/arts/gender-peace-security/ engagement/event-recordings#COVID-19_and_violent_extremism _Gender_perspectives-2.

154 **"Yusuf shows no repentance":** Hannah Beech, "What Indonesia Can Teach the World About Counterterrorism," *Time,* June 7, 2010.

LOSS OF FAITH

161 **"These man, they are not":** The content of the Tumblr accounts of these social media accounts from Syria which I viewed in 2018, at fa-tubalilghuraba.tumblr.com/archive and diary-of-a-muhajirah.tumblr .com, is no longer online.

161 **"build a perfect utopian":** Interview with Scott Atran by Onbehagen,

April 4, 2018, www.human.nl/onbehagen/kijk/interviews/scottatran
.html.

162 **Neuroscientific studies:** "The Adolescent Brain: Beyond Raging Hor-
mones," *Harvard Health* (blog), March 2011, www.health.harvard.edu/
mind-and-mood/the-adolescent-brain-beyond-raging-hormones.

163 **"Joining the 'caliphate' is not":** Charlie Winter, *The Virtual "Caliphate":
Understanding Islamic State's Propaganda Strategy* (Quilliam, July 2015),
core.ac.uk/download/pdf/30671634.pdf.

164 **Nutella and kittens:** Amanda Taub, "No, CNN, Women Are Not Joining
ISIS Because of 'Kittens and Nutella,'" *Vox,* February 18, 2015.

164 *Becoming Mulan?:* Carolyn Hoyle, Alexandra Bradford, and Ross Frenett,
Becoming Mulan? Female Western Migrants to ISIS (Institute for Strategic Dia-
logue, 2015), www.isdglobal.org/wp-content/uploads/2016/02/ISDJ2969
_Becoming_Mulan_01.15_WEB.pdf.

164 **"sub-state *desperadoes*":** Cihan Aksan and Jon Bailes, eds., *Weapon of the
Strong: Conversations on US State Terrorism* (London: Pluto Press, 2013), p. 1.

165 **experiments measuring "sacred values":** Nafees Hamid et al., "Neuroim-
aging 'Will to Fight' for Sacred Values: An Empirical Case Study with Supporters of an Al Qaeda Associate," *Royal Society Open Science* 6, no. 6 (2019),
royalsocietypublishing.org/doi/abs/10.1098/rsos.181585.

167 **"not all radicals":** John G. Horgan and Mary Beth Altier, "The Future of
Terrorist De-Radicalization Programs," *Georgetown Journal of International
Affairs* (Summer–Fall 2012): 88, www.academia.edu/3882144/The_Future
_of_Terrorist_De_Radicalization_Programs. See also Stefan Malthaner,
"Radicalization: The Evolution of an Analytical Paradigm," Cambridge
Core, Cambridge University Press, December 4, 2017, www.cambridge
.org/core/journals/european-journal-of-sociology-archives-europeennes
-de-sociologie/article/radicalization/A91A5B84B27365A36ADF79D3
DFFE6C0C.

168 **"bunch of guys" theory:** Marc Sageman, *Understanding Terror Networks*
(Philadelphia: University of Pennsylvania Press, 2004).

169 **"make a value judgment seem":** Clark R. McCauley and Sophia Moskalenko, *Friction: How Conflict Radicalizes Them and Us* (New York: Oxford
University Press, 2017), p. 104.

170 **disillusionment with the group's tactics:** Julie Chernov Hwang, *Why Terrorists Quit: The Disengagement of Indonesian Jihadists* (Ithaca, NY: Cornell
University Press, 2018), p. 50.

170 **"These are just little things":** Peci quoted in John Horgan, "Individual
Disengagement: A Psychological Analysis," in Bjørgo and Horgan, eds.,
Leaving Terrorism Behind, p. 22.

ONLY GOD KNOWS THE HUMAN HEART

178 **"Did you split open his heart?":** Abu Amina Elias, "Hadith on Jihad: Did You Tear Open His Heart to See His Intention?" *Daily Hadith Online,* December 2, 2020, www.abuaminaelias.com/dailyhadithonline/2012/04/19/jihad-tear-open-heart/.

179 **Amir Abdillah was convicted:** "Indonesia Jails Driver over Jakarta Hotel Bomb," BBC News, June 14, 2010, www.bbc.com/news/10310940.

183 **Frank Meeink, a former white supremacist:** Frank Meeink, "Tree of Life, Roots of Rage: 3 Former Extremists Discuss Planting Seeds of Hope in the Context of Rising Hate-based Violence in the United States" (online discussion), Parallel Networks, October 29, 2018, pnetworks.org/tree-of-liferoots-of-rage-3-former-extremists-discuss-planting-seeds-of-hope-in-the-context-of-rising-hate-based-violence-in-the-united-states/.

184 **burns over 45 percent:** Niniek Karmini, "Indonesia Brings Convicted Militants and Victims Together," *Daily Herald* (Chicago), February 26, 2018, www.dailyherald.com/article/20180226/news/302269966.

186 **U.S.-backed repression in East Timor:** Cihan Aksan and Jon Bailes, *Weapon of the Strong: Conversations on US State Terrorism* (London: Pluto Press, 2013), p. 1.

187 **"the Nazi sympathizer next door":** Richard Fausset, "A Voice of Hate in America's Heartland," *New York Times,* November 25, 2017, www.nytimes.com/2017/11/25/us/ohio-hovater-white-nationalist.html.

187 **"You know who had":** Marc Lacey, "Readers Accuse Us of Normalizing a Nazi Sympathizer; We Respond," *New York Times,* November 26, 2017, www.nytimes.com/2017/11/26/reader-center/readers-accuse-us-of-normalizing-a-nazi-sympathizer-we-respond.html.

188 **the *Daily Mail*'s headline:** Freddy Mayhew, "*Daily Mirror* Changes Splash Headline Describing Mosque Killer as 'Angelic Boy,'" *Press Gazette,* March 18, 2019, www.pressgazette.co.uk/daily-mirror-changes-splash-headline-describing-mosque-killer-as-angelic-boy/.

188 **"People mad about this":** Lacey, "Readers Accuse Us."

193 **rebrand themselves as stately:** Bruce Hoffman, "Al-Qaeda's Resurrection," Council on Foreign Relations, March 6, 2018, www.cfr.org/expert-brief/al-qaedas-resurrection.

193 **"brainstorm":** Michael Fürstenberg and Carolin Görzig, "Learning in a Double Loop: The Strategic Transformation of Al-Qaeda," *Perspectives on Terrorism* 14, no. 1 (2020): 26–38, www.jstor.org/stable/pdf/26891983.pdf.

195 **empathy of a violent:** Niccola Milnes, "When Less Empathy is Desirable: The Complexity of Empathy and Intergroup Relationships in Preventing Violent Extremism," wasafirihub.com (blog), November 12, 2018, www.wasafirihub.com/when-less-empathy-is-desirable.

GREAT GAMES

198 **Today Pakistan remains:** *Global Terrorism Index 2019,* November 2019, www.economicsandpeace.org/wp-content/uploads/2020/08/GTI-2019web.pdf.

198 **"somewhat bizarrely":** Secunder Kermani, "Pakistan's Dilemma: What to Do about Anti-India Militants," BBC News, March 9, 2019, www.bbc.com/news/world-asia-47488917.

201 **myth of the predatory Black:** See, for example, Jennifer Wriggins, "Rape, Racism, and the Law," *Harvard Women's Law Journal* 6, no. 103 (1983), digitalcommons.mainelaw.maine.edu/faculty-publications/51.

201 **"raping children regularly":** "Proud Boys," Southern Poverty Law Center, www.splcenter.org/fighting-hate/extremist-files/group/proud-boys.

202 **fulminated against Muslim:** Alejandro Beutel, "The New Zealand Terrorist's Manifesto: A Look at Some of the Key Narratives, Beliefs and Tropes," National Consortium for the Study of Terrorism and Responses to Terrorism, April 30, 2019, www.start.umd.edu/news/new-zealand-terrorists-manifesto-look-some-key-narratives-beliefs-and-tropes.

202 **"I go from one place":** Rudyard Kipling, *Kim* (Garden City, NY: Doubleday, Page), p. 186.

210 **"The history of Pakistan":** Mohammed Hanif, speech to Karachi Literary Festival, London, May 20, 2017.

214 **"kill rather than capture":** Jeremy Scahill, "The Drone Papers," *Intercept,* October 15, 2015, theintercept.com/2015/10/15/the-drone-papers/.

214 **"dull, dirty and dangerous":** Jackie Northam, "Popularity of Drones Takes Off for Many Countries," NPR, July 11, 2011, www.npr.org/2011/07/11/137710942/popularity-of-drones-takes-off-for-many-countries.

214 **"Either shoot to kill":** Grégoire Chamayou, *A Theory of the Drone,* trans. Janet Lloyd (London: Hamish Hamilton, 2015), p. 169.

215 **"patterns of life":** Ann Rogers and John Hill, *Unmanned: Drone Warfare and Global Security* (London: Pluto Press, 2014), p. 85.

THE WORLD'S BEST DERADICALIZATION PROGRAM

217 **rural literacy rate:** "Economic Survey Reveals Pakistan's Literacy Rate Increased to 60%," *News International,* June 11, 2020, www.thenews.com.pk/latest/671198-economic-survey-reveals-pakistans-literacy-rate-increased-to-60.

217 **weddings, dowries, mortgages:** Christopher Boucek, "Saudi Arabia's 'Soft' Counterterrorism Strategy: Prevention, Rehabilitation, and Aftercare," Carnegie Endowment for International Peace, September 22, 2008,

carnegieendowment.org/2008/09/22/saudi-arabia-s-soft-counterterrorism
-strategy-prevention-rehabilitation-and-aftercare-pub-22155.

220 **only 17 percent internet penetration:** "Individuals Using the Internet
(% of Population)—Pakistan," Data, World Bank, 2020, data.worldbank
.org/indicator/IT.NET.USER.ZS?locations=PK.

221 **Some boys were sold:** Cathy Scott-Clark and Adrian Levy, "How to De-
fuse a Human Bomb," *Guardian,* October 15, 2010.

221 **"I'd never seen such hatred":** Christina Lamb, "100% Pass Rate at Boy
Bomber Reform School," *Sunday Times,* April 27, 2013.

227 **After Alexander defeated the Persians:** Mary Renault, *The Nature of Alexander* (London: Alan Lane, 1975), p. 131.

228 **transmitters strapped to the backs:** Krishnadev Calamur, "New Pakistani
Taliban Leader Blamed for Schoolgirl Shooting," NPR, November 7, 2013,
www.npr.org/sections/parallels/2013/11/07/243752189/pakistani-taliban
-pick-leader-blamed-for-schoolgirl-shooting.

230 **on a lunch break:** Ayesha Umar, "Dr. Farooq: The Loss of an Intellectual,"
Express Tribune, October 6, 2010, tribune.com.pk/article/2025/dr-farooq
-the-loss-of-an-intellectual.

231 **gold-plated submachine gun:** Jack Guy, "Saudi Crown Prince Gifted
Golden Submachine Gun in Pakistan," CNN, February 20, 2019.

232 **to counterbalance Iranian influence:** Madiha Afzal, "Saudi Arabia's Hold
on Pakistan," Brookings Institution, May 10, 2019, www.brookings.edu/
research/saudi-arabias-hold-on-pakistan/.

232 **Saudi sources had provided funding:** Bruce Riedel, "Saudi Arabia Is Part
of the Problem and Part of the Solution to Global Jihad," Brookings Institution, July 29, 2016, www.brookings.edu/blog/markaz/2015/11/20/
saudi-arabia-is-part-of-the-problem-and-part-of-the-solution-to-global
-jihad/.

232 **"both the arsonists and the firefighters":** Scott Shane, "Saudis and Extremism: 'Both the Arsonists and the Firefighters,'" *New York Times,* August
25, 2016.

232 **"the most significant source":** "WikiLeaks: Saudis 'Chief Funders of
Sunni Militants,'" BBC News, December 5, 2010.

233 **Robert Pape, a political scientist:** Elliott Balch, "Myth Busting: Robert
Pape on ISIS, Suicide Terrorism, and U.S. Foreign Policy," *Chicago Policy Review,* May 6, 2015, chicagopolicyreview.org/2015/05/05/myth-busting
-robert-pape-on-isis-suicide-terrorism-and-u-s-foreign-policy/.

AMERICAN BLOWBACK

240 **"smashing military victory":** Oleg Syromolotov (Russian deputy minister of foreign affairs), statement at OSCE counterterrorism conference, "The Reverse Flow of Foreign Terrorist Fighters: Challenges for the OSCE Area and Beyond," Rome, May 10–11, 2018.

241 **93 percent of terrorist attacks:** "Global Terrorism Index 2016," Institute for Economics and Peace, November 2016, economicsandpeace.org/wp -content/uploads/2016/11/Global-Terrorism-Index-2016.2.pdf.

241 **"government action":** "Journey to Extremism in Africa: Drivers, Incentives and the Tipping Point for Recruitment," United Nations Development Program, 2017, journey-to-extremism.undp.org/content/ downloads/UNDP-JourneyToExtremism-report-2017-english.pdf.

241 **"global, holistic, multidimensional":** Helen Duffy, " 'Foreign Terrorist Fighters': A Human Rights Approach?" Brill Nijhoff, December 12, 2018, brill.com/view/journals/shrs/29/1-4/article-p120_120.xml?language=en.

241 **"the interconnectedness of human rights":** "Guidelines for Addressing the Threats and Challenges of 'Foreign Terrorist Fighters' within a Human Rights Framework," OSCE, 2020, www.osce.org/odihr/393503.

243 **In her 2015 book:** Sarah Chayes, *Thieves of State: Why Corruption Threatens Global Security* (New York: W. W. Norton, 2015).

244 **"[Corruption] gives credence":** "Testimony to the Senate Foreign Relations Committee: Corruption: Violent Extremism, Kleptocracy and the Dangers of Failing Governance," Carnegie Endowment for International Peace, 2016, carnegieendowment.org/files/Chayes_Testimony_6-30-16 .pdf.

245 **"Out of a hundred Taliban":** Chayes, "Corruption and Terrorism," *op. cit.*

245 **"They'd say, 'If you join' ":** Fatima Akilu, remarks at Thomson Reuters Foundation conference "Is Deradicalization Possible?" London, 2016.

246 **"area of active hostilities":** Jack Serle and Jessica Purkiss, "US Counter Terror Air Strikes Double in Trump's First Year," *Airwars,* December 19, 2017, airwars.org/news-and-investigations/page/2/?belligerent=us -forces&country=somalia.

246 **143 more terror attacks:** Thrall and Goepner, *op. cit.*

246 **U.S. diplomat in Yemen:** Matt Sledge, "Every Yemen Drone Strike Creates 40 to 60 New Enemies for U.S," *HuffPost,* October 24, 2013.

246 **"cause enemies for the United States":** "Former Counterterrorism Czar Richard Clarke: U.S. Drone Program Under Obama 'Got Out of Hand,' " *Democracy Now!,* June 2, 2014, www.democracynow.org/2014/6/2/former _counterterrorism_czar_richard_clarke_us.

246 **"All of these innocent people":** Ed Pilkington and Ewen MacAskill,

"Obama's Drone War a 'Recruitment Tool' for ISIS, Say US Air Force Whistleblowers," *Guardian,* November 18, 2015.

247 **"He's not my son":** Quoted in Henrick Karoliszyn and John Marzulli, "Long Island–Bred Terrorist's Plea Reveals LIRR Plot," *New York Daily News,* April 9, 2018.

247 **"the Forrest Gump of jihad":** Paul Cruickshank, "The Radicalization of an All-American Kid," CNN, May 15, 2010.

248 **chapter 11 discharge:** Bryant Neal Viñas and Mitchell Silber, "Al-Qa'ida's First American Foreign Fighter after 9/11," Combating Terrorism Center at West Point, January 17, 2019, ctc.usma.edu/al-qaidas-first-american-foreign -fighter-9-11/.

251 **"To say that the defendant provided":** "American Al Qaeda Member Turned Informant Avoids Long Sentence," Reuters, May 11, 2017.

253 **Based on his information:** Viñas and Silber, *op. cit.*

254 **"The juxtaposition of Mr. Vinas's atrocious":** Adam Goldman, "Service to Both Al Qaeda and U.S., with Fate Hanging in the Balance," *New York Times,* May 15, 2017.

255 **box of Fruity Pebbles:** Adam Goldman, "He Turned on Al Qaeda and Aided the U.S. Now He's on Food Stamps and Needs a Job," *New York Times,* March 6, 2018.

QUANTUM ENTANGLEMENT

260 **"manifestly unlawful":** Kenneth Propp, "Speech Moderation and Militant Democracy: Should the United States Regulate like Europe Does?" Atlantic Council, February 1, 2021, www.atlanticcouncil.org/blogs/new-atlanticist/ speech-moderation-and-militant-democracy-should-the-united-states -regulate-like-europe-does/.

261 **"a veil of forgetfulness":** J. M. Hawes, *The Shortest History of Germany: From Julius Caesar to Angela Merkel: A Retelling for Our Times* (New York: Ex- periment, 2019), p. 195.

261 **"antifascist schools":** Frederick Taylor, *Exorcising Hitler: The Occupation and Denazification of Germany* (London: Bloomsbury, 2014).

261 **"East Germany put far more":** Susan Neiman, *Learning from the Germans: Race and the Memory of Evil* (New York: Picador, 2020), pp. 98–99.

262 **Jürgen Habermas articulated:** Jeffrey Gedmin, "Right-Wing Populism in Germany: Muslims and Minorities after the 2015 Refugee Crisis," Brook- ings Institution, July 24, 2020, www.brookings.edu/research/right-wing -populism-in-germany-muslims-and-minorities-after-the-2015-refugee -crisis/.

262 **"No other country in the world":** Julia Berczyk and Floris Vermeulen,

"Prevent Abroad: Militant Democracy, Right-Wing Extremism, and the Prevention of Islamic Extremism in Berlin," in *Counter-Radicalization: Critical Perspectives,* ed. Christopher Baker-Beall, Charlotte Heath-Kelly, and Lee Jarvis (Milton Park, UK: Routledge, 2015), pp. 88–105.

262 **some 720, with roughly half:** Lukasz Jurczyszyn et al., *Report on the Comparative Analysis of European Counter-Radicalisation, Counter-Terrorist and De-Radicalisation Policies* (Dialogue About Radicalisation & Equality, 2019), p. 16, www.dare-h2020.org/uploads/1/2/1/7/12176018/_reportcounterradicalisationpolicies_d3.2.pdf.

262 **earliest formal violent extremist:** Witold Mucha, "Polarization, Stigmatization, Radicalization: Counterterrorism and Homeland Security in France and Germany," *Journal for Deradicalization,* 2017, journals.sfu.ca/jd/index.php/jd/article/download/89/79; "We Talk to Extremists, Not About Them," Violence Prevention Network, 2021, violence-prevention-network.de/?lang=en.

262 **Verantwortungspädagogik:** "Breaking Away from Hate and Violence— Education of Responsibility (Verantwortungspädagogik)," Migration and Home Affairs—European Commission, December 11, 2018, ec.europa.eu/home-affairs/node/7422_en.

265 **membership in right-wing:** Michael Herzog zu Mecklenburg and Ian Anthony, "Preventing Violent Extremism in Germany: Coherence and Cooperation in a Decentralized System" (working paper), Stockholm International Peace Research Institute, August 2020," p. 64, www.sipri.org/sites/default/files/2020-08/wp_2005_violent_extremism.pdf.

265 **"biggest threat":** Tony Barber, "Germany Wakes up to the Far-Right Terror Threat," *Financial Times,* December 3, 2020.

270 **since the downfall of the Third Reich:** *Germany's New Nazis,* Panorama, BBC, September 30, 2017, www.ronachanfilms.co.uk/2017/10/16/panorama-germanys-new-nazis-2/.

271 **"I am German when we win":** "Mesut Özil: Arsenal Midfielder Quits Germany over 'Racism and Disrespect,'" BBC Sport, July 23, 2018, www.bbc.com/sport/football/44915730.

271 **"If my theory of relativity":** Albert Einstein, in *The Expanded Quotable Einstein,* ed. Alice Calapice (Princeton: Princeton University Press, 2005), assets.press.princeton.edu/chapters/s6908.pdf.

271 **"spooky action at a distance":** "'Spooky Action at a Distance' Makes Sense—in the Quantum World," *Mind Matters,* December, 2020, mindmatters.ai/2020/12/spooky-action-at-a-distance-makes-sense-in-the-quantum-world/.

271 **"They are built on zero-sum":** Julia Ebner, *The Rage: The Vicious Circle of Islamist and Far-Right Extremism* (London: I. B. Tauris, 2017), p. 28.

273   **Some neo-Nazis have partnered:** Ibid., pp. 181–82.

273   **a quarter of Germans hold:** Esra Özyürek, "Export-Import Theory and the Racialization of Anti-Semitism: Turkish- and Arab-Only Prevention Programs in Germany," LSE Research Online, March 2016, core.ac.uk/download/pdf/188463821.pdf.

274   **"Despite its opposition":** Esra Özyürek, "German Muslims' 'Shocking' Response to the Holocaust," *Haaretz,* February 1, 2021, www.haaretz.com/world-news/german-muslims-shocking-response-to-the-holocaust -1.9500759.

HOW TO DERADICALIZE YOUR TOWN

276   **"unique to the Jewish people":** "Jewish Nation State: Israel Approves Controversial Bill," BBC News, July 19, 2018.

276   **Viktor Orbán's far-right:** Elżbieta M. Goździak, "Using Fear of the 'Other,' Orbán Reshapes Migration Policy in a Hungary Built on Cultural Diversity," *Migration Policy,* October 10, 2019, www.migrationpolicy.org/article/orb%C3%A1n-reshapes-migration-policy-hungary.

276   **"Cosmopolitanism is an expansive":** Kwame Anthony Appiah, "The Importance of Elsewhere," *Foreign Affairs,* March–April 2019.

277   **nearly a third of Mechelaars:** Ryan Heath, "Liberal Mayors Launch Fightback against Populism," *Politico,* December 2, 2016, www.politico.eu/article/liberal-mayors-launch-fightback-against-populism-bart-somers-of -mechelen-francois-decoster/.

278   **His grandfather Ludwig:** Bart Somers, *Mechelen Bouwstenen voor een betere stad* (Antwerp: Houtekiet, 2012).

279   **highest per capita number:** Michael Birnbaum, "Belgian Muslims Face Renewed Anger, Alienation after Attacks in Paris," *Washington Post,* January 15, 2015.

279   **"a laboratory for Belgium":** Hans Bonte, "The Vilvoorde Model as a Response to Radicalism," Strong Cities Network, 2015, strongcitiesnetwork .org/en/wp-content/uploads/sites/5/2017/02/The-Vilvoorde-model-as -a-response-to-radicalism.pdf.

281   **"Do I contradict myself?":** Walt Whitman, "Song of Myself" (1892), Poetry Foundation, www.poetryfoundation.org/poems/45477/song-of -myself-1892-version.

282   **eighteen hundred soldiers:** Alissa de Carbonnel and Robert-Jan Bartunek, "Soldiers on Europe's Streets Dent NATO's Defence Edge," Reuters, September 14, 2017, www.reuters.com/article/europe-attacks-military -idINKCN1BP1C6.

282   **"genuine public sphere":** Lene Hansen, "Reconstructing Desecuritisation:

The Normative-Political in the Copenhagen School and Directions for How to Apply It," *Review of International Studies* 38, no. 3 (2012): 525–46, www.jstor.org/stable/41681477.

283 **green, clean, and safe:** Descriptions of the changes in Mechelen before and after Somers took charge appear in citizens' nominations for the World Mayor Prize, which he won in 2016. See www.worldmayor.com/contest _2016/mechelen-mayor-somers.html.

287 **"The massive influx of foreigners":** "Vlaams Belang Mechelen," Facebook, www.facebook.com/VlaamsBelangMechelen.

290 **"build up a destructive":** Herman Van Goethem, ed., *Kazerne Dossin: Memorial, Museum and Documentation Centre on Holocaust and Human Rights* (Mechelen: Kazerne Dossin, 2012).

290 **"We speak a lot":** Bart Somers, *The Mechelen Model: An Inclusive City* (Barcelona Centre for International Affairs, 2017).

291 **"the continued detention":** "Syria: UN Experts Urge 57 States to Repatriate Women and Children from Squalid Camps," UN Human Rights Council, February 8, 2021, reliefweb.int/report/syrian-arab-republic/syria-un -experts-urge-57-states-repatriate-women-and-children-squalid.

291 **"To turn its back":** Yasmine Ahmed, "The UK Supreme Court Has Failed Shamima Begum," HRW.org (blog), March 2, 2021, www.hrw.org/news/ 2021/03/02/uk-supreme-court-has-failed-shamima-begum.

292 **"Loneliness is the common ground":** Arendt quoted in Maria Popova, "Hannah Arendt on Loneliness as the Common Ground for Terror and How Tyrannical Regimes Use Isolation as a Weapon of Oppression," *Brain Pickings,* September 27, 2020, www.brainpickings.org/2016/12/20/hannah -arendt-origins-of-totalitarianism-loneliness-isolation/.

292 **"architecture of serendipity":** Cass Sunstein, *Going to Extremes: How Like Minds Unite and Divide* (Oxford: Oxford University Press, 2009), p. 80.

293 **1918 flu pandemic:** James Politi, "NY Fed Study Links Spanish Flu to Extremist Voting in 1930s," *Financial Times,* May 5, 2020, blogs.ft.com/the -world/liveblogs/2020-05-05-2/.

293 **Hate crimes and violence:** Ali Rogin and Amna Nawaz, "'We Have Been Through This Before': Why Anti-Asian Hate Crimes Are Rising amid Coronavirus," *PBS NewsHour,* June 25, 2020, www.pbs.org/newshour/ nation/we-have-been-through-this-before-why-anti-asian-hate-crimes-are -rising-amid-coronavirus.

293 **"perfect storm for recruitment":** Miller-Idriss quoted in Hannah Allam, "'A Perfect Storm': Extremists Look for Ways to Exploit Coronavirus Pandemic," NPR, April 16, 2020, www.npr.org/2020/04/16/835343965/-a -perfect-storm-extremists-look-for-ways-to-exploit-coronavirus-pandemic.

294 OUR STREETS FLOOD: Somini Sengupta, "Protesting Climate Change,

Young People Take to Streets in a Global Strike," *New York Times*, September 20, 2019, www.nytimes.com/2019/09/20/climate/global-climate
-strike.html.

294 **"Human beings":** George Orwell, "Review of *Mein Kampf*," *Book Marks*,
April 25, 2017, bookmarks.reviews/george-orwells-1940-review-of-mein
-kampf/.

295 **anthropologist Scott Atran:** Atran quoted in Robert Gebelhoff, "Rethinking the War on Terrorism, with the Help of Science," *Washington Post*,
March 31, 2019.

295 **"absolutely important":** Scott Atran, "Alt-Right or Jihad?," *Aeon*, November 6, 2017, aeon.co/essays/radical-islam-and-the-alt-right-are-not-so
-different.

INDEX

ABOUT THE AUTHOR

CARLA POWER is the author of *If the Oceans Were Ink,* a finalist for both the Pulitzer Prize and the National Book Award. Her childhood was spent in St. Louis, with stints living in Iran, India, Afghanistan, Egypt, and Italy. Having started her journalistic career at *Newsweek* in the 1990s, she has since contributed reportage and essays to numerous publications, including *Time, The New York Times, Foreign Policy, Vogue, Vanity Fair,* and *The Guardian.* She lives with her family in East Sussex, England.

carlapower.com
Twitter: @carlapower

ABOUT THE TYPE

This book was set in Dante, a typeface designed by Giovanni Mardersteig (1892–1977). Conceived as a private type for the Officina Bodoni in Verona, Italy, Dante was originally cut only for hand composition by Charles Malin, the famous Parisian punch cutter, between 1946 and 1952. Its first use was in an edition of Boccaccio's *Trattatello in laude di Dante* that appeared in 1954. The Monotype Corporation's version of Dante followed in 1957. Though modeled on the Aldine type used for Pietro Cardinal Bembo's treatise *De Aetna* in 1495, Dante is a thoroughly modern interpretation of that venerable face.